WILLIAM JAMES
(1771–1837)

The Man who Discovered George Stephenson

Miles Macnair MA

RAILWAY & CANAL HISTORICAL SOCIETY

*This book is dedicated to the memory of Charles Hadfield,
author, canal historian and publisher extraordinary, who dedicated
one of his own classic books to William James.*

First published 2007
by the Railway & Canal Historical Society

www.rchs.org.uk

The Railway & Canal Historical Society was founded in 1954 and incorporated in 1967.
It is a company (No.922300) limited by guarantee and registered in England as a charity (No.256047)
Registered office: 3 West Court, West Street, Oxford OX2 0NP

ISBN 978 0 901461 54 4 (hardback)

ISBN 978 0 901461 55 1 (softback)

Designed and typeset by
Malcolm Preskett
Printed in England by
Biddles Ltd, King's Lynn, Norfolk

TITLE PAGE
The only known portrait of William James, 'engraved by W. Roffe
from a miniature by Chalon'. *National Railway Museum*

Contents

Colour plates (between pages 48 and 49)

Monochrome plates (between pages 112 and 113)

Figures in the text

William James (1771–1837)
A member of a truly visionary
English triumvirate

THE Palmes d'Or, at least in the history of technology, go to those who make a technical advance actually work, and not to the theoreticians. But as James Watt Snr said long ago, we actually learn more from studying the history of failures than from the analysis of such successes as Watt's own steam engine. William James was a member of a vital triumvirate, along with the mineral surveyor William Smith (1769–1839) and the engineer Richard Trevithick (1771–1833). All three encountered major problems on the 'failure front'; James suffered his own imprisonment and bankruptcy in 1822 and 1823; Smith, after his time in another London debtor's prison in 1819, went into exile in the north of England; Trevithick, after his own long exile in South America, ended his days in a pauper's grave in Kent.

Let us first consider their triangular situations in October 1801. The Napoleonic Wars then raged all over Europe, while the all too-short Peace of Amiens lay six months in the future. Smith was busy pioneering the science of mineral prospecting, especially for those, like coal and iron, fuelling the world's first Industrial 'revolution' here. Smith had just issued his printed *Prospectus* for a book on the subject, which he hoped would make his fortune, but when his publisher suffered a double bankruptcy, this project had to be abandoned. Smith was already in close contact with James, who was soon to be busy with the railway projects which were to revolutionise freight and passenger transport. Both were soon in contact with Trevithick, busy pioneering his locomotive, which would help to further James's transport vision. Each man was then a visionary, hoping to lead revolutions in science and technology.

Now we move to June 1819, some years after the end of the long Napoleonic Wars. Smith is in a debtors' prison in London, despite (or because of) the publication of his famous *Geological Map* in 1815. Trevithick is lost in his own long Peruvian exile, amid the civil war there, after his own bankruptcy in February 1811. James too is struggling financially – the Midland iron trade was in deep depression after the end of the wars, and 'country banks now declined to advance money to people [like James previously] of the first credit'. So much for market forces in *laissez faire* England. Their shared vision is nicely expressed in Smith's 1820 reduced *Geological Map of England and Wales*, which now lists 'the principal articles of mineral tonnage' carried on our canals and railways.

All three visionaries have now achieved a place in the pantheon of national achievers. But, as measured by the new *Oxford Dictionary of National Biography* (2004), this has been recognised to a different extent. Smith, the 'father of English geology', and Trevithick, the father of the locomotive, get four pages, but James only two. Why is Henley-in-Arden's most significant son so underrated? This is largely because of the different ways their lives have been chronicled by later biographers. Smith received a fine biography in 1844, from his, by then eminent geologist, nephew John Phillips (1800–1874), soon after Smith died. That book, understandably, avoided discussion of Smith's problems, his mentally-unstable wife, his financial disasters and his imprisonment. Trevithick was equally well served, if a good bit later, first by his engineer son in 1872, 39 years after his death, and then in 1934 by two eminent historians of technology. James, on the other hand, has been by far the least, and worst, served, only through a self-seeking 'cri-de-coeur' biography by his younger daughter, published in 1861, 24 years after he died – and reprinted in 1961 with a careful introduction by Tom Rolt. So we should be delighted that Miles Macnair has here managed to redress the balance and has at last given James the attention he so clearly deserves.

H. S. Torrens

I COULD not have started, let alone finished, this book without the help and encouragement of many people. Foremost is Hugh Torrens, Emeritus Professor of Earth Sciences at Keele University, who has been unstintingly generous in sharing his own voluminous source material and a tower of strength in helping to trawl through libraries and record offices. I also owe a huge debt of gratitude to Dr Michael Lewis for his encouragement and wise suggestions at the final editing stage.

To Nick Billingham I am deeply indebted for references and guidance on the Stratford Canal. Gwyn Howell had fortunately become intrigued by the James / Agar-Robartes correspondence in the Lanhydrock archives and I have drawn extensively and gratefully on his summaries of these letters. Contemporary material to illustrate William James's life is virtually non-existent and therefore I owe a special thanks to Robin Barnes for his delightful water-colour interpretations. My thanks also go to Richard Dean for converting my rough sketches into professional maps, and to Malcolm Preskett for his enthusiastic design.

Many other people have replied to my enquiries with generosity, and I would like to record my thanks to the following:

Vicky Haworth (Robert Stephenson Jnr);
Robert Stephenson Roper
(Robert Stephenson Snr);
Jim Lewis (Glynn family);
Brian Hart (Canterbury & Whitstable Railway);
Adrian Jarvis (Samuel Smiles);
William Hedger (Bexhill);
Robin Watson (Trebinshun);
Paul Holden (National Trust).

Also Alexander Owen for assisting my research at both Lambeth Palace and the National Archives at Kew.

From archivists, curators and librarians across the country I have received courteous and professional help; record offices at Warwick, Stratford-upon-Avon, Birmingham, Sandwell, Liverpool, Preston, Stafford, Worcester, Kent, Kew and Cornwall; the Museum of Freemasonry, the Lanhydrock archives, the Courtney Library in Truro, the National Library of Wales and the libraries at Lambeth Palace, the House of Lords and Lincoln's Inn.

It has been particularly rewarding to meet and correspond with several direct descendants of William James now living in Australia and England. I am very grateful to Susan Gladstone, Joyce Carey, Margaret Cund and Jenni Tyice for details of their family trees. (I regret that limitations of space prevent my including more details on the lives of William James's descendants in the late 19th / early 20th centuries.) It was a privilege to welcome Ken and Bruce James from Australia at the unveiling of the William James memorial plaque at Henley-in-Arden in June 2003. This is also an opportunity for me to thank again my fellow committee members on this project and all the friends and organisations who gave donations.

Finally I want to say an enormous thank you to my wife Juliette, for her tireless proof reading, her perceptive culling of redundant information from early drafts and for putting up with the 'third person in our marriage'.

INTRODUCTION

'History is not what you thought; it is what you can remember.'

W. C. Sellar and R. J. Yeatman, *1066 and All That*

IT HAS often been said that history is largely written by the winners. Under their editorial control, events can be re-interpreted and selected reputations enhanced while inconvenient people may be sidelined or erased completely. It is more difficult to hide giants, because they tend to leave footprints. Readers of modern histories of the Industrial Revolution will find the name of William James mentioned quite frequently but only very briefly – a sentence here, a short paragraph there – before the authors concentrate on the more familiar icons of this extraordinary period of British history.

Yet the phrases used in connection with William James are tantalising and provocative:

- 'A pioneer without reward . . . Of the visionaries, William James was pre-eminent.'[1]
- 'He had a career of such extraordinary diversity . . . that it puts him apart from the rest.'[2]
- 'James foresaw the future . . . James' visionary, single-minded drive led him to attempt too much, too quickly. He was a man before his time.'[3]
- 'This larger than life character . . . who saw too far and moved too quickly, and so failed.'[4]
- 'Entrepreneurs like William James were men as isolated as they were outstanding.'[5]
- 'He had the unique foresight to realise what *could* be done with railways.'[6]
- 'He was among the earliest, if not *the* earliest, of the originators and promoters of the system of passenger transit on railways.'[7]
- 'A vigorous and far-sighted projector.'[8]
- 'That enthusiastic but unlucky advocate.'[9]
- 'Though he did not discover the locomotive, he did what was the next best thing to it, he discovered George Stephenson.'[10]

Who was this man of such visionary talent, energy and influence? Why is he not as well remembered as his peers such as Thomas Telford, Richard Trevithick, Joseph Locke and the Rennie brothers, the Stephensons and the Brunels? Why were there no monuments to him? Did he leave no correspondence? Was he an obscure, lonely eccentric? Why is there only one biography of him, and that

no more than a slim volume, published virtually anonymously in 1861? And why – the key question – has he been virtually airbrushed from history?

Some of the answers to these questions are easy to uncover, others are much more enigmatic. One can be dealt with straight away. Few historians have taken the trouble to look for sources on William James beyond his daughter's biased and fallible – and virtually unreadable – biography *The Two James's and the Two Stephensons* (hereafter abbreviated as EMSP).[11] Yet my own researches have unearthed hundreds of William James's letters, account books, documents and plans that have lain buried in archives, libraries and record offices. This present book, using these previously unpublished sources, sets out to try to answer the other questions by presenting the facts of his extraordinarily varied life before attempting to draw some conclusions. And as such, it may prove to be a helpful resource for future writers.

But when one comes to fit William James into the context of his contemporaries, there is one major problem. Unlike most of them, he was a polymath and therefore belongs in no convenient biographical pigeon-hole. He was a lawyer, a skilful drafter of Parliamentary Bills, a geologist, a surveyor and land-agent; he became a civil engineer and a significant quarry owner, coal-miner and ironmaster. Furthermore, he and his son were far-sighted inventors, but the significance of their patents would only be appreciated decades after his death. He was, in summary, a Regency entrepreneur and risk-taker, colliding with an era that would condemn these activities as mere gambling. In its present form, this book concentrates on his endeavours in the field of transport, and therefore his very significant achievements in many other areas – particularly land agency and estate management – have been condensed and abbreviated. Readers are asked to bear this in mind when drawing their own conclusions about William James's overall contribution to the development of the Industrial (and Agricultural) Revolution.

The Two James's and the Two Stephensons

AN important source of information, opinion and conjecture about James is, inevitably, the only previous biography of him, published in 1861. The author is given only as 'EMSP', but there is no doubt that the person hiding behind these initials was his younger daughter Ellen Matilda Steward James, who had married a Mr Paine. As Tom Rolt wrote in his introduction to the reprint published on its centenary in 1961, 'she obviously believed passionately that her father and brother had been victims of grave injustice. Unfortunately, strong emotion of this kind, however justifiable, seldom goes hand in hand with objective truth.'

One has therefore to be particularly strict, diligent and questioning when making use of this book as a source. She quotes lengthy extracts from letters and reports, which she appears to have had in front of her at the time of writing but can in most cases, unfortunately, no longer be traced. It is sincerely hoped that this present publication may stimulate other researchers to uncover their existence in obscure libraries or family archives.

I have treated these *direct* quotations as primary sources, annotated by the reference EMSP*. Where I have made use of any other material from her book, either as a stimulus for deeper research and analysis or because there appears to be no other way of fleshing out James's life and times, the less emphatic reference EMSP is used.

One word of warning. W. T. Jackman refers to an article of 1857 'in which is found James's diary down to 1808.' [12] This is a fantasy. It refers to three letters to the editor of the *Mining Journal*

(14 November, 5 December, 26 December 1857) from James's son William Henry, doubtless prompted by the recent publication of Smiles's life of Stephenson, in which he poses, and tries to answer, the question 'Who was the *bona fide* originator and founder of our modern Railway System?' He says that he has his father's diary and many other papers to draw on; and much of EMSP is merely an expansion of these three letters. But the diary is not quoted, nor does it now survive.

The Warwick Archives

THE Warwick family archives in the County Record Office at Warwick are a vast resource for James's life between 1800 and 1815. These papers are stored, non-chronologically, in a great number of boxes and cover five centuries. The somewhat abbreviated catalogue itself runs to over 500 pages, with about twenty boxes on each page. Apart from estate accounts, single receipts, assignments and trustee documents, James's two letterbooks – outgoing only – have survived for the years 1802 to 1806. The second of them is a leather-bound volume compiled by his clerk, Joseph Povey, and tooled on the spine with the title 'Book A'. It contains copies of over 700 letters. How it came to be among the Warwick archives is a mystery in itself, since there is a penned note on the inside cover stating that it was 'purchased by Mr Povey', perhaps implying that he had bought it from the liquidators of James's estate. Why is it back among the Earl's archives? It would be wonderful to assume that somewhere else, perhaps among the papers of the Povey family, there lurk companion volumes covering later dates.

ONE

Forebears, Family and a New Career

I F ONE stands on Clopton Bridge at Stratford-upon-Avon, it is not difficult to feel a sense of awe and wonderment that this structure, built 500 years ago in the reign of King Henry VII, still carries the heaviest road transport of the first decade of the twenty-first century. Look a few yards downstream and there is another bridge, an elegant, seven-arch design in brick, which, although strong enough and wide enough to carry a full size railway, is now used only as a tourist footpath (plate 1). At the northern end of the bridge lies the Bancroft canal basin, with a lock connecting it to the river Avon. This bridge and this basin are the surviving echoes of one man's fantastic vision, a dream that saw Stratford-upon-Avon as the epicentre of a revolutionary transport system that would link the Midlands to London and the South Coast; a system that would see trains running on iron rails and hauled by 'iron horses' driven by steam, swiftly transporting not only coal, freight and minerals but passengers as well; and all this a mere five years after the battle of Waterloo. If things had turned out just a little differently, historians would now be associating Stratford-upon-Avon and Moreton-in-Marsh with the dawning of the world's railway systems rather than Stockton, Darlington, Liverpool and Manchester.

Beside the Bancroft basin stands a fine memorial statue to William Shakespeare, and across the Bancroft Garden sits the theatre that bears his name, yet until recently the great visionary and entrepreneur with whom we are concerned has had no memorial.[13] His name was William James.

James was descended from an old family whose roots lay in the Forest of Dean in Gloucestershire. His grandfather, Henry James, married Mary Greaves of Moseley, then a market town a few miles south of Birmingham, and they had one child, William – our subject's father – who was born around 1730. This William, who became a solicitor, married Mary Lucas, the daughter of Simon and Susanna Lucas of Lindsworth Hill,

Kings Norton. Mary Lucas's mother had in later life been converted to catholicism and sold or mortgaged much of her family property to found convents overseas, but they were still a well-off and well-connected family.[14] At some stage, William and Mary James moved to the ancient Warwickshire market town of Henley-in-Arden, and in 1769 they had a son who was baptised with the name of his father but survived only a few months. Then on 13 June 1771 their second son was born, who was also christened William at a ceremony in St John's chapel three weeks later.[15]

Two years before, another boy named William had been born in the remote village of Churchill in Oxfordshire. His father was the village blacksmith, and although his background and upbringing could not have been more different from that of William James, their lives were to impinge in a remarkable way. From his humble origins, William Smith would go on to make discoveries and deductions that would shake the established orthodoxy and change the way in which we view the world around us.

On 13 April 1771, the birth of another boy was recorded in the village of Pool in what was then seen as the wild and inhospitable Celtic outpost of Cornwall. He too would grow up to make epoch-making inventions, the import of which would initially be dismissed by the scientific establishment – but not by William James. They may have met only once, yet that meeting lit a fire of imagination which burned in James for much of his life. That child was named Richard Trevithick.

William James's parents were to have five other children. His first sister, Mary, to whom he became particularly attached, was christened in Henley-in-Arden on 17 May 1774. Anne was born in 1776, Henry in 1779, Susannah in 1781, the first Elizbeth in 1782 (she died in infancy) and the second Elizabeth in 1785.[16] Henry was to make a career for himself at the Treasury, where he was nicknamed 'My Lord Little Shilling' because

9

of his advocacy of certain currency reforms. He died a bachelor at the age of 73 and, until much later, takes virtually no part in this story. James's four sisters, however, have major parts to play, one of which, starting almost in farce, would end in disaster.

The young William James went to school in Warwick before studying law at Lincoln's Inn, and while in London he joined a number of debating societies and became a fluent and persuasive orator.[17] Later on, for example, he proved, unlike the self-educated George Stephenson, a lucid performer in front of parliamentary committees. A biographical notice published in 1840 provides the only physical description we have: 'though corpulent, his manners were elegant and easy.'[18] After James's death, Robert Stephenson told Samuel Smiles, his father's biographer, that James was 'a ready, dashing writer . . . possessed a great deal of taking talent. His fluency of conversation I never heard equalled, and so you would judge from his letters.'[19] (The Stephensons, father and son, are introduced at this early stage in our story because the interplay of personalities and talents between the two families is a vital thread in its development, and for a time in the early 1820s their careers were to become crucially and mutually interdependent.) Some time prior to 1797 James was admitted to the Law Society, and he also became a freemason, which was to be an important influence on his later life. His training done, he returned to Henley-in-Arden to join his father's legal practice.

On 4 September 1793, in the Saxon church at Wootton Wawen a mile south of Henley, William James married Dinah Tarleton. A few months older than her husband, she was the orphaned daughter of William and Mary Tarleton who had both died when she was nine. The Tarleton family owned several farms to the north of Henley-in-Arden and James, an expert and dedicated horseman, would have frequently ridden to hounds across their land. Dinah came to their marriage with a dowry of at least £1,000 and they started their married life living at the 'Yew Trees' on Henley-in-Arden High Street, which William James had bought for £390 (plates 2a and 2b). The young couple enjoyed a high social standing; an invitation to dinner at Wootton Hall from Sir Edward and Lady Smythe – 'Lady Smythe will send the carriage at 2 o'clock' – still survives among the few personal papers of William James that have come down to us.[20] This invitation must have been of particular significance; perhaps it was to introduce the young couple to Bernard Dewes of Wellesbourne Hall, who was soon to set

James's career on its course to wealth and fortune. Perhaps one of the guests was the spendthrift Earl of Warwick, another character who was to play a major role in James's life and through whom James would enjoy the trust and friendship of many great families.

Sadly, we have no precise description of what Dinah James looked like; James referred to her as 'my angel wife' and, when speaking to their children, he would, according to their daughter Ellen, use the phrase 'that saint, your mother'. In recollecting her mother some years after her death, Ellen would write that 'all who were acquainted with this lady agree in testifying, that if ever these appellations were appropriately conferred on any mortal, her holy, meek, and retiring disposition, combined with the spiritual beauty of her fine and expressive countenance, seemed to make these terms not unsuitable to her.'[21] She would have to endure the stresses and strains of living with what modern generations would call a complete workaholic and, moreover, one who would spend weeks at a time travelling away from home. To this extent, theirs was a very modern marriage. Not that James did not feel these pressures as well. He was often ill, and later on he suffered a number of physical accidents, but his correspondence shows that he would return to his work and his travelling at the first possible moment, frequently summoning his long-suffering clerk to take letters from his sickbed.

In those early years, however, there is nothing to suggest that life for the young James family was anything but prosperous, amiable and comfortable. Their first son was born on 29 January 1796 and christened William Henry. The law practice of James and his father, the local JP, had a fair amount to occupy them, especially with local disputes between landlords and tenants arising from the provisions of Enclosure Acts. William James Snr was a wealthy man, the impact of his rash speculations in canal shares still to come. James's four younger sisters were as yet unmarried, and there was no hint yet of the ferocious family vendetta which would later explode. But in 1793 Britain had gone to war with France, and the next thirty years were to see the greatest upheavals to the nation's currency, coinage and finances that had ever been recorded. They would be exciting times for entrepreneurs prepared to take risks, and for inventors who could bring engineering innovation to bear on the burgeoning Industrial Revolution. Though very different from its counterpart across the channel, England was also undergoing its own social revolution, stimulated

Fig.1: **An example of William James's personal 'letter head'.** Henley-in-Arden Heritage Centre

by a rapid rise in the population, a significant redistribution of the national wealth, and the emergence of the middle classes. And in 1797 James embarked on a new shift in his career, which would involve him in managing the estates of some of the leading members of the aristocracy, in the course of which he was to become one of the richest commoners in the realm

1797 was a year of financial panic, partly induced by the landing of a small force of French troops at Milford Haven on the coast of Wales and not helped by mutinies within the Royal Navy at both Spithead and the Nore. There was a massive run on the banks, the value of speculative canal shares collapsed and William James Snr was forced to sell his ancestral home at Soilwell House in the Forest of Dean to try to cover his commit-ments.[22] Life in the James family suddenly became more earnest and young William, then 28, sought a new career on his own as one of the new breed of professional land agents on behalf of Bernard Dewes of Wellesbourne Hall, Warwickshire.

The role of the land-agent in Georgian England was complementary to that of estate stewards and bailiffs, but with one big distinction. While the latter usually worked exclusively for one employer, the agent was a freelance professional, often with business interests of his own. 'Estate improvements of a more scientific nature meant that the people occupying these positions had to be something more than glorified husbandmen.'[23]

'His extensive knowledge in very varied practical departments made his services valued throughout several counties. He had large knowledge of mines, of plantations, of various branches of

valuation and measurement, of all that is essential to the management of large estates. He was held by those competent to judge as unique amongst land agents for his manifold knowledge and experience, which enabled him to save the special fees usually paid by landowners for special opinions on the different questions incidental to the proprietorship of land.'

This quotation (from Fortescue 1915) is an almost perfect description of William James and the multi-faceted talents that he could offer to landowners. Apart from the buying and selling of land, estate owners required three things. The first involved improving the productivity of surface land, largely through drainage, but also by introducing new crops. Among these, the most important innovation at the end of the 18th century was probably the turnip, which allowed English farmers to over-winter their dairy herds rather than sending them to slaughter, and this lowly root vegetable would give English agricul-ture a significant advantage over its counterparts in Europe. James himself was an enthusiastic exponent of the cultivation of flax and the use of burnt straw as a fertiliser.[24] The second essential factor was recognising the potential for exploiting minerals below the surface. James became an eager self-taught student of geology, although at the start of the 19th century, as will be seen in Chapter 5, it was a very imperfect science. A third aspect, closely linked to the second, involved improving methods of transporting the products of mines and agriculture to the market place. All of these factors impinged on the legal framework of tenancies, way-leaves and manorial statutes, so that an expert knowledge of the law, and the professional authority to act, were further bonuses which James could offer potential clients. As pointed out in the quotation, being able to offer all these facilities in a single package, combined with charm, elegant manners and a ready wit, made James's services particularly sought after – services for which he could charge substantial fees.

By the end of the 18th century, the agrarian revolution in England was in its maturity, driven by a need (exacerbated by the wartime reduction in imports) to increase production to feed an expanding population and by the desire of landowners to increase their income. Much of the land within every parish was appropriately referred to by the Anglo-Saxon term 'waste'. The drive for higher productivity had two main thrusts: firstly to bring increasing areas of waste land under cultivation – or forestry – and secondly to create enclosed or hedged fields which physically separated livestock from crops.

Historians are divided about the rights and wrongs of the Enclosure Acts and their impact on rural communities. Those with a largely political agenda deplore the end of 'commoning' and a peasant class living, often marginally, by self-sufficiency; they tend to argue that Enclosure merely increased the assets and incomes of the great estates and the landed gentry, whilst driving villagers back into serfdom. Those historians who look at the total economic consequences argue that the whole package of reforms, of which the Enclosures were merely a part, not only helped to achieve the dramatic improvement in national prosperity that set England apart from her continental neighbours, but also strengthened the yeoman farming concept and, for the first time, offered paid employment to a new class of agricultural workers. There also arose a market in land itself.

Either way, it is undeniable that the physical landscape of the countryside was radically altered and, furthermore, the management of estates in their new configurations needed a more professional approach. A country legal practice like that of James and his father would have had much to occupy it. New patterns of land tenure, with new rental arrangements, had to be negotiated, and long-forgotten wills had to be traced and proved. Equally important, certain ancient rights had to be protected against unscrupulous landlords. Spasmodic riots through-out the previous two centuries demonstrated what could happen if the processes were not carried out with sensitivity.

There was another very important implication of the Enclosure Acts. For the first time, land could be compulsorily purchased with the sanction of Parliament, a process liable to involve bureaucratic error, legal red tape and, inevitably, the stench of corruption. One aspect of practical land improvement became particularly important, and that was drainage. Every land agent worth his salt had to become competent at surveying, establishing datum points and laying out a level so that drainage ditches could be dug economically and the water induced to flow away in the right direction under all weather conditions. On a larger scale, this became a skill that was essential in canal design, and in the last decade of the 18th century England was swept up in the Canal Mania. This phenomenon, together with James's particular involvement in this aspect of the Industrial Revolution, will occupy a later chapter, but here we are more concerned with his father. Not since the South Sea Bubble of 1720 had so many private individuals seen such a golden investment opportunity. Short-term fortunes were made and lost, and unfortunately William James Snr was a substantial loser.

The Dewes were 'an ancient family of good character and position but modest fortune' and John Dewes had acquired Wellesbourne Hall and its estate in about 1748. By 1797 in had passed down through the Granville family to Bernard Dewes.[25] James, his wife Dinah and their baby son William Henry moved to take up residence in the village, which lies four miles east of Stratford-upon-Avon and about seven miles due south of Warwick. It is likely that they went to live in the 'Little House' in Chestnut Square, still referred to unofficially as the Agent's House,[26] and it was here that their second son, John Henry, was born on 9 June 1798.[27]

James had hardly started to get to grips with the problems of Bernard Dewes's inheritance – like many estates of the time it was heavily mortgaged – when he was invited, in his capacity as a lawyer, to take on an important civic role as Deputy Recorder for the town of Warwick. It would be the start of a long and complex involvement with the eccentric Earl of Warwick. In November 1798, the Earl replied to James's acceptance:

I have just received your letter, and think myself very fortunate in procuring that activity and efficient assistance on which I depend from you, to bring the very disgraceful state of the corporation into some order. Firmness and activity are wanted, and, I trust, will be found ready to be exerted in such a manner as must tend to the future interest of the public, as well as the individuals in the town of Warwick. I am, with much regard, dear Sir, your faithful servant, Warwick.[28]

As in many medieval towns, the Corporation of Warwick was largely chosen from the gentry, who saw their main role to be sponsors and trustees of public buildings. The 1720s had seen the construction of the handsome classical Shire Hall and, although it was not a large building, the cost had run wildly over budget, prompting a group of local people to bring a suit in Chancery against the Corporation for misappropriation of funds. Not only did they win, but the commissioners ordered the Corporation to refund £4,000 into the charity fund and, when this proved impossible, the building was sequestered, forcing the mayor and corporation to hold their meetings at a local inn until 1770.[29]

James must have made a considerable success in sorting out the embarrassing finances of the Corporation, because in 1801 he was appointed as one of two land agents for the immense Warwick estates. But before plunging into this very productive and highly stressful phase in James's career, it is important to look at some of the financial background to the period and how the government was coping, or not coping, with an economy suddenly thrown onto a war footing.

William Pitt had been a dedicated and considerably successful economic reformer as Chancellor of the Exchequer (adopting many of the ideas perpetrated by Adam Smith in 'The Wealth of Nations') before becoming prime-minister in 1783. Determined to reduce the National Debt by means of annual payments into a sinking fund, he brought in a number of reforms to stimulate revenue from customs duties and excise – the main source of government income – not by raising levels of duty, but by stimulating trade and tackling the inefficiencies arising from corruption. He was slow to reverse his economic course, but a collapse of revenue and the panic run on the banks in 1797 forced the government into two crucial steps. The first was the suspension of convertibility, the automatic right for holders of Bank of England notes to convert them into specie. It was announced at the time that this draconian step, enshrined in the Bank Restriction Act, was only temporary and that convertibility would be restored the moment the war ended. The second – highly unpopular –

step was the introduction of income tax, which, after a brief phoney period of self-assessment, became in 1799 a graduated charge of up to 10 per cent on all incomes over £60 per annum. As far as James was concerned, this tax provided a major stimulus to demands for his services, as his clients reeled under the triple blows of reduced purchasing power, curtailed income and accelerating inflation. On top of this were the peer pressures to maintain an increasingly extravagant lifestyle, involving duplicate establishments in London or Bath, classical enhancements to their houses and landscapes, and the purchase of works of art, not to mention the demands of fashion in terms of fine clothes, porcelain dinner services and the other luxury consumer goods now coming onto the market. During the years of the Napoleonic wars, England suffered its greatest period of inflation since Tudor times, average commodity prices rose by 92 per cent,[30] and one of the many side-effects of this corrosive infection was the virtual elimination of the supply of coinage. At the time, most coins were silver, and as the ingot price of the metal rose above the face value, coins were taken out of circulation to be melted down.

As a result of all these factors, the prime method of settling any financial transaction became the Bill of Exchange. Debtors and creditors exchanged pieces of hand-written paper stating the value of a transaction and the terms of settlement. They often got lost. Copies got confused with originals, clerks inevitably made errors and the mail, particularly in country areas, was sometimes unreliable. Debts incurred by one party would sometimes be settled by promissory notes given by a third party, who was not necessarily involved in the original transaction at all. Country banks issued small-denomination banknotes (another form of promissory note) which helped smooth the settlement process somewhat, but these partnerships often proved to be less than robust. It was a most imperfect environment for conducting any sort of business, susceptible to numerous abuses of forgery, fraud and default, but there was no alternative and James, like everyone else, had to learn how to live with it. When he got involved in the books of account for the Earl of Warwick, they were in complete and almost terminal chaos. Furthermore – and this is essential to our understanding of what happened next – no one took the trouble to inform James of the somewhat draconian terms of the trusts under which the estates were entailed, terms which the Earl very largely chose to ignore.

TWO

Warwick – The Early Years
(1800–1802)

OR the sixteen years from 1798 to 1814, William James was deeply involved with the affairs of the Earl of Warwick, and although the relationship between these two strong personalities started with mutual respect and friendship, it would finally deteriorate into acrimony and litigation. Professionally, it is the best documented of any period in James's career, since the private papers of the Warwick family were deposited, in all their non-chronological chaos, in the County Record Office at Warwick when the Castle was sold to Madame Tussaud's in 1978.[31]

George Greville, the ninth Baron and second Earl of Warwick of the second foundation, was born in 1752 and succeeded to the title on the death of his father in 1773 (plate 3a). He had married his first wife, Georgiana Peachey, in 1771, but the following year she died tragically, aged twenty, giving birth to their son and heir, also christened George Greville. After her death the Earl suffered a major character change, and in his own words became 'the most solitary and wretched of human beings',[32] while elsewhere he has been described as 'passing across the pages of history like some forlorn ghost trying to make its presence felt in the contemporary world.'[33] In the years after his first wife's death, he spent over £100,000 on the fabric of Warwick Castle. He added lavishly to the already large collection of paintings and furniture, including the purchase of the Warwick Vase from his uncle Sir William Hamilton, as well as building the fine road bridge over the Avon below the castle.

In 1774, with the idea of cheering him up, some of his gambling friends had taken him to Newmarket and introduced him to the excitement of horseracing. He was very quickly hooked. He acquired a string of fine thoroughbreds and the following year enjoyed considerable success as an owner. Encouraged by his apparent judgment and skill in this risky sport, he somehow entered into a wager with Richard Vernon (later MP for Newmarket and known as the 'Father of the English turf') for the phenomenal sum of £50,000 – or approximately £3 million in today's money. He lost. Now it so happened that Richard Vernon had three extremely pretty daughters, and it was not long before an engagement was announced between the Earl and Henrietta Vernon. She was sixteen when they married in July 1776, and she came to the marriage with what one can only describe as a negative dowry, an understanding that her father would not press for settlement of the wager.[34]

The new Countess of Warwick bore her husband a son, Henry Richard, in March 1779, and later a second son, Charles, followed by another son and no less than six daughters. If the Earl really thought that his luck had changed, he was to suffer another terrible blow in 1786, when his first son, George Greville, died at Winkton in Hampshire on 22 April. Suddenly the Vernon grandson, Henry Richard, was now Lord Broke and the heir to the earldom, and the Vernons became much more interested in ensuring that he had something positive to inherit before his father squandered it all away. New trustees were appointed in the persons of the Earl of Upper Ossory and the Earl of Galloway, both cousins of the Countess.

Perhaps the terms of this original Trust Deed of 6 March 1788 still gave the Earl of Warwick too much latitude, because in May 1800 a new memorandum was drawn up by the Earl of Galloway and signed, somewhat casually, by the Earl of Warwick. It started off by stating that his personal debts were estimated at about £40,000, 'but of which no correct account has yet been made out.' This was followed by clauses saying that the ongoing income of the estates was unquantified and that there were outstanding charges against the estate of at least £12,000. Disposals were to be made to pay off the Earl's personal debts, and he had to make a new will guaranteeing to leave Lord Broke not only the property assets but also 'all his movable property, which shall be in and about Warwick Castle, its buildings and gardens.' Crucially, there is no mention of trees and standing timber. In the meantime, the Earl refused to recognise the financial restraints imposed on him and entered an undertaking in 1800 to buy from the executors of Lord Bagot the 2,500-acre Tachbrook Estate, part of which adjoined the castle grounds on the south side of the river, overlooked by the main rooms in the castle. Future generations and present-day visitors should be grateful to him for protecting this view, but at the time it caused yet more mayhem. The total purchase price was apparently something of the order of £100,000, with an initial down payment of £15,160.

It was at this time that the Trustees split the Warwick land agency in two, with William James given responsibility for the 'Outer Estates'. The management of the 'Home Estates' was the responsibility of John Casper Vancouver, the elder brother of George Vancouver, a famous explorer and circumnavigator after whom the city of Vancouver is named. Vancouver came from a Norfolk family and owned a 1,300-acre farm in Suffolk, as well as a major share in some brickworks in Hackney, Middlesex. James and Vancouver would not get on; James saw Vancouver as an overpaid dilettante and Vancouver probably considered James to be merely a small-town bean counter.

James wrote an initial report on his proposals for improving the Outer Estates which involved selling off the purely agricultural holdings and concentrating on the only one with any mineral prospects – in Somerset. The Earl replied enthusiastically:

If I could be surprised at either your activity, zeal, or ability, I should have been completely so, when I read your last letter . . . It would be unfair to your family to take you away; but if other business calls you here, Lord Galloway will, I am sure, be happy to see you, for his sentiments and mine, with regard to you, are the same . . . I could not occupy myself more to my satisfaction than in studying your plans, which are extensive, but, I am persuaded, founded on the certain basis of sound good sense and ability; and as such I feel their value, and that of their author.[35]

At this meeting James was asked by Lord Galloway to try to quantify the rental income that should be generated by all the estates and get a more accurate estimate of the Earl's personal indebtedness.

In addition, the Earl had another civic role for James, though in effect a very military one. The Earl, as Lord Lieutenant of Warwickshire, had already raised four troops of eighty men each to form the Warwickshire Fencible Cavalry in 1794, plus a further four troops of Yeomanry Cavalry, with Bernard Dewes of Wellesbourne as one of the lieutenants. But by 1801 'the apprehension of invasion necessitated further precautions for Home Defense'[36] and James was now appointed as Commandant Major of the Warwick Provisional Cavalry. Discipline was strict and James seems to have taken up the challenge with his characteristic eagerness and determination. His daughter claimed that this was achieved 'at a great expense to himself,' and whether she was referring to financial expense or further demands on his health and stamina, the reality was that he suffered on both counts. As an example of his commitment, she wrote that, after a day's military duties, he would often ride the thirty-odd miles into Staffordshire to inspect the coal mine he owned up there – and still be back again the following morning for exercises with his men.[37]

The Earl wrote to James on 28 July 1801:[38]

I hereby promise to William James, Esq., to pay to him the sum of one hundred and fifty pounds per annum, until he obtains through my interest that sum from Government, in consideration of the services which he has rendered me and my family, and in addition to his agency.[39]

James certainly never got a penny of it from the Earl, so he took his claim to 'Government', writing on 30 August the following year to a Mr Hemans at the War Office in Whitehall:

Dear Sir, I am sorry I am not favoured by you with an answer to my last letter as I am hourly disused for the several Bills due from the Volunteers to the tradesmen and others.

Balance due to me on the pay list
to Dec 24th 1801   £76 13 4

Since that time, officer's pay   £65 0 10

Exclusive of our demand for the General Account terminating 1801 – and the clothing of the Men. Pray, my dear Hemans, answer my letter by return of post.

The trouble was that, by the time he wrote, the Treaty of Amiens had been signed the previous March and everyone assumed that the war against Napoleon was over. Since he was not commissioned on the Army List, James would not strictly be entitled to officer's pay anyway, but he had taken the Earl at his word and he felt he had to try to get some recompense for all his expenses. His family was still trying, years after his death. At the time of the eventual disbandment of his cavalry, James was presented by his fellow officers with a sword worth one hundred guineas, and the Earl wrote to him stating that 'H.R.H. The Duke of York has laid your name before his Majesty for his approbation.'[40]

James had received another honour in March 1802 when he was elected a member of the Royal Society of Arts, Manufactures and Commerce,[41] while the previous year he had been elected as High Bailiff of the Court Leet at Henley-in-Arden, a post he would hold for eighteen years. Yet despite all these other distractions, plus the work of land agency, he still continued his law practice. He had rented an office in Warwick High Street[42] which resulted, according to his daughter, in 'an immense increase in new business', so in 1802 he took on a partner to share the load, a solicitor named Henry Hughes of Warwick.[43] James's somewhat headstrong character was not suited to partnerships and in 1803 he dissolved the arrangement, avowing that he would in the future concentrate solely on land agency. Requests for his services were flooding in from other clients introduced by the Earl, including several of the latter's relations, the Prince Regent himself and the Archbishop of Canterbury. Not for the last time he took on far too much.

Furthermore, James still had ongoing commitments to the Dewes family. Wellesbourne was heavily mortgaged, partly to pay for the purchase of canal shares, and in February 1802 James wrote to Bernard Dewes at length to explain the measures he intended to take to pay off some creditors and obtain new sources of credit:[44]

I have seen several friends who say they shall shortly have Money to put out at interest and I will not fail to engage all I can for you. The Warwick Canal shares are now worth £125 per share and they are not expected to advance much . . . The Napton shares are worth about £130 per share but are expected to advance in value by midsummer. The Stourbridge Canal shares are now £280, but are expected to rise, as also the other shares, as soon as the definitive Treaty is signed,[45] unless too great a quantity is brought to Market, which probably may be the case. I have spoken to two Gents about the coal in your

Swadlingcote Estate, who promised to consider its situation and will shortly give me an answer.

Bernard Dewes replied with instructions to go ahead and on 25 February James wrote to a public notary in Birmingham named Edward Smith, with whom he would have a long and eventually traumatic association.[46] James suggests that they should share the commission.

Though a Land Agent by profession, I do not wish at all to interfere with the sale of canal shares, and therefore shall constantly apply to you on the subject, if we can agree on terms. In giving up sales of this kind, of course, I relinquish a branch of business to another Gent, and it appears but reasonable that I should have some compensation or advantage in that which immediately refers to my own clients and friends.

Among James's other achievements for the Dewes family it is also recorded – a hint of things to come – that he was urging the construction of a 'rail-road' from their Swadlincote colliery to the Ashby Canal.[47]

Deciding that he was unlikely to return to live in Henley-in-Arden, James offered to sell back to William Mills of Barford the 'Yew Trees', the house where he and Dinah had spent the first years of their marriage. On 15 December 1802 he wrote to Mills reminding him that he had originally paid £390 and had spent at least £80 on improvements.

Since the time I purchased it, property at Henley has certainly increased in value.[48] As it has been my intention for some time to sell it unless my father had chosen to have resided there, I have refused several offers of letting . . . have no doubt that it will readily let for £30 per annum. The price I expect to receive is £450 clear of all expenses.[49]

The sale was not quite that straightforward, because one can gather from a letter James wrote the following January to a Mr Lea, attorney of Henley-in-Arden, that a part of his wife's dowry might have been entailed with the original purchase. James could boast that it was irrelevant anyway, because he had:

built a fortune in mines and estates, that has enabled me to make an arrangement which will most amply supply my wife with the comforts of life in case I meet with a premature death; which, on account of the risks I run in exploring mines, bogs and desert places, and the great exertions I am constantly necessitated to make – to meet the wishes of my numerous friends – will most probably be my fate.[50]

As we will see, he would survive these physical dangers (sometimes only just) and outlive his wife, yet it was she who eventually had to sacrifice the last remnants of her dowry in an attempt to avert financial disaster.

Throughout 1802 and 1803, James increasingly refers in his letters to bouts of ill-health, probably brought on both by stress and by the quite incredible amount of travelling he had to do. In August 1802, at the request of Joseph Yates, he made his first visit to Lancashire. The Yates family, based at New Peel Hall, had inherited the eastern portion of the Peel estate near Little Hulton in 1737 and soon afterwards had started to exploit the underground coal assets. Joseph Yates had also taken mining leases on other parts of the estate including those owned by the Revd Mr Kenyon, who resided at Old Peel Hall, together with a property called Common Head Farm.[51] The reason why Yates invited James to the county was that the Duke of Bridgewater had made him an offer of £14,000 for his property and the various mining concessions; he needed the services of the man with a growing reputation for valuing mineral rights.

Coal mining was already a well-established industry in the region, and the installation of flash-locks on the rivers Mersey and Irwell in 1735 had had a dramatic effect on carriage costs. Between Liverpool and Manchester, rates on the new navigation were reduced to around 12s per ton compared to the packhorse rate of £2. The availability of water was, however, always a problem and this, combined with both the rapid growth of industry and the population of Manchester, led to a proposal for a true canal from the Wigan coalfield via Leigh and Salford, which was presented to Parliament in 1754.[52] It failed, and the reason it failed was the committed opposition of landowners along the route, led by Lord Stanley. As William James would find to his discomfort a few years later, this would not be the last time that landed interests would fight to scupper improved transport links.

One family on the other hand were passionate supporters of the proposal: the Egertons of Worsley. Scroop Egerton, the fourth Earl of Bridgewater, had been elevated to a dukedom in 1720, but as a result of tragic mortality among his thirteen offspring, it was Francis Egerton, the fifth

and youngest son, who inherited the title at the age of twelve in 1748. He was a strange child. Suffering desperate ill health and believed by some to be mentally defective, he was placed under the guardianship of his cousin the Duke of Bedford and his brother-in-law Earl Gower, who sent him initially to Eton and then off on the Grand Tour. While in France he saw what Charles Hadfield has described as the 'first modern canal in the world', the Languedoc Canal which linked the Atlantic to the Mediterranean. This remarkable waterway stretched for 150 miles, had numerous locks and aqueducts and had been completed by Louis XIV in 1681. It made a big impression on the young man. Meanwhile, his estates in England were being managed by an outstandingly capable pair of brothers, Thomas and John Gilbert.[53] Francis Egerton assumed full responsibility for the Worsley Estates in 1757 and, having sown his wild oats in London society and on Newmarket Heath and suffered two unfortunate love affairs, threw himself into increasing the output from the Worsley collieries and improving the means of transporting it to the markets of Manchester and Liverpool. In achieving these aims, he was to become one of the pre-eminent entrepreneurs of his age.

By the time William James came to stay on the neighbouring estate in 1802, the Duke had completed his canal from Worsley to Manchester and Runcorn a quarter of a century before. From its very inception, he had introduced the revolutionary concept of taking the canal right inside his underground mine-workings. This served three purposes: not only direct transport access, but also a means of both draining the mines and providing a reservoir of water for the canal. The designs were prepared by John Gilbert and supervised personally by the Duke himself, who had adopted a lifestyle much closer to that of his workers than of his aristocratic neighbours – much to their embarrassment. And there was talk of an even more remarkable invention, an inclined plane deep within the mines, whereby counterbalanced barges could be taken from one level to another without the use of conventional locks.

James was determined to see these wonders for himself. On 10 September 1802 he sought permission from the Duke to visit the workings. It was only granted, rather grudgingly, on the strict understanding that he did not bring his clerk with him, that he was escorted by John Gilbert's successor in the land agency, Benjamin Southern, and that he made no sketches.[54] Perhaps the Duke felt that the new generation of canal proprietors had learnt too much from his pioneering work. In previous years he had certainly been more open in allowing visitors access, and 'Worsley had become the focus of attention for other industrialists and a tourist attraction for the learned and the curious', but he was now in the last year of his life and becoming increasingly cantankerous.[55]

The tour of the underground workings, the twin tunnels – extending over twelve miles – and Gilbert's inclined plane was only a part of James's programme for the weeks he spent in Lancashire that year. He journeyed the whole length of the canal and would certainly have been impressed by the hugely expensive aqueduct over the river Irwell at Barton. He studied the various Acts of Parliament that had had to be pushed through in order to complete the canal. He enquired about the costs of the venture and why it had taken seventeen years to complete. He listened to the complaints of the boatmen about shortage of water at some times of the year. But his main interests were to assess the feasibility of 'laying lines of rail-road' in the region and calculating the potential demands for coal traffic across the whole county. He and his clerk looked at possible routes for railways from Peel to Leigh, and from the Bridgewater Canal to Bolton, Wigan and the Leeds & Liverpool canal. He discussed these possibilities with the Manchester, Bolton & Bury Canal's engineer John Nightingale and the Leeds & Liverpool's engineer Samuel Fletcher[56] and the following year he returned to Lancashire to carry out more detailed surveys. This was the origin of the Bolton & Leigh Railway.

Returning south on 14 September, James wrote to Joseph Yates in some urgency, strongly advising him to refuse the Duke of Bridgewater's miserly offer of £14,000. 'I have seen sufficient of your estate to convince me that it is worth at least £67,000.'[57] He urged that Yates should do nothing until the end of October when he promised to send his full report. If he could save his clients that sort of money, no wonder his services were in increasing demand.

But James's over-riding conclusion from these visits was the need for a direct railway linking Liverpool to Manchester and bypassing the river and canal navigations completely. At the time, the concept was utterly impossible. But here was sown the seed of one of the defining ventures of the 19th century, to which James would return in 1821. As we will see in a later chapter, he would

invest his energies, time and money into this project – and nearly lose his life – only to have the laurels snatched away from him by others.

The Duke of Bridgewater had encountered fierce opposition to his canal from the turnpike trusts as well as from several landowners; any new competitive transport system would have to overcome similar objectors, but now joined by the entrenched canal proprietors as well. James returned south to file his Lancashire experiences at the back of his mind and seek new patrons for his transport revolution. He also took back the memory of a fearsome place which bordered the southern edge of the Worsley and Peel estates, an enormous peat bog which covered 6,000 acres and into which a man could sink without trace. It was called Chat Moss, and twenty years later it would very nearly kill him.

When James had reviewed all the 'Outer' Warwick estates (in Gloucestershire, Northamptonshire, Somerset, Middlesex and rural Warwickshire) he very quickly came to the conclusion that the only area of long-term potential value for its minerals lay at Clutton. This was on the northwest corner of the Somerset coalfield, which was already recognised and exploited, and promised to be a source of serious wealth. The acreages near Wellingborough in Northamptonshire and at Frocester in Gloucestershire had no mineral interests, nor did the farms around Alcester in Warwickshire. The Hackney estate, bordering Vancouver's brick-fields, might have some long-term promise for housing development, but it could be tucked away for now without immediate expenditure. As James understood his brief, he was to use the income generated from these diverse properties for essential maintenance and some improvements, and to invest the balance – and the proceeds of sales – in maximising the potential at Clutton. As far as he was concerned, he was in charge of a self-contained portfolio, without having to subsidise the affairs of the Home Estates or become involved with the politics at the Castle. Those were Vancouver's concern, though James was irritated to note the enormous sums of money being lavished on Vancouver's grace-and-favour residence at Tachbrook House. The relationship between the two agents was becoming increasingly strained. James also assumed that the Earl was a free agent to authorise plans submitted to him; he still had no idea of the restrictive terms of the various trusts. He was about to receive a rude shock.

THREE

Clutton, Resignation and 'The Finest Situation in the Kingdom' (1803–1805)

CLUTTON was an exciting prospect, but there were two immediate problems. First, the mining concessions had been leased out on most unsatisfactory terms – the freeholds would have to be bought back. Secondly, there was very poor access. Although the closest coalmine to Bristol on the map, Clutton was actually the furthest in terms of existing communications, namely the Somerset Coal Canal.

This waterway was adding to the prosperity of other mines in the coalfield at Paulton, Timsbury and Radstock, but Clutton, several hundred feet above its western end, did not even have a connection to it. James concluded that what was needed was a direct railroad from Clutton to the river Avon at Keynsham, and the first step was to try to purchase land around Chelwood which would open a route down to the valley of the river Chew. Early in 1803, he started urgent and secret negotiations with the owner, the Rt. Hon. J. Hiley Addington MP, brother of the then Prime Minister, Henry Addington.[58]

On 3 April 1803 James wrote to the Earl of Warwick in great excitement.

> I have the satisfaction to inform your Lordship that I have succeeded in purchasing Mr Addington's Estate adjoining to Clutton, by which I will prove to the conviction of my bitterest enemy that I have obtained to your Lordship a clear bonus of at least £20,000 in its present state. Its ultimate value is too magnificent for me to state at this time. I am alarmed myself at its magnitude . . . I shall have the honour to report to your Lordship respecting this Estate as soon as I have surveyed it again, but I have seen sufficient to convince me that it will be more wise to sell Warwick Castle than to part with Chelwood on any terms . . . The whole purchase money is £13,650, which includes timber, of which £5,000 may remain upon mortgage.

> I am convinced that there are mines of lime and coal of great value in the Estate.[59]

James had also negotiated way-leaves through other properties covering three miles of his intended railroad, which would open up the markets in Bristol and Bath for 'all the coals which can be drawn' and 'from being the last in the market, will meet the trade on better terms than any other mines on the Somerset Coal canal.' New mines were opening in South Wales to supply the Bristol market, but if the

> vast plan which I have projected for your Lordship is successful, I am convinced that those very Coal-masters who have proposed the destruction of your Clutton works will in some future period be soliciting permission to bring their coals through your 'funnel' and along the rail-road at a large tonnage, rather than navigate them along the Coal Canal.

His scheme would revolutionise the whole economics of the Somerset coalfield. He praises the endeavours of the Duke of Bridgewater, despite their immense cost. 'The next greatest work in this Kingdom will be at Clutton – we shall also have many difficulties to encounter – but we shall not sink one fiftieth part of the capital' expended by the Duke.

In an earlier letter, the Earl had evidently mentioned some invention by an impoverished Mr Eckhardt, which inspired James to launch into one of his masonic homilies.

> The machine which Mr Eckhart proposes is a most invaluable discovery, and is applicable to all the purposes that your Lordship describes.[60] It is a disgrace to the Government of any country that such men should ever feel distress, but it is so ordered by the Allwise Being that the men who are the greatest Benefactors of the human race should be the worst provided for, and for

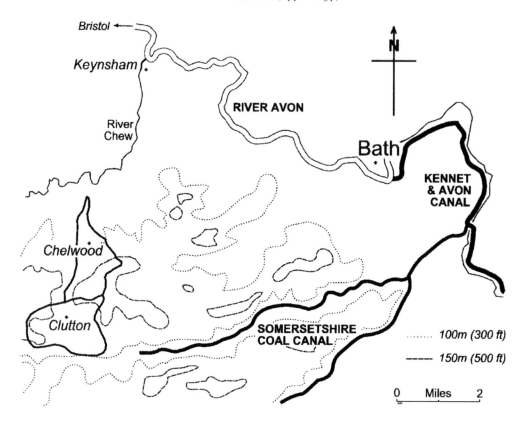

Fig.2: **The location of the Earl of Warwick's estate at Clutton, illustrating the importance of the Chelwood estate on the route of James's proposed railway to Keynsham and the impracticality of linking the Clutton mines to the Somersetshire Coal Canal.**

the wisest of reasons. For so indolent are we in our affluent circumstances, that excepting a few astronomers and painters, it is almost a truism that Genius is reared in the cradle of adversity.

This rather pompous paragraph, and the one that follows, are included here for three reasons. Firstly, James will return to this theme about the lack of recognition for 'initiators' at the very end of his life, and then with a very personal axe to grind. The second is that he now feels that he has himself joined the ranks of those in affluent circumstances. And the third is that he makes one of the most ridiculous commitments of his whole life.

I thank God I have been enabled to make a very ample fortune for my children and I

am content . . . My head and my heart are constantly fixed at Clutton and *I never intend to embark in new speculations.*

By early July 1804, personal relationships within the Warwick agencies were reaching boiling point. On 7 July James wrote to John Forster, of Messrs Forster, Cooke & Frere, the trustees' solicitor at Lincoln's Inn, London, expressing his concerns that Vancouver is assuming more and more extravagant control over the Earl's affairs while his own loyalty and hard work to rectify the Earl's finances are being sidelined. He then asks for instructions to proceed with the sale of the Frocester estate, already approved by the Earl, and goes on to suggest that the Wellingborough estate should also be earmarked for sale, along with the outlying estates in Warwickshire. He estimates that all these properties might raise as much as £170,000, 'ample to pay the debts and [secure] the fortunes of the younger children.'

> I have not a doubt that there is property of the value of many hundreds of pounds within Warwick itself, which is not known to belong to the family. The Evidence Room is in the greatest confusion, scarcely a tithe distinct, and there is no perfect plan of any part of the Estate. I was going to arrange the evidences, deeds etc and make a correct inventory, also specifying the Tythes, but I have been so constantly and eternally interrupted by Mr Vancouver, tormenting me with his squabbles, that I never can be at peace in the county.

The reason this letter is discussed here in some detail is that it shows that James was developing a sound financial strategy. He mirrored this with his other clients; but if he was not in overall control he wanted to have nothing to do with it.

James now had a revealing meeting in London with John Forster, who explained to him all the restrictions of the various trusts. Luckily, James and Forster got on well; they not only respected each other, they became good friends and over the years Forster would recommend James to a number of his other clients. Forster pointed out that there was no way that the trustees would agree to a quick sale of the Outer Estates until a complete review of the outstanding liabilities had been prepared. So in July 1803 the trustees drew up yet another long document to try once again to regularise the Earl's affairs, and now they appointed James as 'Receiver of All Rents'. He had finally and convincingly beaten his 'worst enemy' and Vancouver, if he was to keep his job, had to deliver to him a gross rental income of £7,500 a year and full accounts.

James's new status had solved his major problem, but in the short term he had the acute embarrassment of having to admit to Addington that he could not yet deliver the cash for the deal on which they had shaken hands. This was very painful to a man of James's high principles, but Addington seems to have been amazingly forbearing until completion finally took place in the summer of 1804. He even confided to James that he was looking for a new home and perhaps James could keep his eye open for something suitable. It just so happened that James had recently received the details of a most interesting estate in South Wales, near the town of Brecon. It was called Trebinshun, and to James it looked a very interesting bargain. He therefore negotiated

an exclusive deal with the vendors whereby he could offer it on to Addington, with the option of buying the adjoining farmland known as Little Trebinshun. Admittedly the house needed modernising, but it lay in a peaceful valley, there were 300 acres of good pasture-land with fine views over the Brecon Beacons, and James believed it fitted the bill perfectly. James, in informing Addington of this, added an interesting slant on contemporary politics.

> You will be pleased to observe that I have contracted to give £7,000 for the absolute purchase of the fee simple and inheritance of the Estate called Great Trebinshun. I am just returned from a journey to Manchester and Birmingham . . . I have had the opportunity of ascertaining the sentiment of the principal persons at those places on the reconciliation which has been effected between your brother and Mr Pitt. Opinion is unanimous in hailing the event as a great accession of strength to the King's Government.

In December 1803 James returned prematurely from a trip to Yorkshire. He was by his own account dangerously ill, yet from his sickbed he continued to dictate a stream of letters to his clerk, Joseph Povey. One of the most urgent was to Vancouver, pressing for the £3,750 'as ordered by the arbitrators to be paid' and in March 1804 he had to write again, asking him to 'supply rentals and arrears as early as possible, specifying not only rents, but species and extent of tenements.' Both requests fell on stony ground. Matters finally came to a head in June 1804 when James wrote a very long letter to the Earl tendering his resignation.[61] It starts by saying that he had sold part of the Frocester estate for £13,020 while increasing the rent from the remainder by £200 per annum. He then urges that the Earl should not be unduly alarmed by 'the immense debt which I have particularized in my report, and which I am convinced does not include the whole of the debts due from your father.' Further sales could bring in a fortune, though he implores the Earl not to be hassled into a forced sale of the Hackney estate, which was being proposed by a Mr Butt,[62] a proposition which James suggests is made either from 'ignorance or sinister design . . . and injurious to your Lordship and the family.' Then the elastic snaps. He is clearly on the verge of a nervous breakdown.

> I have now devoted the best years of my life to the service of your Lordship's family,

[and you must know] that I have been attentive to your interests and made my best exertions to serve you. I have sacrificed every comfort of my life as a husband and parent . . . but to endure eternal anxiety, to be subjected to mortification, insults and injuries, without the power to remedy them, is a state of misery and degradation to which I hope I shall never again be forced to submit. I'm compelled by the duty I owe to my family and my own character, to notify your Lordship and through you to my invaluable friends and the Trustees that I shall be very greatly obliged by you all if you will please accept my resignation . . . I must plainly state that my health and feelings will not allow much longer this state of complete misery. God forbid that your Lordship should think that my intentions are to create confusion greater than we are at present submitted to. I entreat your Lordship to excuse this long letter and consider me at all times, Your obedient and humble servant, W. James.

As well as this passage, which occupies only a fraction of it, the letter states that James had devoted the entire year (1803) to the Warwick business, apart from a mere sixteen days for his other clients (although one has to say that this is a whopping understatement). He suggests that to cover all the aspects of his present role it would be necessary to appoint three separate individuals, with a warning to beware of the 'scavengers of the present day.'[63] His concern about missing out on his family life is also revealing – his wife had borne him another son on 16 November 1802 and, in honour of the Earl who agreed to be a godfather, the child had been christened George Walter. According to James's daughter, the Earl offered to give the child a christening present of Myton House, just outside Leamington Spa, and its surrounding park. She says that 'her father's principles would not allow him to accept the gift' but the real reason, of course, was that the Earl was absolutely forbidden to do any such thing under the restrictions of the trust.[64]

On 29 June 1804 the trustees duly met. They had before them James's latest estimate of the Earl's debts, which amounted to 'at least £108,000, exclusive of the £50,000 portion charged upon the estate,' and his calculation that the estates would yield an income — net of expenses, repayment of mortgages and maintenance charges – of only £2,064, which was about £7,000 short of the total of the annuities awarded to the Warwick

family and other retainers. At the conclusion of the meeting they drew up a minute to the affect that unless the family agreed to a sharp reduction in the annuities and the Earl agreed to his adopting a plan of 'retirement', they would have no option but 'to seek their own discharge and surrender into the hands of the Court of Chancery,' which would result in 'extreme embarrassment and distress, and the most ruinous and degrading consequences.'

One wonders whether James really wanted his resignation to be accepted, or whether he was merely holding a pistol to the trustees' heads and hoping that it might go off in Vancouver's face. He had a number of other irons in the fire. He wrote to Addington on 21 July with more details about how Trebinshun might be financed, ending with a warning that it might be difficult to communicate with him over the next two weeks. He was going up to Manchester, then Durham, Yorkshire and Lincolnshire, but a letter might find him if addressed via John Hall at Scarborough; in August he would be visiting North Wales, South Wales and Somerset.

Addington replied to James that he was extremely grateful for the offer of Trebinshun, but could not take the matter further since he had independently contracted to buy an alternative property at Langford Court near Bristol. Released from his obligation to his client, James was now free to conclude the purchase on his own behalf; he could think about relocating his family far from the exasperations of Warwick and starting a completely new phase in his career. While he waited for the trustees' decision, he wrote to one of his clerks, John Kershaw, on 11 August in a mood of scarcely contained excitement.[65]

As I have never treated you merely as a clerk or assistant, but considered you in the light of a friend, I shall communicate to you a matter of the greatest confidence, relying on your secrecy that no person should be informed of my intention. Having the offer of some large agencies in Wales and perceiving that I cannot render for Lord Warwick any efficient service so long as a certain person influences his conduct, I have been for some time looking out for a situation in that Country, and have at length found one, which I have purchased. I offered it to my friend Mr Addington, but he cannot accept it on account of the Title to another Estate. This I am very glad of, as it has afforded me the opportunity of showing my disposition to serve him and at the

same time of ultimately serving myself.
The Estate I have purchased consists of a
good mansion house and farm-house
adjoining and 300 acres of land of excellent
quality, and about 40 acres of woodland.
The house is at present uninhabited and
wants some repairs.

One of the agencies he refers to was with Sir
Edward Smythe, who had let Wootton Hall and
taken over his family's estate at Acton Burnell in
Shropshire. They had corresponded in July, and
one paragraph is illuminating as it shows that
James was anxious to dissociate himself from
his own father's reputation for rash speculation.
'Having had no correspondence with my father
for many years on business, you may be assured
that I am free from his prejudices.'

James completed the purchase of Trebinshun
in October and he wrote to Addington on the
27th in a buoyant mood, stating that he thought
Trebinshun was 'the finest situation in the
kingdom' and that he and his wife were hoping to
move in by Christmas. Now perhaps he could
look forward to enjoying the life of a country
squire. His mine at Wednesbury was bringing in
a decent income, he had several land agencies
with clients who were far less complicated and
demanding than the Earl of Warwick (including
the first overtures from the Earl of Dartmouth at
Sandwell Hall, West Bromwich) and he had plans
to rebuild Trebinshun as an elegant mansion in
the contemporary style. Perhaps he would have
time to explore his idea that the massive coalfields of the valleys south of the Brecon Beacons
might extend further north, to lie hidden below
his own fields

Thus ended a turbulent year. Napoleon was
dominating Europe, England was back on invasion
alert and James had (he thought) resigned from
his responsibilities to the Warwick family, but his
main concern in the run-up to Christmas was that
the fires should be lit in the grates at Trebinshun
and that the beds should be well aired.

James's retirement was not to last long. In early
1805 yet another trust memorandum was drawn
up for the Earl of Warwick's somewhat enforced
signature and James, perhaps reluctantly, perhaps
with some satisfaction, was persuaded to continue
not only as Receiver of Rents but also as the sole
agent for all the Warwick estates. He negotiated
some new terms which allowed him a fixed
salary for the first year of £300 plus £50 for his
clerk. There was certainly an understanding
about a limit on the time he would devote to the
Warwick affairs. He was already renting an
office in London at 14 Carey Street, and now he
relocated into larger and more prestigious premises
around the corner in New Boswell Court,
Lincoln's Inn.[66] These offices and apartments
would become his base every spring, when it was
important for his clients' business that he was
close to the seat of government. He charged half
the rent, £29 2s, against the Warwick Trust, plus
one guinea per day expenses. One of the days he
clocked up was for 'Attending Lord Warwick
about an indenture at Hill Street House and the
difficulties he labours under for want of money.'[67]
At least the Earl did eventually, in 1805, get one
legal opinion in his favour: counsel ruled that he
was entitled to the proceeds of any sales of timber
from properties sold to settle his debts, and James
would recall this precedent when he took on his
next agency, the one that would both make him
and eventually break him.

James had made his first review of the estates
of the Earl of Dartmouth in early 1805, although
he had to confess that his report was delayed
because he had been 'grievously afflicted with an
abscess in my head which affects my sight and
hearing, occasioned by exposure to cold and severe
weather.'[68] The Earl's seat was at Sandwell Park,
West Bromwich, a few miles north-west of Birmingham, and there the 'Home Estates' extended over
a large acreage in South Staffordshire around
Wednesbury, a region where there were already a
number of early coal mines, including that
owned by James himself. The Earl also had a
number of outlying properties. Typically, the
whole lot was heavily mortgaged, and equally
typically, James took an immediate dislike to the
incumbent steward, a Mr Wright, who James
considered to be both indolent and inefficient.
James's plan for the Earl was based on his hallmark
strategy of selling the outlying properties and
concentrating the resources on exploiting the
coal. But, as he had found at Warwick, there were
major snags, since the outlying estates were
entailed either to mortgagees, the Court of
Chancery or complex trusts. There was however
one potential source of instant revenue, and
James latched on to the precedent established for
the Earl of Warwick – selling the timber. On 8
April 1805 the standing timber at Friar's Park and
Hill Farm was put up for auction in five lots and,
as anticipated, the bidders had got together to
form a ring, each agreeing not to bid against the
others. James would have none of this nonsense,
as he recounted to the Earl the following day.

I have been so long used to find the Estates
of the Nobility surrounded by a lot of

interested and ignorant men that I always calculate upon their combinations and conspiracies against any measure I suggest. It requires a considerable degree of firmness in a Principal, and a certain degree of patience and consistency in an Agent, to force down old practices and break asunder the bands of prejudice which fetter most ancient estates.

James had taken the precaution of having each lot independently valued and told the bidders that he had set a reserve on each, sufficient to allow genuine buyers a fair profit, but not the cosy 'rip-off' margins they had been accustomed to. As another part of his master plan, James suggested that his clerk, John Kershaw, should be appointed to the role of Home Steward. 'His timidity is very great, but I have a strong idea that he will be found equal to the task.' The appointment would prove to be a great success and Kershaw later married the governess to the Earl's children.

Over the next three years James supervised, from a distance, slow but steady improvements in the Dartmouth finances, though the major exploitation of the fabulous West Bromwich 'ten yard' coal seam would be undertaken not by the Earl as principal, but by James himself as a leasing contractor, taking on – with borrowed money – the financial responsibility for the heavy capital investment. This phase of James's career is so important, so crucial, that it deserves separate consideration, and it will be covered in Chapter 8.

At Warwick, there were a few loose ends to tidy up. Vancouver had persuaded the Earl to join him in two extravagant speculations. One involved a coalmining venture near Llanelly in South Wales,[69] the other a factory at Tachbrook to make a new form of soap for the navy, patented by the Earl himself and which supposedly worked in salt water. This was based on fuller's earth, a seam of which had been discovered by Vancouver during drainage operations nearby. He had brought in a Dutchman by the name of Van Doornik who proved to be a complete crook, effectively stealing the patents for his own use, and the whole venture proved a fiasco. James found himself having to extricate the Earl from a contract to supply fuller's earth to the felt works at Atherstone owned by Abraham Bracebridge.

In early 1806 James received a very significant increment to his authority. Yet another set of trust deeds was drawn up by indentures dated 22 April, with James effectively given power of attorney over 'all Manor-ships, Tenements etc. in the Counties of Warwick, Somerset, Gloucester, Northampton and Middlesex.'[70] He was charged – by the trustees, not the Earl – 'to make and effect all necessary and proper repairs and improvements in and upon such estates.'

James now instigated the drawing-up of the first detailed map and plan of the town of Warwick.[71] This had a dual purpose, because by recording the owners and residents in each individual property, it made the task of rent and tithe assessment much easier. James himself is shown to be both the proprietor and occupier of a large house and grounds in Old Mill Lane, opposite St John's House.[72] It was an elegant family residence, with extensive gardens and an ornamental lake on which the young William Henry would later carry out his own engineering experiments with boat propulsion. James is also recorded as being the owner or tenant of several other properties around Coton End.

James would never return to live at Trebinshun. The builders moved in during the spring of 1805 and rebuilt the main part of the house as the classical Georgian mansion that exists today, later described as a residence fit for 'a family of respectability, a very large sum having been lately spent upon it, with every regard to comfort and convenience'[73] (plate 3b). He rented it to Capt Edward Hamilton RN, later Admiral Sir Edward, and eventually sold the whole estate to him in 1814 for 'upwards of £20,000.'[74]

James was shortly about to embark on an extraordinary 'adventure', and, to appreciate why he did this, it is helpful to understand rather more about the way in which he and his contemporaries viewed the physical world around them. He was becoming increasingly preoccupied with the business of locating and exploiting the minerals that lay beneath his clients' land. This needed new skills, new ways of looking at a landscape, and James was already a self-taught practitioner in the art and primitive science of geology.

FOUR

Fossils, Strata
and a Venture in Sussex
(1806)

WILLIAM JAMES'S perception and understanding of the physical world around
him would have been very different
from ours. About 520 million years ago, geologists
now believe, the rock formations that were
eventually to form the basis of England and Wales
were located on the edge of a vast continent near
the South Pole. This is classified as the Cambrian
period and the continent is called by the
somewhat Tolkeinesque name of Gondwana.
Scotland, as always, was quite distinct, lying on
the southern edge of another continent, Laurentia,
several thousand miles nearer the equator on the
opposite side of the Iapetus Ocean.[75]

Over the following geological periods, tectonic-
plate movements saw these two separate land
structures migrate northward. They are believed
to have met and joined, near the equator, in the
so-called Devonian period, about 380–400 million
years ago. Life was evolving fast in this era, with
fish and molluscs in the rivers and oceans, and
plants on the land. Certain insects had even
developed the ability to fly, which provided
plants with an enhanced route for pollination.
Without predation from grazing animals, all
forms of plant life prospered luxuriantly. For the
next 100 million years much of the British Isles lay
under tropical swamps, building up layer after
layer of rotting vegetation, itself to be buried and
compressed under new sediments as the
continents re-coalesced in the Permian and
Triassic periods. Forced against each other by the
seething tectonic power-house, layers of existing
rocks and minerals sheared and folded, fused and
shattered in a massive process of metamorphosis.
The plant material became coal and anthracite.
Where the structure and permeability of the
surrounding rocks allowed, the more volatile
products of decomposition became trapped as
pockets of natural gas, while the intermediate
products, rich in chemicals, produced the oil fields.

It is now understood that, every hundred
million years or so, some cataclysmic disaster

occurred, destroying virtually all life species
existing at that time. A few massive meteor or
comet strikes are known to have occurred,
causing overwhelming climate changes of which
the most famous, at the end of the Cretaceous
period, probably led to the extinction of the
dinosaurs. Other extinctions may have been
caused by huge volcanic activity, resulting in the
release of clouds of sulphur dioxide and other
poisonous gases. Pockets of life would survive,
but the plants and animals of the succeeding
era would be distinct from those that came before.
Basic life cycles remained the same however;
birth, growth, reproduction and finally death.
The bodies of marine animals sank into the
sediments of oceans and lagoons, streams and
swamps, to be petrified under successive layers
of silt into what we understand to be fossils.

The earth underwent long, slow cycles of
temperature change. Ice ages came and went,
interspersed with periods of high average
temperatures that turned soil into deserts and
evaporated oceans into salt-pans. Floods and
gales, hurricanes and howling sandstorms
eroded the surface of the earth; creeping glaciers
transported shattered mountain-tops into rock-
strewn valleys.

To William James and his generation, however,
the landscape of Britain was a wonder and a
mystery, its beauty and variety yet another
manifestation of the infinite power and wisdom
of Almighty God. Although men like James
Hutton[76] had begun to question whether the
process of structural evolution might have taken
a very long time, most people accepted Bishop
Ussher's analysis that the world had been created
in 4004BC.

Quite a number of people started collecting
fossils as objects of curiosity, the beautiful great
snail-like ammonites found along the cliffs of
Dorset enhancing many a fashionable gallery
among the works of art collected on a Grand
Tour of the continent. Another incidental effect of

the war with France was that the 'Grand Tour' became virtually impossible, so the gentry had to turn their attention to travelling in their own country. The Peak and Lake Districts, the Yorkshire Dales and the Cotswolds encountered their first tourist boom. Everywhere there seemed to be different types of rock, different-coloured building stones. Furthermore, in many places there were local entrepreneurial traders offering those strange fossils for sale as souvenirs.

There was one particular fossil collector whose life was to impinge on that of William James in a most significant way, and whose career was to have a number of uncanny parallels with his, though their backgrounds and upbringing could hardly have been more different. He was William Smith, the farm labourer in Oxfordshire, born the eldest son of a blacksmith just two years before James in 1769.

It is not known how or when they first met, but by 1799 William Smith had developed some revolutionary ideas on how rocks were formed, the sequences in which they had been deposited, and how they might be dated by the presence, or absence, of fossils in different layers or strata. His experiences from cutting the Somersetshire Coal Canal, and from descending mine shafts in the nearby coalfields, convinced him that there was a pattern to the way that different strata succeeded each other. The landscape of the region south of Bath showed evidence of a tortured birth – outcrops of various rock formations thrusting themselves through the surface, sometimes in gently sloping inclinations, sometimes in almost vertical waves. And the pattern of layers seemed to be repeated, both underground and at similar outcrops maybe several miles away. Wherever a seam of coal occurred, for example, the type of rock immediately above it always appeared to be the same. Below it, although the rock type was different from that above, the consistency remained. By mapping the various outcrops and the angles at which they declined, might it not be possible to predict what lay under the surface at considerable distances away, and, moreover, at what depth? Was this pattern repeated elsewhere, not just in Somerset? Could one, perhaps, by tracing and studying surface outcrops, produce a map of the basic geology of the whole country? William Smith had set out to check whether his instincts were right, travelling as far as he could afford to, and by 1800, he was sufficiently encouraged by his findings to decide on publishing a map of his results. To pay for it, he started a subscription list, which William James had heard about through the grapevine of the

various Agricultural Societies that were springing up in every county. He had already received a copy of Smith's pioneering report of 1799, *Order of the Strata in the Vicinity of Bath . . . of such Shells etc occupying a series of 23 of the principal strata which are enumerated therein.*[77]

Unselfish in his encouragement of the talents of others, James was quick to recognise that such a map might be extremely useful to anyone involved in estate management, and he apparently solicited support for William Smith from some of his professional colleagues. But he had major reservations about the way Smith was going about his great project. Some of these were practical matters of confidentiality, some were concerns that an 'innocent' would be exploited by people less scrupulous than James,[78] while others arose from a righteous and rather pompous indignation that this 'peasant' was questioning fundamental tenets of the Christian faith.

His first letter to Smith that has survived is dated 7 Oct 1800,[79] and it throws some fascinating light, not always flattering, on the 29-year-old William James whose colleagues, one suspects, must have found him rather a prig. He warns Smith about the character of most land agents – 'I hate the whole tribe of them, believing and knowing them to be a set of scoundrels' – and then, admitting that he is perhaps 'singular in his moral views', he launches into a sermon about retaining 'Integrity, Rectitude and Honour'. Finally he becomes more political, detecting in Smith a possibly dangerous radicalism of the sort that had fuelled the French Revolution. The bloody horrors of the Reign of Terror, the public executions and the massacre of the French aristocracy were fresh in everyone's mind. '*Beware of Democratic Principles*' he warns, before signing off with effusions of friendship and an invitation to visit him.

In November 1801, when Smith was working at Woburn Abbey with John Farey (who will reappear shortly in a 'nemesis' role), he wrote to James that he hoped to see him soon and that he had encouraging news about his observations and the subscription list.

My different journeys into Norfolk, North Wales, Staffordshire etc have enabled me to complete such an accurate outline of the various Strata as you will be much pleased to see. I have got a very respectable list of subscribers and shall be glad to add such names as you have been kind enough to collect, and remain, Sir, Your very much obliged servant, Wm Smith.

It seems likely that James's next letter to Smith (now describing himself as a land surveyor and living, very much beyond his means, at 15 Buckingham Street, London) was written on 25 January 1805. It is another sermon, however kindly meant, and one can detect a strong masonic undercurrent to its language. His tone is benignly patronising. He warns Smith of the dangers of 'World Making', of trying to devise theories from his observations of strata without recognising that the Creator moves in mysterious and unpredictable ways. The example James quotes about the location of coal seams is particularly piquant, because the following year he would embark on a scheme of potentially national importance. He set out to open a new coal mine – in Sussex.

To present-day readers, and to many of William James's contemporaries, the very idea of sinking a coal mine on the coast of Sussex would appear to be palpable lunacy. But when in 1805 workmen digging wells for a new military barracks near Bexhill hit a layer of black carbonaceous material, James agreed with a local entrepreneur, Joseph Routledge, that this might be the clue to a more extensive coal resource beneath. And there were several compelling reasons why he urged immediate, and expensive, action.[80]

The first was that Sussex desperately needed a new source of fuel. Until the 18th century the Weald of Sussex and Kent was the most important iron-producing region in the whole country, but by 1800 the industry was in terminal decline because all the local timber to manufacture charcoal had been destroyed.[81] The focus on iron-making had migrated to Shropshire, South Wales and the Black Country and, until disrupted by the war, more than half of domestic consumption was supplied by imports from Sweden and Russia. If coal was found in quantity, the entire local economy would be rejuvenated. More immediately, there was an urgent military demand for millions of bricks. In 1804, with the Sussex coast on invasion alert, the government was building a string of defensive Martello towers in addition to the new barracks and, although the clay for the bricks was no problem, the fuel to fire them was.

Secondly, 1,124 acres of the land around Bexhill[82] – including that requisitioned for the barracks – was owned by the Duchess of Dorset, the wife of William James's wealthy client and friend Charles, Baron Whitworth. The friendship would later be cemented when he became godfather to the James's fourth son, born on 25 March 1808 and christened Frederick Whitworth Tarleton

James. Whitworth had had a successful diplomatic career as ambassador at the court of Catherine the Great in St Petersburg, but was sacked by her son Paul in 1800 after a row about Malta. In 1801 Whitworth had married the widowed Duchess of Dorset, whose mother had herself married Lord Liverpool the second time around. As beneficiary from the Duke's death in 1799, she had the enormous annual income of £13,000. After the Peace of Amiens in 1802 Whitworth was appointed ambassador to Paris, his wife giving her French hosts the impression of a typical haughty aristocrat 'with tight lips and a square, determined jaw.'[83] Despite his diplomatic skills, Whitworth became involved in a number of high-profile rows with Napoleon before finally being given his passport the week before war was resumed in May 1803.

By October 1805, James had completed an extensive survey of the coastal region of Sussex and Kent and had explored the wells already sunk. The following month he submitted to the Duchess a sixteen-page report on his findings, covering the deposits of iron ore (which were already known to exist) and his impression that he had found ample evidence of the possibility of underground layers of coal, though he admitted these were based only on 'superficial indications'. He was probably also influenced by earlier suggestions from others that coal might lie under land at Ashdown Park and St Leonard's Forest. There were no surface outcrops as there were in Somerset to help plot the location of coal seams, and he was humble enough to admit that 'at present our knowledge on the subject is so very limited that the wisest Man and most experienced Miner must confess he is just beginning to learn.' Whether any coal seams were thick enough to be recovered at a profit could only be determined by sinking shafts, but he concluded that if he was right,

the income . . . would be immense . . .
from the Value [these mines] will give
to the surface of the Bexhill estate, by
the establishment of an Harbour and
of Furnaces, Foundries and other
Manufactories which prevail in a County
abounding, as I conceive this does, with
valuable minerals. Then we may say to
our political Enemy we also have a Coast
of Iron!

His fee for the survey and report was £95, and at the end of November he travelled to London to discuss the next moves with the Duchess, Lord Whitworth and their solicitor – John Forster again. James had two concerns. The first was one of secrecy, because he feared that opposition to the scheme might be stirred up in the north-east, if coal interests there felt their supplies to London threatened by a successful outcome. Secondly, he was anxious that they should somehow involve Sir Horace Mann, who owned neighbouring estates between Bexhill and Hastings. As he wrote to Forster on 28 January 1806, 'I do not approve of exciting a spirit of adventure in the Natives until we have secured all the land'. It was agreed that an Act of Parliament should be sought to enable mining leases to be granted, and James and Forster drafted the Bill, which was examined by a House of Lords committee in April 1806. When James appeared before this committee he was, for security reasons, deliberately less emphatic about the prospects for coal than he had been in his report to the Duchess, but he gave greater emphasis to the prospects for minerals in general. The following month the House of Commons passed the Bill, unamended, and the Sussex Mining Company was officially on its way, although trial borings had already been started in anticipation of a successful outcome.

There were eleven shareholders in the syndicate, of whom ten can be identified, which suggests that somebody had two shares.

1. John Bagnall (1759–1829), an iron- and coal-master from West Bromwich.
2. Samuel Bill (1773–1847), a coal merchant from West Bromwich and a lifelong friend and confidant of James, for whom he worked as agent at the Pelsall colliery at Walsall from 1813. He would suffer bankruptcy in 1821 and will recur later in the story. Bill was to be the mining manager at Bexhill.
3. Samuel Fereday (1758–1839) of Ettingshall Park, Staffordshire, banker, coal owner and iron-master who also went bankrupt, in 1817 and again in 1821. He fled, like many men in his position, to France, possibly owing James a lot of money.
4. John Forster (1752–1834), the company solicitor.
5. Mr Peyton. The identity of this enigmatic character is unknown. From documents of 1809, he clearly had a legal interest in the structure of the partnership; he may have been a nominee from the government, which would have had a keen strategic interest in the outcome,[84] or he might have represented the interests of the company bankers.

6. Josiah Routledge (1791–1822), who had been instrumental in suggesting to the Dorset trustees that William James should be called in initially. He died in Dieppe in 1822, which suggests that he too may have gone bankrupt.
7. Nicholas Vansittart MP (1766-1851), then secretary to the Treasury. He would not only become James's partner in two collieries in West Bromwich, but also Chancellor of the Exchequer 1812–23.
8. Arabella Diana, Duchess of Dorset.
9. Charles, Baron Whitworth.
10. William James.

The first workings were on the cliff-tops to the south-east of the town. Trial borings were made by the somewhat crude method of sinking a narrow shaft with large crowbars (boring bars), a process that pulverised the rock and made it difficult to detect any subtle changes in strata. But the speculators, egged on by their own enthusiasm and that which echoed back to them in the local press, were already committed to making an expensive full-size shaft in parallel. Encouragement also came from no less a luminary than Matthew Boulton, James Watt's partner. 'Cursory observations which I was enabled to make,' he said, 'incline me strongly to think that there are coal measures at Bexhill.'[85]

In June 1806 the borers penetrated what appeared to be a 3ft seam of coal at a depth of 164ft, but the sea flooded in and now they would have to invest in steam-powered pumping engines. The first of these, probably the one which, to save time, was transferred from James's colliery in Staffordshire,[86] proved totally inadequate and was replaced by a much larger, more expensive engine of 80 horsepower, probably from Boulton's Soho Works in Birmingham. But it was a losing battle and the first shaft was abandoned, to be replaced by another nearly 100ft higher up on Bexhill Down at the northern extremity of the Dorset estate. This was almost a mile inland, surely far enough from the sea to avoid the flooding problem, even if the shaft had to be considerably deeper. This second shaft was well under way when John Farey arrived on the scene in September. This polymath was undertaking a 'stratigraphic cross-section' of the county on behalf of Sir Joseph Banks, the President of the Royal Society, and his first impressions were very favourable.

William James . . . is a miner of the first repute. These works have proceeded with a degree of spirit and enterprise which has placed all the eastern parts of the county on the tip-toe of expectation ... We sincerely hope that no circumstance will occur to damp the ardour of the parties in this interesting search after an article of such general interest as fossil coal.[87]

But when he examined the specimens of material from the borings, he became far more guarded, as he wrote in a letter to his friend William Smith on 29 September describing his visit to 'these quixotic works.' He concludes that the carbonaceous material is not real coal anyway, merely 'bituminous wood' and that below it there is only 'sandy or grit rock'.

James meanwhile was desperate to press on with the second shaft, writing to his friend and iron-smith William Whitmore in Birmingham with urgent requests for more boring rods.[88] 'Conceiving this a very important crisis, I am, I confess very anxious to get the hole proved in my presence. I have been excessively ill with agueish symptoms; violent fever arising from exposure over Lambeth Marsh' (see Chapter 6). 'I still continue extremely unwell, but have not time to rest myself ... I must work night and day until I recover this time.'

James could not have ignored an acrimonious correspondence which was occupying the pages of the *Monthly Magazine*, the *Agriculturist Magazine* and the *Sussex Weekly Advertiser* in early 1807. John Farey was now saying, at first anonymously, that the venturers in the Sussex Mining Company, by ignoring the lessons of stratigraphy expounded by himself and William Smith, were wasting their time. On the other hand, Cater Rand, a schoolmaster, engineer, surveyor and self-appointed local expert, was trumpeting that their cause was 'laudable' and that Farey 'was lugging in what he does not understand, in a most illiberal, invidious and un-gentlemanly style.' Public arguments continued through 1808 and into 1809, Farey noticing with hardly concealed self-righteousness the 'error which has occasioned the useless expenditure ... of thousands of pounds ... in the vicinity of Bexhill.'[89]

In July 1809 Samuel Bill reported to the proprietors on the strata encountered at various depths by a third sinking at Cooden, which had gone down to 451ft but still without striking coal. John Forster had by now declared his intention to pull out of the venture and, at a further meeting in August, James presented the (almost) terminal accounts. The problem of flooding had continued, and the pumping engines had cost £120 a week in fuel costs alone and were worn out, although they were still on the asset register

at near their purchase price. Income was nil. Total costs had amounted to £30,754 and calls of only £700 per share had been made, leaving shareholders and their bankers with substantial outstanding liabilities. For some this would prove to be the last straw, although the account books of Knole (the Sackville family seat in Kent) note the payment of £1,200 to the Sussex Mining Co in 1809 almost as if it was a mere item of petty cash.[90] James was not really embarrassed either. He had been paid £200 for various land agency services to the Duchess in 1807, followed by £300 per annum in 1808 and 1809, and he was about to get a commission from the sale of a local property.[91]

The coal venture at Bexhill had been an unmitigated disaster, but it was only one of numerous projects occupying James in the years 1806–09, projects which would range from Warwick to South Wales and London to Cornwall and would ignite his first visions of a network of arterial railways across the country.

There is an ironic footnote to the Bexhill saga. On 5 May 1809 Leonard Horner wrote to G. B. Greenhough, president of the newly formed Geological Society:[92]

> At Warwick ... my brother Dr Winthrop[93] introduced me to a man he thought might be a useful honorary member of the Geological Society, he having a great reputation among the gentry in the neighbourhood. He is a 'land doctor', a solicitor and calls himself mineral surveyor. I found him however to possess a great deal of conceit and very little knowledge. What he had was so confused that I should be afraid to place any reliance upon the truth of his observations. I understand he is the man who has set the good people of Sussex in search of coal. I said nothing of the GS as I am satisfied he could be of no use.

In spite of this unflattering assessment of his capabilities, James was duly elected as an ordinary member of the Geological Society on 3 January 1812.[94] John Forster was elected later in the same year. This honour was never granted to either William Smith or John Farey, the chief critic of the Bexhill debacle, on the basis that they were 'too practical and un-gentlemanly',[95] though both James and Smith, in pursuit of their different careers, had equally to suffer the agonies of long-distance road travel. Because Smith, it is said, covered 10,000 miles a year,[96] and James probably not much less, it is relevant at this stage to recognise the discomforts and inconveniences they both had to endure.

FIVE

Roads, Ruts and Rails

Throughout his career, James was a prodigious traveller on the roads of England and Wales. Every month he spent several days – and nights – in a variety of horse-drawn carriages, traversing the length and breadth of the country, firstly on behalf of his widespread clients and latterly on his own account. These carriages had primitive suspensions, ran on roads of very variable quality, and were subject to delays from a myriad of sources, particularly the weather. Accidents caused by broken wheels or overworked horses were a constant hazard. Charles Dickens, when a young journalist, described the tortures of a long journey by stagecoach as comparable to being 'racked'. Maximum speed would be that of a trotting horse. To a man of James's restless vision, it must have seemed not only desirable but essential to devise a better alternative. Time spent travelling between appointments was time wasted, and as early as 1808 his thoughts were already turning to a national network of iron railroads. Rapid passenger transport was high on his agenda, and here he was unique among his contemporary – and now more famous – railway pioneers, who concentrated their attention on freight and mineral traffic to the exclusion of people.

Admittedly, the roads themselves were slowly improving. Their maintenance was originally a parochial responsibility, each parish electing two unpaid surveyors for the year, who supervised 'statute' labour supplied by the parishioners themselves on a scale depending on the value of their land-holdings or the number of horses they owned. This might be a reasonably satisfactory state of affairs at the centre of each separate community, but fell down at the peripheries and left the through routes that linked parishes virtually untended and in a poor state of maintenance. Neither was there any incentive to build new roads. These problems were largely addressed by the creation of the turnpike trusts, which had the right to raise tolls from users.

The first had been set up along part of the Great North Road as early as 1663; by 1750 Parliament had authorised 143 trusts, and over the next twenty years, by which time the turnpike road map of England and Wales looked uncannily like railway maps of a century later, this number rose to 519. In 1838 there were 1,116 trusts controlling 22,000 miles of road, and the last trust was established as late as 1864.[97]

Naturally the early trusts were mainly concentrated on roads radiating from London and the larger provincial towns and cities, and typically covered distances of under ten miles. By 1750, however, turnpike trusts were much larger affairs, nearly half having responsibility for lengths of thirty miles or more. Revenue came from tolls and from subsidies from the parishes, but capital for new roads and major route improvements was raised by way of loans from individual investors, often local landowners who appreciated a safe and unspeculative return on their money while at the same time seeing the practical benefits of improved local transport. The trusts were non-profitmaking organisations, the original enabling Act prescribing the rate at which tolls could be charged. Agricultural traffic and the carriage of building materials were exempt, and the trusts were licensed for a limited number of years, usually 21.

The quality of individual managements naturally varied, and the contemporary press was full of tirades against inefficient trusts which squandered their revenue on corrupt staff, legal costs and the servicing of their loans, rather than spending it on repairs. The very fragmentation of the trusts meant that there was no unifying authority and no standards for road construction and maintenance. Certain individual surveyors would make a name for themselves, the most famous undoubtedly being John Loudon McAdam who successfully extolled the virtues of good drainage, graded materials and a compacted convex surface that allowed surface water to run off into the verges. Thomas Telford believed in a more expensive structural philosophy, insisting on solid foundations and large engineering projects to shorten routes by way of new bridges, cuttings and embankments – a return to the road-building concepts of the Romans. These principles he was able to follow in his two great road projects, the Holyhead road and the main arteries into the Highlands of Scotland, but these were funded by central Government for largely political motives. James would later secure the services of Thomas Telford on his first long-distance railway scheme.

Good or bad, the turnpike trusts did oversee a revolution in the road network of England and Wales and, to a lesser extent perhaps, the lowlands of Scotland. The result was a radical improvement in the productivity of horse-drawn vehicles, in cartage costs, and in transit speeds.[98] At least in summer; in winter, even the better turnpike roads deteriorated into quagmires and minor roads became virtually impassable. In real terms, road freight charges fell throughout the 18th century, from about 15d per ton/mile in 1700 to around 10d by 1760 and nearer 7d in the 1790s. Passenger fares stayed more constant, but this was compensated for by dramatic reductions in journey times. In 1750, a journey by stagecoach from London to Cambridge, Ipswich or Dover took about 24 hours. By 1821 these times had been halved. Birmingham and Bath, accessible in 36 hours in 1750, could by 1821 be reached in eighteen hours, and the fastest mail coach to Bristol took just under twelve. But the most dramatic improvements were over the longer distances to the north. Over the same period, the timings to York and Liverpool were reduced from 80 hours to 30, whereas the improvement on the Exeter route was a more modest 30 per cent. These were the best times, given favourable weather, and few journeys could be guaranteed to run to a reliable timetable.

Mail coaches had been introduced into England in 1784 by a theatrical entrepreneur named John Palmer, and they competed with the stagecoaches which were mainly operated by chains of inn-keepers. The 'Mails' charged passengers a higher fare which reflected speed (six horses as opposed to four, changed every ten miles), security (every mail coach had an armed guard), and higher depreciation (coaches had to be replaced every three years). At the height of the coaching era, the quickest were averaging just over ten miles per hour, the fastest scheduled run being that of the Shrewsbury Wonder which averaged 10¾ miles per hour over its 158-mile journey. The annual mileage run by mail coaches in Great Britain reached its peak in 1837, the year of James's death, at the quite staggering total of 6,643,217 miles.[99] These statistics, known because of the centralised bureaucracy of the Post Office, take no account of the unregulated mileage achieved by the stage-coaching industry. And to put Stratford-upon-Avon in context, it is recorded that at least 24 coaches passed daily through the town in 1817, the main routes being from London to Birmingham, Shrewsbury and on to Chester and Holyhead.[100]

There were other dreamers, apart from James, who wondered whether horse-drawn railways might provide an attractive alternative to ordinary roads; men like William Thomas had suggested such things in 1800, James Anderson in 1801 and Richard Lovell Edgeworth in 1802.[101] A few were even beginning to wonder if the novel use of steam power might not be applied to replacing the horse. Pre-eminent among these was the Cornish engineer and exact contemporary of James, Richard Trevithick, who made and tested his first steam road locomotive in 1801, interestingly enough some years before his much more famous and pioneering machine for use on a railway which will appear later in this chapter.[102]

As James endured hour after hour of time-wasting discomfort, he would see the canals from the windows of his cramped carriage. He would watch the barges queuing at the locks and the horses ponderously dragging their loads along the towpaths. At the coaching inns, he would be assailed with tales of the problems caused by the boat people, often an unruly crowd who lived a poor vagabond life and who were not above a bit of poaching and pilfering as they made their way through estates and communities. The whole transport process was insecure and inefficient and, from the corpulent James's viewpoint, slow and damnably uncomfortable. He would devote much of his life to doing something about it.

'It is known that as early as 1799, at the period George Stephenson was so praiseworthily learning his letters at 3d a week, Mr James was engaged in laying out plans for railroads.'[103]

By 1801, when James was 30 years old, simple railways had been in use for virtually two centuries and were already, in some areas, an established part of the industrial scene.[104] Most were in the coalfields, privately owned, part and parcel of a colliery's equipment and designed to transport its coal to the nearest navigable water, whether sea, river or, increasingly now, canal.

Some served ironworks or stone quarries, but very few carried any other traffic. The concept of the public railway which, like an inland navigation or turnpike, was available upon payment of tolls to anyone with freight to carry, was only just emerging. Since the 1770s the principle had been implicit in lines built as feeders by canal companies, but the independent public railway appeared only in 1798 with the Lake Lock Rail Road near Wakefield, and the Surrey Iron Railway Act of 1801 incorporated the very first dedicated railway company.[105]

Unless the mine or quarry lay actually on navigable water, these early lines provided the only alternative to road transport which, for heavy bulk traffic, was hideously inefficient and expensive. They were modest in scale, rarely more than ten miles in length, and horses supplied the normal traction; a single horse could pull a load of anything from one to three tons, far more than by road and, what was more, in virtually all weathers. For downhill traffic in hilly country, inclined planes, rope-worked and counter-balanced, had long been employed and, for uphill haulage on steep gradients, fixed steam engines were just being introduced.

Waggon wheels were traditionally flanged, running on timber rails pinned to timber sleepers. But by 1801 wooden rails were being replaced by short lengths of cast iron held, usually, on stone blocks. These rails now came in two forms. The 'edge rail', of various cross-sections, still carried flanged wheels and was the norm on Tyneside, which was the principal cradle of the railway. Elsewhere there was battle royal, which the relatively new-fangled plateway looked like winning. This had L-shaped plates to carry unflanged wheels and was already dominant in the Midlands and South Wales. This is no place to argue their rival merits; suffice it to say that, by a Darwinian survival of the fittest and with some help from the Stephensons, the flanged wheel and edge rail ultimately prevailed. But, with the inherent brittleness of cast iron, both types were subject to frequent breakages, especially under the weight and pounding of locomotives. The much tougher wrought iron, although tried as early as 1805, was then far too expensive and inconsistent in quality. As we will see in Chapter 10, James was one of the first to appreciate the virtues of wrought-iron rails, which would be pivotal to his future railway schemes.

Terminology varied, and was woolly. The normal name in the Midlands was 'railroad' or 'railway' (with or without a hyphen), on Tyneside 'waggonway', in South Wales 'tramroad'. To put their scale in context, it has been estimated that in Britain, by 1830, these early railways totalled some 1,500 miles, of which about 350 were in South Wales and several hundred in the north-east.[106] For comparison, the canal network peaked at rather over 3,000 miles, the latterday railway network at 24,000.

In 1802 James visited collieries around Donisthorpe in Leicestershire on behalf of Bernard Dewes 'tracing crops of veins, and furnishing observations of mines and intended rail-roads.'[107] In that year he also, as noted earlier, travelled to Lancashire and suggested various railways in the area of Leigh, Ashton and Ellenbrook. It was probably in about 1803 that James laid down his own first line of rails to link one of his early Staffordshire collieries to the canal system. There were numerous others that he would have known about and possibly visited. In the Midlands alone there were celebrated examples of canal feeders at Caldon Low near Stoke-on-Trent, the Little Eaton Gangway, the Peak Forest, and the Ashby and Ticknall Tramroads, all of which, built in the 1790s or very shortly afterwards, continued to operate virtually unaltered until well into the 20th century.

The South Wales valleys were another area thick with tramroads, on one of which, on 13 February 1804, an epoch-making event took place. Richard Trevithick, developing from his steam road locomotive which had so alarmed his neighbours in Camborne on Christmas Day 1801, had devised the first locomotive to run on rails.[108] For a very short time this primitive machine clattered down the tramroad which linked Penydarren and other ironworks around Merthyr Tydfil to Abercynon on the Glamorganshire Canal.[109] Its single horizontal cylinder was buried in the boiler, and its piston, with the enormous stroke of 4ft 6in, drove the wheels by cast-iron gears. Trevithick wrote a week after the first run – and this was a crucial point in the light of subsequent arguments about who invented the blast-pipe – 'the fire burns much better when the [exhaust] steam goes up the Chimney than what it do when the engine is Idle'. On the first public run on 21 February the locomotive hauled, at walking pace, five trams loaded with ten tons of iron and seventy men down the nine miles to Abercynon. Over the following five months it made a few more trips, but it broke too many of the cast-iron plates to be viable as a railway locomotive. It was in fact intended from the start as a demonstration of the versatility of Trevithick's high-pressure steam engine; and already, at intervals during its period on the tramroad, it had, with its wheels removed, powered static machinery. And that was its subsequent function for the rest of its life.[110]

Was William James present at that historic first run? His daughter, Ellen Paine, wrote that 'Trevithick's [locomotive] was the first he viewed at Camborne, in Cornwall . . . in 1803.'[111] There is no corroboration in Trevithick's correspondence, nor is it mentioned in any surviving letter from James. Her source was perhaps Smiles: 'The idea of railway locomotion haunted him [James] like a passion. He went to Camborne, in Cornwall, to see Trevethick [sic] upon the subject, in 1803, and witnessed the performances of his engine at Merthyr Tydvill in the following year.'[112] But Ellen Paine, significantly, does not mention the Merthyr visit.

What is much more plausible is that James witnessed Trevithick's next truly public demonstration of a steam locomotive, in north London in 1808. For this famous venture, a little locomotive and a single open carriage were set up on a circular track on undeveloped ground near the site of the later Euston station.[113] A high wooden paling was erected around the track, which had a diameter of about 60 yards, and the public was charged 2s a head to enter and, hopefully, be flabbergasted. The show ran for just a few weeks in September 1808, until one day 'a rail broke and occasioned the engine to fly off at a tangent and overturn.'[114] This first accident on a steam-hauled passenger railway may have contributed to the fact that the enterprise was a commercial disaster and it never ran again. Richard Trevithick probably never designed another railway locomotive.[115]

There is a further reason why this pioneering experiment was a flop. *The Times* had whetted its readers' appetite with a paragraph on 8 July: 'We are credibly informed that there is a Steam Engine now preparing to run against any horse, mare or gelding that may be produced.' The whole affair was promoted to the public, according to a contemporary article in the *Observer*, as the venue of a race to settle a wager, Trevithick having thrown down a challenge that his locomotive could out-run any horse over a period of 24 hours. The locomotive was even called *Catch-Me-Who-Can*. But no such race ever took place; the public felt conned and the press dismissed the whole entertainment as an amusing but impractical fairground toy.[116]

James, however, was utterly captivated by what he now saw as the future potential of this first whimsical experiment *(plate 4)*. It was as if he had been present a century later at the Wright brothers' first tentative powered flight at Kitty

Hawk and had begun to envisage what this could lead to; that in a few years time man would fly across the English Channel in a monoplane (also to win a wager) and that within a few more decades airliners would be flying passengers on commercial routes around the world. Certainly from 1808 onwards the extent of his vision expanded – if one could build a railway nine miles long, why not a hundred miles? Or three hundred miles? It was merely a matter of scale; and of a lot of money. But one aspect was now an integral part of all his future plans: the motive power would be the steam locomotive. He could already dream of someone, somewhere, being able to build such machines that would be powerful enough to haul trains not only on the level, but up modest slopes as well, and at speeds much greater than even the fastest mail-coach. If he could go into partnership with such a person, he would surely become even more famous than James Watt, while canals would look like a transient phase in transport evolution.

Such a partner was not going to be Richard Trevithick, who had lost faith in his own brainchild, fallen out with his partners in the venture (one of whom embezzled his funds), and retired back to Cornwall where in 1809 he fell ill with typhoid and was soon afterwards declared bankrupt. He had been given encouragement and honest support by the Cornish scientist and MP Davies Giddy,[117] who will recur in this story much later on, but for now it is necessary to return to 1808 and introduce James's fantastic vision of the General Railroad Company.

His journey to Lancashire in 1802 had persuaded him that there was enormous potential for railways in the booming industrial conurbations of that region, and he sketched the first possible routes of a line linking Liverpool with Manchester and Bolton. That same year, as recorded in an earlier chapter, he inspected the Duke of Bridgewater's pioneering canal but, on listening to customers' complaints about its inadequacies, he drew up his first plans for a network of railways that would effectively bypass it. Further south, he heard of plans for a canal between Warwick and Coventry and set out to survey an alternative railway route, on which he then reported to the Earl of Warwick who gave his tacit approval to investigate further. He had also, that December, projected the railway in Somerset to link the Earl's mining prospects at Clutton with the Avon at Keynsham, once he had bought Chelwood.[118]

He had been active in other counties too. In 1804–5 he was employed by Robert Myddelton

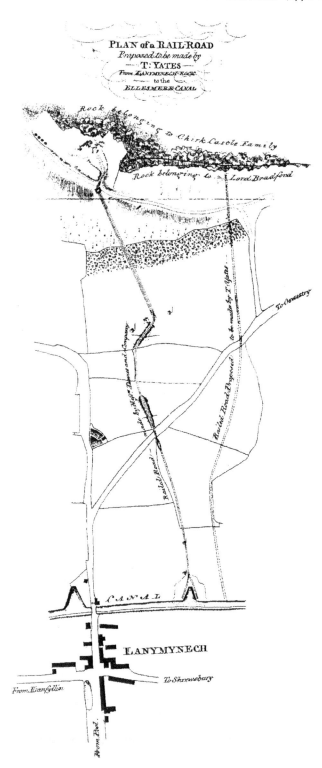

Biddulph of Chirk Castle in Denbigh-shire to advise on a short railway being laid to the Ellesmere Canal by a fellow land-agent, Richard Jebb, who was leasing the limestone quarries at Llanymynech on the Shropshire/Montgomeryshire border. James told Biddulph of his hopes 'to see this estate producing for its owners a princely income'.[119] (see fig.3, left)

He studied routes for possible railways for the Hon. Charles Agar in Cornwall and in Flintshire for Sir Thomas Hanmer, plus another in Staffordshire from Walsall to Erdington on behalf of the Earl of Dartmouth.[120] He could already appreciate the advantages of horse-drawn railways over canals, and when he added the potential which he now recognised in the steam locomotive, the scale of his concepts exploded. What was needed, he wrote, was a huge new company to survey, promote and build railways wherever they were required, not just for goods haulage but for long-distance passenger traffic as well: a company which would employ all the professional staff required to deal with land purchase, way-leaves, parliamentary approval and the raising of finance, one which would then put out construction contracts and finally run the things – under his direction. This was to be the General Railroad Company, and James appreciated that it would require a monumental amount of capital. His first estimate was £1 million.[121]

The concept was so wildly in advance of its time that it would need nearly twenty years to gestate and mature. The iron horse had crept very briefly from the primordial soup of technology. James believed that it would not really emerge again until greater attention was paid to the design and manufacture of a strong, flexible and enduring iron road.

Fig.3: **Plan of the railroad on the Chirk Castle estate at Llanymynech. (This map also includes the second line proposed by T. Yates in 1822 – see chapter 12.)**
Courtesy NLW Chirk Castle MS.

SIX

London, a Funeral
and the Archbishop
(1806–1815)

URING the decade up to 1816, James's extraordinary career followed a number of parallel but fascinating courses. Two of his major investment projects – the river Avon and the Stratford Canal, and his coalmines and other industrial enterprises – deserve chapters (7 and 8) of their own. But first we must return to conclude matters at Warwick.

With the Earl effectively banished from Warwick Castle after 1806, James had to accept responsibility for seeing that the contents of the castle itself and the ornaments in the grounds were secure, a job made more difficult by a stream of visitors. Some visits were official, like that in September by the Prince of Wales and his brother the Duke of Clarence, but most were strictly unofficial, as the housekeeper, Mrs Hume, organised clandestine tours of the property to make a little pocket-money. In 1809, desperate for money from somewhere and labouring under the almost paranoid impression that his advisers were siphoning off funds that were rightly his, the Earl demanded that James's accounts for the previous three years be re-audited. He wrote to the Earl of Upper Ossory, now the sole senior trustee:

The reports of Mr James . . . have been cursorily looked over by Mr Vancouver, whose letter to me on a further tax on my income I have thought proper to send to your Lordship. For the reasons contained in Mr Vancouver's letter, I do hereby and in the most positive terms indict and protest against the expenditure of any more money by Mr James in repairs and improvements until his former charges for these and other purposes are examined and allowed by me.[122]

Old wounds were being reopened, old rivalries exploited. Messrs Bird and Wedge duly carried out this task, noting that 'the affairs of the agency are much perplexed . . . with continuing difficulties

arising from the pressure of creditors.' They concluded as follows:

We the undersigned being acquainted with the Earl of Warwick's Estates and knowing its cares, and having perused Mr James's rental books thereof and considered the trouble and exertions which he has made, and the clerks and permanent expenses he has sustained as agent thereof, do declare his charges for salary . . . at £850 . . . to be a moderate Compensation and Satisfaction for the same – and having perused his charges for necessary expenses within stated for 1804–1808, we do declare them to be necessary and proper to be allowed; and this our opinion we shall at all times be ready to verify, from our personal knowledge of his zeal and exertions to serve Lord Warwick and his family.

Signed Jn. Bird & John Wedge 14th day of January 1810.[123]

Finally in July 1813 the Earl made his last despairing throw of the dice. By now he had persuaded his wife and the younger children, who were not receiving much by way of annuities, to join him in a case in Chancery against the Earl of Upper Ossory, Lord Broke (his oldest surviving son and the major beneficiary of the trust), and William James. It was eventually heard on 30 July 1814.[124] The plaintiffs' case was that in nine years the rental income had amounted to £50,000 and that James had spent £40,000 on repairs and improvements, taxes and debt repayments, of which £28,000 had been expended without the Earl's specific authority. It also claimed (despite the testimony of Messrs Bird and Wedge) that James had produced no accounts, that he had used the rental income for his own speculative purposes, and that James's affairs 'were in a state of complexity, confusion and embarrassment.' (One has to feel that this was a supreme example of the pot trying to blacken the reputation of the kettle.) They asked the court to rule that James be removed; that a proper person be appointed to examine whether the present tenants were paying the right amount of rent and, if not, to evict them; and that most of the trees and timber on the plaintiffs' estates be felled and sold. Here the Earl was obviously clutching at the possible lifeline thrown him by the opinion of 1805, though he was subtle enough to state that the reason for this request was for 'the preservation and improvement of the rest' of the trees.

The Earl of Upper Ossory stated in defence that James 'enjoyed the entire confidence of all the parties to the original indenture of appointment and that he had recently deposited with the trustees, voluntarily, security to the value of £10,000 and upwards', including ten of his shares in the Stratford Canal.[125] Furthermore an auditor, William Alexander, had been appointed in 1808 and had passed all the accounts up to Michaelmas 1812. The court's ruling was brief and concluded that 'there are no grounds for removing the said William James from the receivership of the estates.'

It appears that about this time he did withdraw himself from the personal management of the Warwick business, handing it over to one of his clerks, although he was still presenting the 'Book of Accounts' as late as 1819. He was no longer living in Warwick, having bought a new family house in West Bromwich to be closer to his coalmining and foundry investments, while the Stratford Canal, of which he was a major shareholder and deputy chairman, was occupying much of his time. The Earl's coal deposits at Clutton, on the edge of the rich Somerset coalfield, were still not yielding their potential for lack of investment. In 1814 they were generating only £617 a year. James had written to the trustees' solicitors in August 1812 urging them to try to form a company 'with the command of sufficient capital'. This he estimated at £30,000 'to complete the communication and the works proper to bring this valuable property into income'. Once completed – and this he suggested might take five years – he estimated an initial output of 1,500 tons per week, which should yield an annual income of £5,500 based on a pithead selling price of 10s per ton and a royalty of one eighth.[126]

Although James retained the freehold of his large house and garden in St John's, he did in the spring of 1814 sell – to the Earl's Trustees – his peripheral property interests in Warwick.[127] These consisted of four lots which he valued at £7,650, but he agreed on £6,000 for quick settlement as he

urgently needed the money for investment in his Black Country enterprises.

Elsewhere, another era was drawing to an end. Emma Hamilton, the widow of the Earl of Warwick's late uncle and Admiral Nelson's mistress, died in penury on 15 January 1815, the nation having turned a deaf ear to Nelson's dying wish. Olivia Serres wrote that 'Lord W. often lamented the patriotic Emma's distress, and at the period of the latter misfortunes of her life, advised measures likely to interest the country in her favour.'[128] The Earl himself died, suddenly, in May 1816. He was 64. The Earl of Upper Ossory died of apoplexy on 1 February 1818, leaving five illegitimate children. The Countess of Warwick lived to the age of 78 and died at Brighton in 1838, having outlived William James by just over a year.

Outside Warwickshire, James carried out land agency duties for a very long list of important people right across the country. In the prevailing financial climate, nearly all of them wanted to sell property, and James's role was often made more difficult and stressful by the lack of buyers. The Earl of Aboyne asked James to sell his English estates at Ranton Abbey in Staffordshire, which James estimated to have a proper value of £80,000, while warning that it might be difficult to achieve this because the land was poorly drained and all the farms were tenanted. When he did put the estate up for auction there was not one single bid. His valuation services were much in demand – he told Humfrey Arden of Sutton Coldfield that he could not spare the time to value his estate in Derbyshire because he had to sell properties worth £300,000 by Christmas and, anyway, he would not undertake valuations unless he were the sole agent. He was permanently trying to sell off property for Bernard Dewes to reduce his mortgage burden.

James himself made one significant property investment when he purchased the Manor of Snowford. This consisted of nearly 1,000 acres of land lying a few miles to the east of Leamington Spa, alongside the Fosse Way. It included 'Lodge Farm, Snowford Grange Farm, Middle Farm and Town Farm, and many fields, closes etc which are named; also three undivided fourth parts of the Manor of Long Itchington.'[129] The precise purchase price and the motivation behind the purchase are unknown, but there might be a clue in the geology of the area. Beneath the surface lies an extensive bed of limestone particularly suitable for calcining into what would later be known as Portland Cement. Present-day travellers down the A423 through the village of Long Itchington, on the eastern borders of the Manor lands, can hardly avoid seeing the extensive Rugby Portland Cement works and its associated quarries. James may have recognised the future potential of this part of Warwickshire, and on 9 June 1813 he sold it to the Earl of Aylesford for the princely sum of £54,661 – about £3 million at current rates.[130]

James carried out a number of valuations and assessments for Lord St John of Melchbourne, and in June 1809 wrote a long report for Lord Willoughby de Broke on the best way of exploiting his coal resources near Bristol.[131] Some of his most significant clients were in London and particularly Lambeth; but before looking at the projects here, which would occupy him from 1804 to 1812, we must consider some family matters.

The births of the James' two daughters were joyous occasions; the delicate Marianna was born on 2 July 1806, while on 9 January 1809 there arrived the robust Ellen, who will emerge much later as the chief torchbearer of her father's reputation after he died. But, back in Henley-in-Arden in February 1807, a melancholy event took place which would have very far-reaching and devastating consequences.

William James's father was now in his 70s, and his latter years had been blighted by unsuccessful speculations in canal shares. However, very prudently, he had had the foresight to assign some of his property interests to his eldest son, keeping them out of the reach of his creditors to whom he appeared to be a humbled destitute. James was by his father's bedside as he started to lose his grip on life, and he wrote to his sister Anne in London on 15 February, urging her to come as quickly as she could to join the family before the inevitable end. 'His extremities are cold and lifeless, the spectacle is most edifying to those whose nerves can stand so awful and solemn an occasion – the Lamp of Life is gradually extinguished, the Lustre of his Brilliant Eye is gone.'[132] Their father's dying concern was that he could not provide for his four unmarried daughters – Mary, Anne, Susannah and Elizabeth – and William made a solemn promise that he would look after his sisters and provide them with dowries; with one crucial caveat. As the new head of the family he was responsible for their moral as well as their financial well-being, and he intimated that any dowry would need to be linked to his blessing on the marriage, and, crucially, to his critical approval of the bridegroom.

William James Snr., described as 'Gentleman of Henley-in-Arden', died on 17 February 1807

and was buried at Wootton Wawen, letters of administration being granted to his eldest son at Worcester on 17 July, with responsibility for distributing his few remaining chattels and adopting his outstanding debts of £4,000.[133]

* * * * *

DOWNSTREAM from Lambeth Palace, the historic London residence of the Archbishop of Canterbury, the area of land on the south bank of the Thames between Westminster and Blackfriars bridges was known as the Lambeth Marsh. It was worth little in the Archbishop's property portfolio, but if the land could be reclaimed it was potentially a most valuable asset. The first tasks were to establish a better river embankment and a comprehensive drainage scheme, and in 1804 James was invited to submit proposals. They would occupy him on and off for the next seven years. The drainage proposals themselves were straightforward; he suggested a number of parallel cuts bordered by raised roadways to be connected by the occasional wooden bridge. He left the implementation to others. But his overall vision was much, much more ambitious. He saw this project as just one part of a grand scheme to redesign the whole region, with particular emphasis on better transport links. Here he was motivated by the fact that the land adjoining Lambeth Marsh to the south, at Camberwell, was largely owned by another client, Lord Holland, a nephew of the Earl of Upper Ossory.

There was already one canal and one railway which impinged on the region. To the east, the Grand Surrey Canal, authorised in 1801, ran from the Thames at Rotherhithe to Camberwell, and was authorised to terminate at Mitcham on the river Wandle. There it was intended to link up with the Surrey Iron Railway, which had been incorporated in 1801 to build a double-track plateway from a basin on the Thames at Wandsworth and along the Wandle valley to Croydon.[134] This concern was ground-breaking. It was the first to be established under the parliamentary standing orders drawn up in 1799 to regulate 'the making of Ways or Roads usually called Railways or Dram Roads'. Apart from the very different Lake Lock it was, as we have seen, the first public railway in the world, and the original surveyor, William Jessop, envisaged the route being eventually extended to Reigate and onwards to the south coast.[135] James, intrigued by this concept, became an early shareholder. The bulk of the traffic was 'lime, chalk, flint, fullers' earth and agricultural products from its neighbourhood to London; and in return to take from thence coals and manure for the supply of the country through which it passes'.[136] It never carried passengers.

For James's purposes, the canal and the railway were both too far away from his new prime site which would emerge once Lambeth Marsh had been reclaimed. He had wider horizons, already involving a railway link to the north, and for this he suggested to the Archbishop's solicitors the need for a tunnel from Lambeth to Scotland Yard under the river Thames – or, better still, a new bridge across it. He argued that the precise

location was important: it should be aligned as a direct extrapolation of the Tottenham Court Road.

Part of the site at the southern end of the bridge should be earmarked for the terminus of a new railway to the south coast, but, crucially, the rails could be extended over the new bridge as well, opening up an important north-south transport link. Today, commuters are reconciled to the fact that the London railway termini form a ring around the city, but James believed this was quite unnecessary. Why not design a railway straight through the West End, while it was still being developed? His idea for the new bridge was

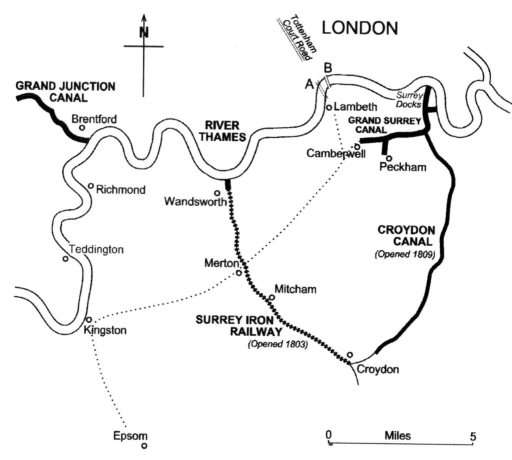

Fig.4: **South London. 1821.**
This shows the canals south of the Thames and the route of the Surrey Iron Railway in relation to Lambeth. Also James's new railway proposals for the Grand Surrey Canal company *c.*1822 – see chapter 12.
..... William James' proposed railway extension to the Grand Surrey Canal
A: William James' suggested location for a new Thames Bridge aligned with Tottenham Court Road
B: John Rennies's 'Strand' (later 'Waterloo') Bridge, opened 1817

indeed adopted in other quarters. A public company was formed with wildly speculative enthusiasm, but, without his input, the selected location was slightly further east and at a different angle. Waterloo Bridge was opened on the anniversary of the battle in 1817. Promoted by the enthusiastic George Dodd as the 'Strand Bridge' and built by John Rennie, its foundation stone had been laid in 1811. It was the first and the longest of Rennie's three London bridges, and had the unique characteristic of a precisely level roadway – as if intended to carry a railway line. It cost the shareholders the equivalent of £1 million.

James's great plans for south London went further still. For Lord Thurlow he promotes a number of Enclosure Bills at Dulwich, together with a new turnpike road from there to London.[137] For the Archbishop he undertakes a number of other surveys and valuations. He goes up to Blackburn to report on a possible coalmine in the grounds of the rectory; in 1807 he advises on the purchase of land adjoining the Croydon Turnpike (for £1,500) and there are other assignments at Saddleworth and Rochdale. He has to balance conflicts of interests. 'I cannot consistently with my character advise the Archbishop to take any steps either to let or improve the strip of land at Lambeth Wyke, until negotiations have been completed with Lord Holland.'[138] He has to deal with the ponderous bureaucracy of the Archbishop's staff, but at the same time they have to deal with the fact that he is seldom on hand, with letters being forwarded to all corners of the country. James just has too many other projects on at the same time. He increasingly pleads excuses for non-delivery – he is off surveying Lord Thurlow's estates, he is busy, he is ill, he is unavailable. Frere's replies become more sarcastic. 'A month's further delay will occasion the loss of a quarter session . . . your head is worth comparatively little, I conceive, unless you lend to a certain extent your hand to execute.' It seems that James's contract was terminated in 1812.

Not that James was probably too concerned, because in that year he was more than fully occupied with the business of other clients, including the Duke of Northumberland – another cousin of the Earl of Warwick. James's appointment as agent and receiver for the Duke's estates had, once again, been sealed over the font. The James' fifth son was born on 31 May 1810, and in honour of his godfather was christened Alfred Percy.[139] James's most important project for the Duke was legislation for the enclosure of waste land at Hounslow, Twickenham, Heston and Isleworth, and the Bills required careful handling through Parliament. James needed an impressive chairman to head the drafting committee, and on 1 January 1812 he wrote to Sir Joseph Banks, the eminent explorer, botanist and President of the Royal Society, imploring him to cancel all other engagements for the following day. 'I am quite certain his Grace would consider himself very much indebted to you for this fresh instance of your readiness to sacrifice your time and ease to this measure.'[140] It is an indication of both James's status and his self-confidence that he could ask for the services of one of the most distinguished authorities of his day. He ended the letter, 'I shall be at Isleworth at 12 o'clock, when I trust that you may be enabled to favour us with your attendance.'

With achievements like this, James's reputation was riding high, and the application of his drive and determination, combined with his legal expertise, would now be called on to rescue a major civil engineering project in Warwickshire from penury and stagnation. It has been noted earlier in this chapter that James was the owner of ten 'old' shares in the Stratford Canal Company, and although he recorded their nominal value as £1,500 – the amount he had been called on to pay for them – the truth was that they were almost worthless. The project had ground to a halt. Bernard Dewes, the chairman, could think of no one better than James to take on the daunting task of reviving it. And James, once committed, would not be content until he had brought it to a successful conclusion.

SEVEN

Waterways
and the Emperor's Nugget
(1809–1816)

O N 24 June 1816, the high-point of his brief involvement with water transport, William James sailed in triumph down the final section of the Stratford Canal. Why did he commit so much time, energy and money to a mode of transport he was already shunting into a backwater? Perhaps he felt a sense of duty to the people of the communities in which he had been brought up; perhaps he felt an obligation to the chairman, Bernard Dewes; perhaps he believed it would still form a vital link in an integrated transport system, or perhaps he was trying to redeem some value from a shareholding that had gone sour. In some ways it proved to be his most successfully completed venture but also one of his most ruinous investments.

The river Avon meanders its way across the south Warwickshire plain (the Upper Avon) and then along the Vale of Evesham until it flows into the Severn at Tewkesbury (the Lower Avon). Together, these two stretches amount to about 43 miles of waterway. Southwards from Stratford-upon-Avon, the river had been rendered navigable to barges of one sort or another since the mid-seventeenth century, though not in the opposite direction up to Warwick itself. Over the years, numerous watermills had been built along its banks, the larger ones protecting their water level by building weirs across the stream.

The driving force behind the need to make the river navigable in the early 1600s was, naturally, trade. The main promoters were the merchants of an increasingly prosperous Stratford, and the single individual who decided to do something about it was a thrusting young man from the village of Fladbury named William Sandys. If he was to spend a lot of his money – it eventually totalled over £20,000 – on locks and sluices to bypass the mill weirs, on purchasing the adjoining land necessary to achieve this, and on dredging, to guarantee a financial return he needed the right to charge tolls. This he bought by Royal Letters Patent granted to him in 1636. As a result

of the political upheavals of the Civil War and then the Restoration, these were back in the Royal gift in 1664, passing from the Duke of York to Lord Windsor (later the Earl of Plymouth). He in turn leased it to a syndicate that included a remarkable entrepreneur named Andrew Yarranton,[141] who had made a considerable success of smelting iron at Astley, a few miles south of Stourport in Worcestershire, the project being financed by a £500 reward for his military services on behalf of the Parliamentarians in the Civil War.

But his investment in the Avon navigation suffered a major set-back in 1674 when there were bread riots in Stratford-upon-Avon, the granaries were torched, and the locks on the river were vandalised. He concluded that poverty was best tackled by new industries, new opportunities for employment, and new methods of distributing farm produce across the country. He was the first to contemplate some sort of canal link between the Warwickshire Avon (via the Warwickshire Stour) and the Thames (via the river Cherwell). Like William James a hundred and fifty years later, he had a dream of making Stratford the hub of a new transport network. But Yarranton's vision went further still. He drew up plans for two completely new industrial communities on the southern outskirts of the town, with granaries, flax mills and linen weaving workshops to rival any on the continent. These would be called New Haarlem (opposite where the theatre now stands) and New Brunswick (at the confluence of the Avon and the Stour at Milcote). Had Yarranton not been killed in a brawl in 1684, Stratford might truly have become the nursery of the Industrial Revolution.

By this time, the head-lease of the Avon Navigation had passed from Lord Windsor to his widow. When she died in 1717, the rights to the Upper Avon tolls went to one son, those from the Lower Avon to another. In 1696 she had been receiving £400 a year on tolls from coal traffic alone. By 1751, annual traffic amounted to about 12,000 tons, mainly grain and flour downstream and Shropshire and Forest of Dean coal upstream from the Severn. Neither Sandys nor the Windsors, nor indeed any of the subsequent lessors, ever got around to installing a tow-path. Flat-bottomed barges of up to 30-ton capacity relied on sail power or, if the wind failed, teams of men hauling along the bank. By 1793, the tolls on the Upper Avon were effectively owned by a Thomas Ramell and those on the Lower Avon by the Perrott family. The coming of the canals in the latter part of the 18th century actually enhanced the prospects for trade on the two Avon navigations. No canal offered a directly competitive route, while the Worcester & Birmingham Canal, authorised in 1791, would in theory deliver traffic from the coal mines of South Staffordshire onto the Severn as well.[142]

The development of the canal network in the West Midlands has been covered by several authors, including the doyen of canal historians, Charles Hadfield, and more recently such writers as Nick Billingham.[143] The situation as it was in 1790 can be summarised as follows. The Trent & Mersey Canal linked those two rivers and provided a vital link between the east and the west coasts and, from a junction with it, the Staffordshire & Worcestershire Canal ran past Wolverhampton and the Wednesbury coalfield to join the upper Severn at Stourport. From another junction, the Coventry Canal brought a link to that city from the north-west. The Birmingham Canal Navigation and its network of local branches was in effect a branch off the Staffs & Worcs, terminating at Newhall Hill close to the city centre. Much of the land to the north of the cathedral in Birmingham was owned by Charles Colmore, who played a duplicitous game with the canal company which had, in its turn, made it clear that it was driven mainly by the desire for profits rather than providing any sort of a public service. Colmore demanded an extortionate price for his land on which the canal basins would be dug (now covered by the local headquarters of BT and the Post Office Tower), while opposing any deviation from the line prescribed by the Act of Parliament. This delayed the completion of the canal for two years, but eventually the company was forced to pay up.[144]

This cantankerous and litigious body fought many battles to try to maintain what it considered to be its monopoly rights in the area, most of which led to pyrrhic victories because they merely stimulated more and more competitors, like the Dudley canals, to bypass its region of influence. When the Birmingham & Fazeley Canal was opened in 1790, there was for the first time a reasonable inland route between Birmingham and London, via the Coventry and Oxford Canals and the river Thames. There was thought to be sufficient demand for another link between Birmingham and the Severn to justify the promotion of a new cut between the two, leading to the Worcester & Birmingham Canal Act of 1791. Typically, this was strenuously opposed by the Birmingham Canal company, who insisted on a physical barrier (the infamous Worcester Bar) between them where they abutted near the Farmer's Gate Locks, at what is now known as the Gas Street basin.

All these developments were detrimental to the trade of both Warwick and Stratford-upon-Avon. 'Since the canal from Birmingham to Coventry has been compleated, the land carriage from Bristol and Worcester through Warwick and Stratford had decreased by three fourths.'[145] To try to rectify this situation, for a time the two towns planned joint schemes, such as a canal linking them both to the Coventry Canal, or an extension of the Avon Navigation up to Warwick itself. Then the Dudley Canal decided to thrust a tunnel through the south-west corner of Birmingham territory and establish a direct link with the Worcester & Birmingham at Selly Oak. The Warwick/Stratford alliance saw the opportunity to make a new and more direct canal from King's Norton, near this junction, skirting Birmingham to the south. Furthermore, moves in 1792 to build a new Grand Junction Canal from Brentford near London to the Oxford Canal at Braunston in Northamptonshire, which bypassed the unsatisfactory section of the Upper Thames, opened up the possibility of Warwick becoming a through trading post on the way to London, if their south Birmingham canal also had an extension from Braunston to Warwick. The Dudley Canal people were ardent supporters, because this offered massive new outlets for coal from Wednesbury and Dudley. The Worcester & Birmingham promoters encouraged the idea as well, since it would lead to increased traffic over their northern section. Stratford, envisaged as being on the end of a short branch, was bound to benefit substantially.

Finally, the obstinate Birmingham Canal company realised that it would be the principal loser from this scheme and, in a major volte-face, wooed and seduced the Warwick promoters to join them in a direct line between their two towns, and the Birmingham & Warwick Canal was conceived. It was authorised in 1793. Suddenly the Stratford promoters found themselves on their own. In the same year they sought authorisation to press ahead with the scheme from King's Norton via Lapworth to the centre of Stratford. Amazingly, but out of fear of upsetting their essential supporter, the Worcester & Birmingham, it was not envisaged that the Stratford Canal should have a direct connection with the river Avon.

The first Stratford Canal Navigation Act was passed on 28 March 1793, six months before William James married Dinah Tarleton. He and his father would certainly have studied the plans for the route, which was to pass within sight of the church where the wedding took place. As he stood at the altar, could he have had the slightest inkling that he would one day be in charge of the whole undertaking, that he would eventually become the largest single shareholder, that he would on the one hand rescue it from never being completed, and on the other hand become an instrument that made it, and most other canals, virtually redundant? The Jameses, father and son, would have been asked by clients for advice on whether to subscribe for shares, though in the climate of the pre-war Canal Mania (fourteen schemes had been floated in 1791–2, and no fewer than twenty in 1793, involving nearly £3 million of shareholder capital) the question was more likely to have been how to get hold of as many shares as possible. William James Snr managed to scramble five shares of £100 each, but – and this was the good news – only £5 had to paid up-front. Before the calls on the balance were made, other investors, squeezed out of the first offering, might decide it was worth paying a premium of perhaps £40 to get on the register, in which case the initial investors could make a profit of 350 per cent. This block of shares joined William James Snr.'s canal portfolio, which included six in the Worcester & Birmingham. His mistake over the next two years was to become a buyer of more (premium) shares, rather than a seller.[146]

The building of the canals opened up further money-making opportunities. Apart from improving river navigations and cutting new waterways across the landscape, this investment whirlwind involved ancillary schemes of wharfage, warehousing and fleets of barges. One such scheme was to involve James's brother-in-law, John Tarleton. In May 1800 he, together with nine partners, formed the Stratford-upon-Avon and Henley-in-Arden Boat Company.[147] The capital was divided into ten £200 shares, and the objective of the partnership was to act as 'carriers and dealers in Coal, Coak (sic), Lime, Graingoods,

Wares and Merchandises upon the Stratford-upon-Avon, Worcester, Birmingham and Netherton canal navigations.' They would also undertake 'the purchasing or taking leases of any lands or grounds adjacent . . . and building or erecting wharfs, warehouses, engines or other thereon.' The partners were spread as far afield as Stafford, Handsworth, Birmingham and Stratford, and it is very likely that the partnership document was drawn up by James, who may well have been instrumental in incorporating the name of Henley-in-Arden into the title. James, although not an original subscriber, soon acquired one share, which he sold for £300 in 1802.[148]

Of the Stratford Canal's initial capital of £120,000, two thirds was raised from within Warwickshire. Negotiations were held with the Oxford Canal to drive an extension from Stratford to Fenny Compton in preference to the Warwick route for the Grand Junction enterprise, but Stratford lost out to the slightly more northern route. Then came the arguments about a direct link with the rival Birmingham & Warwick near Lapworth (which the Dudley Canal agreed to subsidise), although the Stratford interests were anxious that this should not be done until the canal had reached the town. They were not in a good bargaining position to trade tolls, so it was finally decided to adjust the line to take the Stratford Canal as close to the Birmingham & Warwick as feasible. The link at Kingswood was, and is, only 400 yards long. The levels at this junction were important, so that accusations of poaching water when boats passed from one to the other would be avoided. Somehow the key interchange lock on the Stratford Canal was constructed in the wrong place – an error that would later prove a very costly mistake.

Early ambitions of the Stratford Canal had included branches to quarries at both Tanworth-in-Arden and Temple Grafton and making the cut wide enough for barges rather than narrow boats, as witnessed by the width of the King's Norton tunnel, but when both the Worcester & Birmingham and the Birmingham & Warwick opted for the cheaper narrow alternative, the Stratford cut was built to the same width. Even with this lower-cost option and the absence of locks on the first ten miles to Hockley Heath, in 1807 the money ran out. Other vital links were running behind schedule. The Dudley Canal tunnel would not be open for another year, the Birmingham & Warwick for another two, and the western section of the ill-fated Worcester & Birmingham would not reach the Severn until 1815.

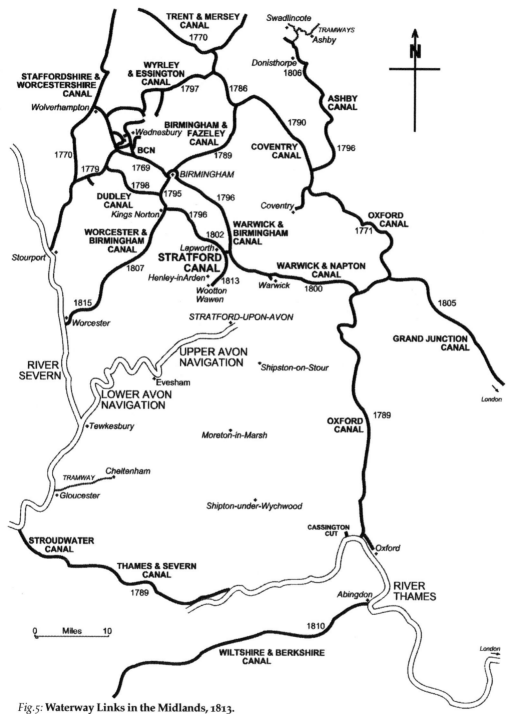

TRENT & MERSEY CANAL
1770

Swadlincote
TRAMWAYS
Ashby

Donisthorpe
1806

STAFFORDSHIRE & WORCESTERSHIRE CANAL

WYRLEY & ESSINGTON CANAL
1797   1786

ASHBY CANAL

Wolverhampton

1790

BIRMINGHAM & FAZELEY CANAL

Wednesbury

COVENTRY CANAL
1796

1770

BCN

1779

1769

1789

1798

BIRMINGHAM

1795

1796

Coventry

OXFORD CANAL
1771

DUDLEY CANAL

Kings Norton

1796

WARWICK & BIRMINGHAM CANAL

Stourport

WORCESTER & BIRMINGHAM CANAL

1802

Lapworth

STRATFORD CANAL

WARWICK & NAPTON CANAL

1807

Henley-inArden

1813

Warwick   1800

Wootton Wawen

1805

1815

Worcester

STRATFORD-UPON-AVON

GRAND JUNCTION CANAL

RIVER SEVERN

UPPER AVON NAVIGATION

Shipston-on-Stour

Evesham

London

LOWER AVON NAVIGATION

Tewkesbury

1789

Moreton-in-Marsh

OXFORD CANAL

TRAMWAY   Cheltenham

Gloucester

Shipton-under-Wychwood

CASSINGTON CUT

Oxford

STROUDWATER CANAL

THAMES & SEVERN CANAL

RIVER THAMES

1789

Abingdon

0   Miles   10

1810

London

WILTSHIRE & BERKSHIRE CANAL

Fig.5: **Waterway Links in the Midlands, 1813.**
This highlights the isolation of Stratford-upon-Avon prior to the completion of the Stratford Canal and the lack of good transport access to the Cotswold plateau around Moreton-in-Marsh.

There were continual cash crises. Several share-holders were reluctant to pay the calls due (£150 had already been demanded on every £100 share) but, with extra loans at high interest rates, the cut did slowly struggle southwards. By 1808 it had reached Wootton Wawen, still six miles short of its objective, but now at least it was able to tap into traffic to the market town of Alcester. James, who had done some surveying for the company in its early years, was by 1800 a shareholder (ten shares) and joined the management committee briefly during 1805. He was invited back in 1808, and over the next twelve years was to hold various appointments, sometimes as chairman, sometimes as supervisor, on both the general and works committees.

Now at last the Stratford Canal had a man in charge who was determined to finish it one way or another, and he applied his restless energy to yet another major project. It was estimated that the company needed another £90,000 to complete and in 1809 James was authorised to launch a new share issue on the disillusioned investors, this time at £40 per share, followed, when this failed to get any takers, by yet another one, on an even deeper discount, at £30 per share. This too failed to attract many subscribers and the whole project stalled for four years. Indeed it might never have been resurrected if James had not pledged to purchase another 156 shares for himself plus 50 in the name of his son William Henry.

James did have an ulterior motive in pressing for the canal's completion. By now he owned substantial coal-mining and iron-foundry interests in West Bromwich and any route that would open new markets was of interest. But his main reason lay at Wilmcote, half way between Wootton Wawen and Stratford, where he owned a large limestone quarry. He had a temporary wooden tramway built from there to Wootton Wawen to transport his stone, which was sold either as building slabs or for lime-burning in the kilns at King's Norton. It is possible that at this stage he even considered converting the whole southern section of the canal to a permanent railway, since he was becoming increasingly convinced that here lay the future of inland transport, at the same time as he was becoming more and more disillusioned with the inherent problems of canal operation, dominant among which was the difficulty of ensuring a reliable source of water at the summit.

In 1809 there arrived on the committee table a somewhat distracting proposition which involved a possible extension to the south. The Wiltshire & Berkshire Canal was about to be completed from near Bath to Abingdon on the Thames. If another canal was taken from Stratford to Abingdon, here was the opportunity for an alternative inland route from the Midlands to London and Bristol. Would the Stratford Company join the Wilts & Berks in promoting this Central Junction Canal? James's fellow proprietors looked at this prize only briefly, considering that they already had more than enough on their plate, but James's imagination was fired – again – and he filed the idea at the back of mind to be reworked, in a different form, at a later date. The board also dismissed the idea of proceeding with the two branches off the canal that had been authorised in the original Act.[149]

Around the year 1810, while the Stratford Canal lay in limbo, James made a significant investment in the heart of Birmingham, by taking a long lease from Charles Colmore on the land adjoining the basins where the Birmingham Canal terminated at Newhall Hill. 'The greater portion of this hill he removed, at an immense expense, and upon its site formed a series of wharves, which he connected by a short branch of canal with the Birmingham & Fazeley Canal.' It was also the natural site for the terminus of a railway he was plotting, which would tunnel through the remainder of the hill and achieve a direct link with his mines in South Staffordshire, 'with a view of breaking up the very powerful monopoly of the Birmingham Canal Company'.[150] This was envisaged as his Central Union Railroad, to be discussed later.

In 1813, before going back to shareholders of the Stratford Canal with alternative proposals for raising money by debentures, James drew up a list of the problems and opportunities that lay before them, and tried to quantify the costs and the benefits. On 8 October he presented his report.[151] It started by explaining why the costs of the stretch from Lapworth to Wootton Wawen had overshot the original estimate by £22,000 (50 per cent). Principal items included rectifying the site of the last lock on the spur to the Birmingham & Warwick, which 'by some unaccountable mistake or negligence' had been cut in the wrong place. The construction of the locks south of Lapworth 'in swampy ground because of bad weather' had necessitated 'the laying down of a rail-road extending nearly seven miles back to the brick-yards,' which had cost an extra £6,300. (He had been fascinated to see how the wooden sleepers virtually floated on the boggy ground. He filed the memory and would revive it when he next encountered the awesome Chat Moss in Lancashire. The brickworks railroad track was reused to form the temporary line from Wootton to Wilmcote, with James himself buying surplus material for use within his quarries there.)

He summarised what still needed to be done and how he proposed to save construction costs:

a) A new reservoir was urgently needed on the summit level. The £9,000 earmarked for this in the original budget had been diverted to deal with extra costs on making the cut itself. (This reservoir was eventually built at Earlswood, but because of lack of funds not completed until 1821. Even though its area was 85 acres and its capacity 34 million cubic feet, in dry summers the company still had to buy water from the Worcester & Birmingham.)

b) The cut had not only to be extended to Stratford but, despite upsetting the still uncompleted Worcester & Birmingham, linked to the river Avon. Of three options considered, the middle one at the Bancroft near the town centre had been chosen, with Stratford Corporation offering a £2,000 loan as an inducement.

c) Apart from the costs of the new locks into the river, the largest single item was the aqueduct over the Edstone valley, estimated at £9,000. Here James recommended a construction technique using a trough built up from cast-iron plates, as pioneered on the Pontcysyllte aqueduct on the Ellesmere Canal and already applied to the much shorter aqueduct at Wootton Wawen. The cost would be far less than a conventional brick and stone structure. It was not the only aspect where the potential of cast iron was exploited. The cost of over-bridges was reduced from £500 to £320 each by employing iron cantilevers, the open slot between them avoiding the need to un-harness the towrope.

The new estimates came to £69,600. It was proposed that £40,000 of this should be funded from the 1,000 £30 shares not taken up from the 1809 issue, plus 330 extra, which should pay for the construction as far as Wilmcote – James's highest priority. By then it was hoped that revenue would be not less than £6,500 per annum, ample to secure loans at 5 per cent to cover the balance if necessary.

James concluded his presentation with a robust call for optimism:

It will appear that nature has pointed out this line of canal as the central communication through this kingdom. The Wash and the Bristol Channel, with the eastern and western ports of the kingdom, could only be united by this Canal and the river Avon, and their produce reciprocally inter-changed ... every intelligent mind, on a deliberate view of the subject, must be convinced that a line of Canal was scarcely ever projected which held out greater prospects of advantage to the Subscribers and the Public.

Brave oratory, and it certainly needed all his powers of persuasion to get this issue subscribed. Maybe because he wanted to show by example that he was personally prepared to put his money where his mouth was, or maybe because he had to underwrite the last tranche, James himself subscribed for a further 39 shares, taking his holding to 205 *(plate 9a)*. He was now the largest shareholder, with six more shares than Bernard Dewes. His holding had cost him £2,675 so far, with commitments to pay a further £4,875 over the next few years. What must have seemed to a man of his means to be a modest liability in 1813 would look rather different a few years later.[152]

Perhaps convinced by his own eloquence, James then made a further indirect investment in the success of the operation – he bought the shares in the Upper Avon Navigation from the executors of Major Fitzthomas, only a portion of which, unfortunately, were freehold. He also had to agree to hand on tolls demanded by the owner of the Lower Avon, George Perrott, who had for a time been a fellow-director of the Stratford Canal Company.

The race against the Worcester & Birmingham was now on. The navvies were put back to work, but even if the finance for completing the canal was largely in place, delays and obstructions beset the work on the ground. And to complete the funding, the company had to resort to selling annuities, 'the ultimate financial degradation for corporations'.[153] There were long debates about the route the canal should take on its last leg into Stratford, James finally winning the argument for taking it virtually along the course of the Guild stream, but instead of entering the Avon upstream of Clopton Bridge, a final turn to the right took it under the turnpike road and past the old archery grounds. James had been deputised to negotiate with the Duke of Dorset's executors for the purchase of the land along the route through Wilmcote and now he had to do the same for the riverbank area at the Bancroft. Since James still acted on occasion for the Duchess, there were inevitable conflicts of interest, and the minute books reflect continuous confusions about

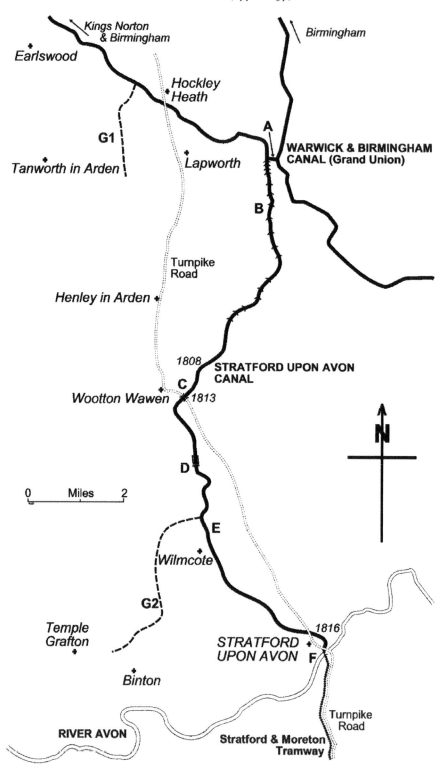

Kings Norton
& Birmingham

Earlswood

Birmingham

Hockley
Heath

A

G1

WARWICK & BIRMINGHAM
CANAL (Grand Union)

Tanworth in Arden

Lapworth

B

Turnpike
Road

Henley in Arden

1808

STRATFORD UPON AVON
CANAL

C

Wootton Wawen   1813

N

D

0   Miles   2

E

Wilmcote

G2

Temple
Grafton

1816

STRATFORD
UPON AVON   F

Binton

RIVER AVON

Turnpike
Road

Stratford & Moreton
Tramway

payments into and out of James's accounts both with her and the canal company.[154]

The company was also involved in expensive litigation. The Dowager Lady Smythe, who had retired from Wootton Hall to Austy Manor on the other side of the canal at Wootton, took strong objection to the aqueduct over the turnpike road, which, she claimed among other things, ruined her view. She also inferred that part of it had been built on a plot of land that had not been part of the original purchase from her family – although approved by her land-agent – and even tried to get a suit in Chancery for an ejectment order. The company stoutly defended its position and empowered James to lead the defence.[155]

> The Committee cannot but feel the greatest regret at this fresh proof of her Ladyship's hostile designs against the Company, but as this suit is instituted evidently to ruin the concern (which was projected and prosecuted under the advice and auspices of her late respectable father, Peter Holford Esq. and in which upwards of £200,000 has been expended) it is the bounden duty of the Committee to defend the Company's property.

James must have suffered ambivalent feelings about this duty, because he and his wife, when they first married, had received generous hospitality from the Smythe family. Finally, however, the case was decided in the company's favour and hefty costs were awarded against Lady Smythe.

A cast-iron plaque to commemorate the opening of the contentious Wootton aqueduct in October 1813 was attached to the southern elevation, listing the major officers of the company at the time, including William James as deputy chairman[156] (plates 5a and 5b).

Fig.6: **The Stratford Canal in relation to the river Avon, the Warwick & Birmingham Canal and the Oxford to Birmingham turnpike road.**

A Junction to Warwick & Birmingham Canal
B Locks built with the assistance of the railroad
C Wootton Wawen aqueduct
D Edstone aqueduct
E William James's Wilmcote quarries
F Stratford-upon-Avon, terminus of both the canal and James's Central Junction Railway, later the Stratford & Moreton Tramway
G Proposed branches, never built, to quarries at Tanworth-in-Arden and Temple Grafton.

The magnificent Edstone aqueduct, the longest aqueduct in England, remains today as one of the most impressive structures on any canal in the country[157] *(plate 6)*.

As the canal struggled southwards, events on the continent were taking a dramatic turn. Napoleon's empire was imploding, and when the allies finally fought their way into Paris at the end of March 1814, twenty-one years of war against France came to an end. Formulating a just and lasting peace would not prove easy, with each of the allies having a different agenda, but at least Napoleon's voluntary, albeit reluctant, abdication removed one problem. Most of his marshals had already deserted his cause and, once he renounced the succession of his heirs, the way was clear for the restoration of the Bourbon monarchy in the person of Louis XVIII. Napoleon was sent into exile in the role of governor of the sovereign principality of Elba and he was even allowed to take with him an army of six hundred men.

* * * * *

Elba is an infertile mountainous island off the west coast of Italy, covering an area of 86 square miles. Napoleon very quickly became bored. 'The administration of his tiny principality and household, to which he addressed himself with the same solemn thoroughness as if he were still ruling an Empire, was insufficient to occupy his time; his rides and excursions, his miniscule army, his monotonous evenings in the company of his sisters and his mother . . . were hardly sufficient to satisfy his insatiable urge for activity.'[158] On his rides he noticed that the inhospitable soil was mixed with outcrops of a reddish-brown rock, which one of his companions suggested might be a valuable source of iron ore. A sample was gathered and dispatched to England for the opinion of the one geologist of whom anyone on his retinue had heard – William James. According to his daughter, fragments of this sample were preserved by his family, though sadly no traces seem to have survived.[159]

Whether James had a chance to reply is not recorded, but on 26 February 1815 Napoleon embarked on his ship *L'Inconstant* and, accompanied by his entire army dispersed on a number of smaller vessels, set sail for the south of France, landing near Antibes four days later. It was an outstanding gamble, yet as the troops sent to arrest him merely rallied to his standard and as his march up the Rhône valley turned into a triumphal progress, his confidence grew in direct proportion to the panic afflicting the new government in Paris. The allies, still largely at loggerheads over the political map of peacetime Europe and with the Congress of Vienna still in session, suddenly had to face up to a rekindling of hostilities. And in London, their Lordships at the Admiralty were faced with the urgent need to mobilise an invasion fleet to ship the army overseas again for another continental campaign. The previous year, when the peace had apparently been finally won, the troops had been released; Navy ships had been dispersed back to their various dockyards, some for much needed overhaul, others to be scrapped. Military spending of all sorts was cut to the bone. Now, suddenly, an army and the means of transporting and supplying it had to be assembled at very short notice; everything was in the wrong place. As we all know, the miracle was achieved. Marshal Blücher did appear just in time, the infantry squares did hold and a combination of courageous command and individual bravery won a glorious victory on a battlefield outside Brussels. But as the Duke of Wellington famously observed, it had all been a 'damned close run thing.'

One person on whom the lessons of the mobilisation panic had not been wasted was William James. He wrote to the Prince Regent ('with whom, as well as the Duke of York, he was on somewhat familiar terms') pointing out the advantages of building one of his railways from the Medway to Portsmouth, providing a direct link between the country's two largest dockyards.[160] By developing his ideas of 'advanced locomotion' it would be possible to move men and material between these two key sites within hours rather than weeks. The amount of supporting stores could be reduced dramatically; no longer would it be necessary to maintain duplicate sets of sails, spars and rigging at both locations; officers and men could be transferred within a day, and, although he envisaged the whole project as a military initiative, if the public were allowed to travel on it in peacetime, this would bring in additional revenue of as much as £2,000 per annum. He does not quantify the likely cost, which would have been immense and fundable only out of the public purse. But if the government had thought it was worth spending £230,000 on building the Royal Military Canal in Kent, merely as a defensive measure against the threat of invasion and with no subsequent commercial value, surely such a strategic investment would be worthwhile. The government did not follow up the idea, but a few years later James was to develop and expand it into an even bolder scheme.

* * * * *

IN TOTAL, the building of the Stratford Canal had absorbed about £297,000, compared to the original estimate of £120,000. The committee wrote to James 'acknowledging his general services in promoting the Interest of the Canal and his great exertions towards completing the same,' although they raised concerns about the somewhat haphazard and chaotic way in which he had kept the books of accounts.[161]

The final grand opening of the Stratford Canal took place on 24 June 1816. By this time, the Worcester & Birmingham, the rival and at the same time the partner, the concern that had contributed to William James Snr's ruin, had been open for six months. Behind the directors' boat came a convoy of barges loaded with coal, the bunting was out and the ceremony was greeted with 'the rejoicings of many thousand people'.[162] James must have relished the accolades of the crowds and on that cold overcast summer's day, with the Napoleonic war finally ended, he could allow himself a justified sense of pride and achievement.

He needed to enjoy a moment of success, because in the coalfields of South Staffordshire, where he was now chairman of the coal-masters' federation, there was poverty and destitution. Not only were some of his miners facing starvation but he was personally losing a lot of money.

Plate 1: **The railway bridge at Stratford-upon-Avon, the most impressive relic of the Central Junction Railway scheme of 1820, whose terminus was at the Bancroft canal basin just off the left of the picture.** Author

Plate 2a: **The 'Yew Trees', High Street, Henley-in-Arden, William and Dinah James's home from 1793 to 1797. The plaque is on the front elevation.** Author

Plate 2b: **The William James memorial plaque, unveiled by Professor Hugh Torrens on James's birthday, 13 June, in 2003. The ceremony was attended by a number of James's descendants, some from Australia.** Author

WILLIAM JAMES
BORN HENLEY-IN-ARDEN
13 JUNE 1771
DIED BODMIN 10 MARCH 1837

LAWYER, SURVEYOR, LAND AGENT
AND TRANSPORT VISIONARY, PROPRIETOR
OF THE STRATFORD CANAL, PROMOTER OF
THE STRATFORD-MORETON TRAMWAY AND
INSTIGATOR OF THE LIVERPOOL AND
MANCHESTER RAILWAY

'FATHER OF THE
RAILWAY SYSTEM'

Plate 3a: George Greville, Earl of Warwick (1752–1816), the only portrait of him in adult life. From a bust in Warwick Castle. Author

Plate 3b: Trebinshun House, Brecon, rebuilt by James to its present style in 1805. Author

Plate 4: **James, notebook in hand, inspecting Richard Trevithick's *Catch-me-who-can* in September 1808. There are differing opinions about the actual design, this interpretation favouring that of Farey/Francis Trevithick/John Addyman rather than the 1962 model in the National Railway Museum, York. From a painting by Robin Barnes 2000.** Author

Plate 5a: **Stratford-on-Avon Canal. The cast-iron trough aqueduct at Wootton Wawen opened in 1813. Half the plaque fell off in 2001 and was replaced with an aluminium replica.** Author

Plate 5b: **The original cast-iron plaque, subsequently re-erected on a wall opposite the towpath.** Author

THIS AQUEDUCT,
was erected by
THE STRATFORD CANAL COMP.Y
in October, 1813,
BERNARD DEWES Esq.R CHAIRMAN.
W. JAMES Esq.R DEP.Y CHAIRMAN.
W. WHITMORE ENGINEER.

Plate 6: **James's aqueduct at Edstone – the longest in England.**
Ten years earlier Pontcysyllte Aqueduct on the Ellesmere
Canal had been built to a similar concept, but with an
overhanging towpath. Author

Plate 7a: The seminal meeting of William James (second from left) and
William Henry James (third from left) with George Stephenson and his
son Robert, Killingworth, July 1821. From a painting by Robin Barnes 2003.
Author

Plate 7b: 'What might have been, 1'
A scene, had James had his way, on the Central Junction Railway in 1824,
with a train headed by a 'Land-Agent' locomotive built by Robert
Stephenson & Co. From a painting by Robin Barnes 2003. Author

Plate 8a: '**What might have been, 2**'
'**Chittapratt' dropping its fire outside Cox's timber-yard, Bancroft Basin,
Stratford-upon-Avon, if James had been allowed to buy Robert Wilson's
locomotive in 1825. Two passenger carriages are suggested on the elevated
track leading onto the bridge. From a painting by Robin Barnes 2007.** Author

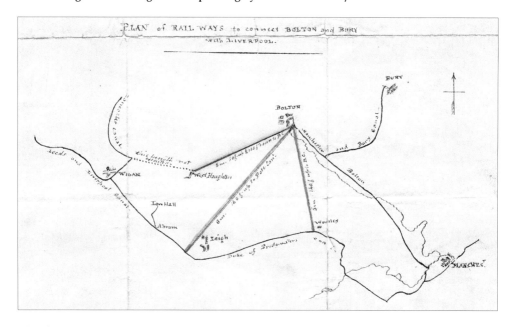

Plate 8b: **James's first sketches of possible
routes for railways from Bolton, 1802.**
Courtesy of Lancashire Record Office
and the Hulton archives. DDHU 6/5

EIGHT

Coalmines, Corn and Politics (1816–1820)

To understand the problems and predicaments that William James faced in 1816, one needs to go back a few years to trace his involvement in the coal and iron industries of South Staffordshire. It seems that this started as early as 1802 with an investment he may have acquired from his father, and Ellen Paine mentions 'his coalmine' when writing about her father's commitment to the Warwick Provisional Cavalry. Letters to many of his clients from this period show that he was very mindful of the practical problems faced by mining contractors – he was frequently urging landowners to be realistic in drawing up licence agreements and not to be too demanding in seeking early returns. He could advise from experience on both sides of the fence. It was as a result of his land agency for the Earl of Dartmouth[163] that James became a major coalmine proprietor in the West Bromwich area of the Midlands. The origins of this, around 1805, are shrouded in a charming piece of family folklore handed down to his children. It implies that James and the Earl were walking one day across West Bromwich Heath, an unproductive part of the Dartmouth estate covered in scrub and gorse but harbouring a large number of rabbits which had become a serious pest, migrating into cultivated parts of the Earl's Sandwell estate and causing considerable damage. When the Earl asked for his recommendation on how to deal with this plague, James apparently replied that the rabbits could go hang, and that the Earl should concentrate on what went on under the land, because he was convinced that there were extensive strata of coal close beneath the surface. This was to lead to the exploitation of the fabulous West Bromwich 30-foot seam. It may well have been a sighting down a rabbit hole that led James to his conclusion.

At the time, however, the Earl's initial response was apparently to reject the idea out of hand; if James wanted to take on the responsibility himself, then the Earl would make over part of the Heath to him, but Ellen Paine claimed that her father was 'too honourable and conscientious to accept such a liberal gift'.[164] Instead he agreed to take leases, paying a royalty of so much per ton extracted, but adopting the financial responsibility of the heavy initial capital investment. In 1808, he reported to Lord Dartmouth that pits were being sunk at Ball's Hill and he hoped that the next winter's coal supply for Sandwell would come from the estate.[165] To begin with the ventures prospered, and by 1813 James was proprietor of no fewer than six mines in the Midlands, five in Staffordshire and one, the Wyken colliery, on the Oxford Canal just outside Coventry.[166] The latter advertised itself as 'the nearest mine to London and the south country' and this was initially a great advantage when war was disrupting coastal traffic from the north-east. The Staffordshire mines were located at Wednesbury, Ball's Hill and Golden Hill in West Bromwich, and at Pelsall and Birchill, both on the Wyrley & Essington Canal between Walsall and Lichfield. The Birchill Colliery had an associated ironworks and foundry on the same site, while at West Bromwich there were limekilns and brickworks which used the low-quality produce, leaving 'coal of a superior quality' available for sale. In total these mines were producing 2,200 tons per week (*plate 9b*).

James was now a significant and influential coal-master, so, as befitted his standing in the region, he bought another large house, at Hill Top, north-east of West Bromwich.[167] He moved his family to Hill Top and let the house in Warwick.

His unique status at that time has been recognised in the *Victoria County History of Staffordshire*. 'Entrepreneurs like William James of West Bromwich and estate agents such as Thomas Smith of Dudley combined a primary concern for the economy of mining with a wide knowledge of its practice and problems; but these were men as isolated as they were outstanding.' He was also a major employer of labour across the Midlands, with nearly 500 workmen on his payroll at his various coalmines, quarries, foundries, farms, limeworks, wharves and canal carrying operations.[168] He was now in his mid-forties and could look with considerable pride on his achievements. He had driven the Stratford Canal to completion. He had placed clerks on his clients' estates; he had agents running his industrial concerns. He had his prestigious London office at New Boswell Court, and his personal wealth has been estimated as being as much as £150,000, though this figure probably included all the properties that he only held on lease.[169] It has also been calculated that his mailing costs alone came to £500 a year. Now surely he could devote more of his time and energy to his transport dreams, turning his concept of the General Railroad Company into reality.

But as the dismal summer of 1816 passed into September, there were genuinely black clouds looming over the Midlands. The harvest was going to be a disaster. Admittedly the battle of Waterloo the previous summer had finally ended the conflict with France and the secure exile of Napoleon to St Helena had brought wild rejoicing on the streets of London. Now perhaps taxes could be reduced. Trade with the continent could be resumed and, just as important, coastal shipping could ply the Channel and the North Sea without fear of attack and plunder by French privateers. Yet in the heartland of England the mood was very different. There was poverty and despair. Cut off from its supplies of coal from Northumberland and Durham, London had become used to obtaining this fuel from inland sources, even though the transport costs along the slow and incomplete canal network were very high. But the old coastal supply routes were quickly re-established and the Midlands lost this important market, while the local demand for coal and iron also suffered a sharp reduction as the military needs for armaments, chain, horseshoes and other metal products of the Midland ironworks dried up. The price of iron fell from £20 to £8 per ton. Furthermore, men leaving the colours were being discharged onto a labour market swamped by unemployed.

On 7 September 1816 the *Staffordshire Advertiser* carried an article which began:

Distress of the Mining and Manufacturing District, in the Counties of Worcester and Stafford. A numerous and respectable meeting was held at the Dudley Arms Hotel, 20th August 1816, for the purpose of taking into consideration the most efficient means of affording relief to the numerous manufacturing and labouring Poor, who are out of employ, in consequence of the present depressed state of trade.

The Rev Dr Booker was in the chair and a number of resolutions were proposed and unanimously supported, among them being 'the formation of a District association for the above purpose, comprising the Parishes of Dudley, Tipton, Bilston, Darlaston, Wednesbury, West Bromwich, Rowley Regis, Sedgley and Kingswinford.' A committee was formed and it was resolved to obtain 'an accurate statement of those in distress' out of a total population of 83,000 in the nine parishes. A federation was formed of all the colliery owners and ironmasters in the region, and, recognising the urgent need for a powerful spokesman with influence in high places, they elected James as their chairman. He drew up a petition on their behalf to be sent to the Prime Minister, Lord Liverpool, via the local Member of Parliament, Edward John Littleton.[170]

It pointed out that, until 1815, 40,000 men had been directly employed in local industry and many more indirectly, but now there were 13,000 out of work, as well as 8,630 'on the parish'. Capital assets had depreciated by three-quarters of their value and no new investment was being made. The industrialists and their workforces had played a major role in the war effort and were now being made to suffer through cheap imports and prejudicial tariffs. The signatories pleaded that 50,000 tons of coal a year should be allowed duty-free into London from the Midlands and that a proportion of import duty should be reallocated as a direct subsidy. The petition carried the signatures of 24 people, representing all the main collieries and ironworks in the region. James himself signed on behalf of the Ockerhill Colliery, as well as the Ball's Hill and Goldenhill Collieries under the name of James, Vansittart & Co. Two Feredays signed, as well as Samuel Bill, who signed on behalf of the Pelsall Colliery, where he was employed by James as his clerk and overseer.

But before considering Lord Liverpool's response to James's petition, one needs to take a broader view of the problems faced by his administration as it tried to tackle the transition from running the country on a war footing to one based on what looked like a lasting peace, at least on the international front. Its instincts were strongly conservative, its guiding motivation to restore the *status quo* of 1793. But in the intervening years the population had grown dramatically, inflation had escalated and the money supply was now awash with paper, much of which was of speculative value only. For the status of the country in overseas markets, the currency had to be stabilised but, since the suspension of convertibility in 1797, there was no benchmark to establish the true value of money. One of the first issues the Government tried to address was a standard based on the price of gold, so the pound was fixed in May 1816 at the equivalent of 123.25 grains of the precious metal. Convertibility of paper debt was quite another matter. In 1815, all they could say was that convertibility would be restored 'when the conditions were right', with a provisional target date of 1817. And as in all markets in times of uncertainty, this pronouncement led to a collapse of confidence in investment and the start of a deflationary slump. Edward Pease, who would later play an important role as founder of the Stockton & Darlington Railway, wrote in his diary, 'I found everywhere a remarkable torpor at Leeds and Manchester. London seemed palsied by the empty coffers of the bankers.'[171]

If the administration dithered over convertibility, it was certain about one thing. Never again would the nation depend on imports of the staple item of its diet – corn – and, to ensure this, all the marginal land that had been reclaimed for arable farming during wartime had to be kept under cultivation. The logical conclusion of this policy was either to impose a punitive tariff on corn imports or to ban them altogether – except at a price high enough to protect the home producers. This was the case for extreme agricultural protection and it was directly opposed to that of the manufacturers, who wanted to see corn at the lowest price possible, both for subsistence reasons and to take pressure off wage rates in the factories. Just as 20th-century governments found in trying to formulate a Common Agricultural Policy across the European Union, establishing a balance between the vested interests was not easy. The Chancellor of the Exchequer, Nicholas Vansittart, James's erstwhile co-investor in the Bexhill adventure and his current partner in two of the West Bromwich coalmines, argued for a laissez-faire import policy linked to a flat-rate tariff of 8s per quarter. This he claimed would not only bring revenue into the Exchequer, enabling an early reduction in taxes, but would put money into the economies of the central European countries, who would then be able to purchase manufactured goods exported from this country. Although supported by men on the enlightened wing of the Government and economists like Ricardo, this strategy was overruled by the landed interest, and the notorious Corn Laws of 1815 were enacted instead, which set a ban on imports below an intervention price of 80s per quarter, except for a 'colonial preference' level of 67s per quarter granted to the North American

states.[172] These laws would be a major factor in the civil unrest which fermented over the next three years and would in 1819 erupt into the Peterloo massacre.

Two other issues clouded the overall picture. First, imported corn (and iron) could be stored in warehouses without duty payment to await a favourable price opportunity. The second issue revolved around the inescapable fact that the population did not eat corn as such, but the manufactured by-product, namely bread, which involved two further vested interests in the form of the millers and the bakers. Until repealed by legislation subsidiary to the 1815 Corn Law, the selling price of bread had been set by magistrates using a formula which was estimated to give both parties a reasonable margin. Once prices were deregulated, some millers and bakers indulged in profiteering, and it was this aspect of the 1815 legislation that led to the greatest unrest.

Taxation was another matter for heated debate: how to balance the input from direct as opposed to indirect taxation and redefine property taxes at a level which would not penalise investment in agricultural and infrastructure improvements. Furthermore, whatever the arguments in favour of reducing overall taxation to stimulate home demand for the output of the country's factories, there was the small matter of the National Debt to consider. This had reached the staggering figure of £900 million. It was vital to keep the Bank of England on board, which was another reason to procrastinate about the question of convertibility.

By 1816, the generally depressed state of the entire economy and its threat to social stability caused ministers to debate the desirability of direct aid to assist regions of particular destitution. Such measures ran contrary to the ethos of the Tory Government; Lord Liverpool expressed the view of the majority of his administration when he said that this was a treadmill from which it would be difficult to extricate itself, and that free enterprise had to solve its own problems, however painful in the short term. Finally, however, it was agreed to give direct relief to a very few cases under the terms of the Poor Employment Act, to be administered by the Exchequer Bill Loan Commissioners.[173] The first beneficiary of an initial tranche of £1.5 million was Ireland, still an entirely agricultural economy, which received £250,000. The second was the fishing industry of Scotland and the third, influenced by James's eloquent testimonial and undoubtedly promoted in cabinet by Vansittart, was the Midlands iron industry.[174] These two would share another £250,000.

James's petition was not the only one received at the Treasury. Around the country generally, the constraints of the income tax were a pressing issue and nearly 400 petitions for its abolition, signed by 200,000 people, were submitted. Vansittart championed its retention to build up the sinking fund, but the motion was lost in the House of Commons by 38 votes. To fund the expected shortfall (£18 million for 1816–17 alone) the Government would be forced to issue yet more paper in the form of Loan Stock, pushing the date for convertibility further and further into the future. The harvest of 1816 had proved to be even worse than the most pessimistic forecasts, not only in England but across the whole of northern Europe. Even the unpopular Corn Laws could not prevent the price of wheat from rising to 117s a quarter. 1817 was a year of social crisis, with the whole fabric of law and order breaking down across East Anglia and riotous mobs on the streets throughout the Midlands and London itself. Instead of enjoying a prosperity driven by new opportunities opened up by the steam age, the whole country was on the verge of anarchy.

* * * * *

THERE now comes a period in James's career which is not well documented. No correspondence has survived for the years 1816 to 1820, while his daughter has nothing specific to say in her biography except that he was involved in a number of Enclosure Bills on behalf of his clients. We do know that he was still engaged by the Warwick family. His accounts as Receiver for the years 1817–18 show that he was paid a salary of £400, plus valuation fees of £108 and expenses of £158. The 'Home' estates were now showing a profit of £11,315 on rental incomes of £17,535, with the 'Outer' ones contributing a further £3,035 on income of £3,716. Still without a satisfactory transport link, the Clutton mines contributed only £850 to this total.[175]

The opening of the Stratford Canal had increased the trade from James's quarries at Wilmcote. As they expanded in area and the miners dug deeper, the quality of the stone improved dramatically; to such an extent that, for the first time ever, lithographs could be printed off native stone rather than that imported from Germany. In 1818 the Royal Society of Arts awarded the Silver Isis Medal to Mr D. Redman for his 'View of the Wye', printed off stone 'taken from a quarry, the property of Wm. James Esq. of Warwick . . . a member of the Society.'[176]

James was still on the general committee of the Stratford Canal and would remain so until 1821.[177] The role of superintendent had been given to his protégé John Kershaw in 1818, the year in which James was granted a 21-year lease on two warehouses at the Bancroft basin. The canal might be fully open to traffic, but it was beset by creditors and heavily in debt. By December 1819 one of its larger debtors was James himself, to the tune of £1,564 2s 3¾d, and he was being pressed by the company for payment 'to enable them to discharge the pressing claims now made against them.' In spite of selling back to the company 50 of his shares at only £15 each, the balance, rather ominously, remained unpaid. Furthermore, he still had unredeemed promissory notes with his stockbroker, Edward Smith, and the alarm bells might have started to ring even louder when Robert Peel introduced a Bill into Parliament in 1819 that set a timetable for the resumption of cash payments by the Bank of England.

* * * * *

IF LITTLE is recorded of James's detailed activities in the years 1816–1820, it is known that no less than three times in 1816 he visited Middleton colliery near Leeds, saw its rack locomotives on cast-iron rails, and talked to John Blenkinsop, their inventor.[178] While these cumbrous machines might work well enough on slow-speed mineral lines, James knew that they were quite unsuitable for his ideas of express transport. It is also known that he devoted much time and energy to travelling the countryside planning routes for arterial railways. He looked particularly at unrealised canal schemes where investors had already shown their hand, sometimes to the extent of obtaining Acts of Parliament. In the following chapters we will see how he revived the idea of linking the river Stort at Bishop's Stortford with the river Cam at Cambridge, this time with a railway, and a similar opportunity at Canterbury in Kent; how he put forward proposals to the Grand Surrey Canal Company for reactivating their plans to expand to the south-west; and how he re-opened his file on the strategic link between the great dockyards at Chatham and Portsmouth. But one scheme would have had his highest priority, a scheme which promised to bring enormous benefits to the Midlands and enhance the value of his own investments there – and possibly rescue his faltering shareholdings in the Stratford Canal and the Upper Avon. This was the Central Junction Railway, which James envisaged would be nothing less than the first 'Hundred Mile Railway' in the world.[179]

NINE

Great Expectations:
the Hundred-Mile Railway
(1820)

IF THERE had been a lesson to be learnt from the mobilisation panic of 1815, James drew an even more important conclusion from the plight of Midlands industry in the following years. He recognised that poor transport lay at the root of the problem, and that what was needed was a quick, reliable transport link between the Midlands and London. Starting off with a map of existing canals and river navigations of the region, he superimposed the principal coalfields around Birmingham and Coventry, adding areas of quarrying interest on the north edge of the Cotswolds and in the Chilterns. He also recalled the proposal put forward in 1809 for a Central Junction Canal from Stratford-upon-Avon, via Shipston-on-Stour, to the Thames at Abingdon, the eastern terminus of the Wiltshire & Berkshire Canal.

For his Central Junction Railway, James modified this route at the northern end to go from Stratford via Moreton-in-Marsh, an important market town for the Cotswolds (plate 10). It then headed along the valley of the river Evenlode, via Shipton-under-Wychwood, to Summertown on the northern outskirts of Oxford. Thence it followed an almost direct route via Thame, Amersham and Uxbridge to a terminus in London which, interestingly in the light of later history, he suggested should be at Paddington. From this main line he proposed a number of branches, the most important of which was to run to Coventry via Shipston-on-Stour, Leamington Spa and Warwick, and another from Shipton-under-Wychwood to Cheltenham, there to link with the existing Gloucester & Cheltenham Railway, while further branches would run from Burford south to the Thames at Faringdon and from the Duke of Marlborough's estates at Blenheim to join the trunk route at Cassington.[180] By 1820 he had completed a preliminary survey of the section from Stratford to Oxford.

To get things under way he needed a powerful sponsor who could rally support both locally and in the House of Lords. Here he was to have a staunch friend and ally in the form of Lord Redesdale, whose family seat was at Batsford Park just outside Moreton and who (along with the Duchess of Dorset) owned much of the land through which the first section of the railway would pass.[181] During the summer months James discussed the plan with him at length, and together they called a public meeting in Moreton on 14 August 1820.[182] The main case put forward for building the railway was a limited one: to reduce the cost of delivering coal to the town by 8s per ton while avoiding the delays that often occurred on the river Severn and the inadequate road from Evesham. Further benefit would accrue from the lower cost of exporting agricultural and quarry products from the area between Moreton and Stow-on-the-Wold. Thomas Telford had been invited to be a consultant. But James must also have outlined the broader scope of his concept, because Lord Redesdale wrote to him on 26 August with some reservations about how much should be put into the prospectus.[183]

> I cannot say that I am quite so sanguine as you appear to be with respect to the effect of the Moreton Railway, particularly with respect to Moreton itself. At the same time, I think it will be useful to the country in general, and that the extension [to Oxford and beyond] will be useful. I have some doubts whether it is prudent at present to say much upon its extension, which may raise jealousies and opposition . . . I think this is a very narrow view of the subject, but it is a common prejudice . . . I think it most advisable not to urge distant and possibly doubtful advantages.

He also questioned James's assertion that the railway would bring great benefit to the quarry owners at Bourton-on-the-Hill, unless there was a branch directly into the quarries themselves which would 'probably be a great inconvenience to me'. The prospectus was duly published in September 1820 and James spent the next months completing a detailed survey of the route from Stratford to Moreton, while cajoling potential investors to fill the subscription list. Here was the potential showcase for his concepts of advanced locomotion: a commercial railway across typical terrain, using steam locomotives on the new strong wrought-iron rails developed at Bedlington in Northumberland and at that very moment being publicised. If people could see such a railway in operation, even if it was only a few miles long, they would undoubtedly be persuaded that this was indeed the future. The economics could be tested as well as the next generation of locomotives. It is important to realise what a pioneering venture this was, how unique the concept, and how close it came to being a milestone in transport history. Its significance has been submerged by later events and the chronicles of subsequent historians, but, at the time, James was justified in thinking he was about to launch a venture of mould-breaking proportions. No one else was seriously planning railways on this grand scale. He had devised the very first 'high speed' inter-city railway in the world.[184]

In the early weeks of 1821, he concentrated his efforts on drafting the parliamentary Bill. It met little opposition at Westminster except from the Perrott family, who saw threats to their interests in the traffic on the Lower Avon, and it was supported in the Commons by three MPs who were also on the subscription list, namely George Lucy of Charlecote, George Phillips and J. H. Langston. The Central Junction Railway started to become a reality when the Act for the first section, from the canal basin at Stratford-upon-Avon to Moreton-in-Marsh, obtained royal assent on 28 May 1821.[185] It empowered the company to issue 670 shares of £50 each to a total value of £33,500 – the cost of constructing the line as estimated by the local contractor Thomas Baylis – and to raise a further £7,000 by mortgaging the tolls. This sum was to cover the cost of land purchase and parliamentary expenses. There were 56 initial shareholders, including Lord Redesdale (40 shares), five members of the Dudley family (20), James himself and friends (25), Thomas Baylis (50), the three MPs and no fewer than eleven clergymen. Many committee members of the Stratford Canal subscribed, including John Greaves (4) and John Kershaw (5); from the moment James had suggested the project, they had seen the advantages that extra traffic would bring to that concern. But people did not exactly fall over each other to buy shares, and the first subscription list raised commitments of only £21,750.

The form of traction to be employed was not specified in this first Act, the relevant clause merely referring to 'men, horses or otherwise'. It may have been a case of diplomatic expediency on James's part to ease the passage of the Bill; once it was on the statute books, his co-directors and shareholders could surely be persuaded to go along with his radical and far-sighted proposals. Interestingly, there was a clause that stated that where steam engines were erected or set up – which implies stationary ones – a method must be adopted to 'consume and burn the smoke arising therefrom, so as to prevent the same occasioning any nuisance.'

In early May, once he had nursed the Bill through its initial stages, James travelled north to confirm his new rails and ally himself with whichever engineer could best progress his ideas of advanced locomotion. The concept of using steam to power machinery in fixed installations was well established. For a century, the pumping engines designed and built by Thomas Newcomen and later by James Watt had been essential components in lifting water and thus in allowing the deep underground exploitation of coal, copper and other minerals. They were vast. A huge coal-guzzling boiler delivered very low-pressure steam into a cylinder several feet long. As the steam was condensed, creating a partial vacuum, the piston was sucked down the cylinder, communicating its motion to the pump via a massive rocking beam. Towering engine houses, the new cathedrals of the Industrial Revolution, became a familiar feature of the landscape in the major coalfields, and, since the fuel for these engines was virtually free, there was little incentive to make them more efficient. They were only capable, moreover, of driving reciprocating devices such as pumps until 1782 when, with Watt's rotative engine, steam could at last power mills and factories. It is not surprising that it was in remote Cornwall, where coal was very expensive, that the first motivation for a more compact and effective way of utilising the latent power of steam should be born.

Richard Trevithick's conceptual breakthrough was to use high-pressure (as he called it, 'strong') steam. In the very simplest terms, this meant a positive pressure, higher than that of the atmosphere. The higher the pressure, the greater the power derived from a cylinder of given size. But here the demon was unleashed; high-pressure steam, unless contained and controlled, was dangerous and potentially lethal stuff, and boiler design too had to be improved. One of Trevithick's main objectives was to free himself – and industry

– from the iron grip of James Watt who, by rigorously and rudely enforcing his own patents and charging very high royalties for their use, had accumulated a large personal wealth. This stimulated other inventors to wrap up their own ideas, however embryonic, behind the protection of the Patent Office which was, as Samuel Smiles wrote, 'a very costly as well as troublesome affair.'

Most of the steam engines Trevithick built were static, and many – notably those for draining the mines of his native Cornwall – were large. But with the new power available from high-pressure steam, relatively miniature engines became possible. Here too Trevithick was the pioneer. He built a number small enough to be classed as movable, for threshing on the farm, for instance, or powering a chain dredger. And, with miniaturisation, self-propelled vehicles at last entered the realm of practical politics. Trevithick's first full-sized experiments of 1800–02 were with road carriages.

The first steam locomotive – or, as George Stephenson would call it, 'travelling engine' – which certainly ran on rails was Trevithick's of 1804, built, as we have seen, for Penydarren Ironworks in South Wales. Possibly it had a predecessor, for in 1802 he had started to build one for Coalbrookdale in Shropshire; but there is no evidence that this was completed, let alone that it ran. No illustration of the Penydarren engine survives, and so-called replicas of it are based, by default, on a contemporary drawing which almost certainly depicts the Coalbrookdale one.[186] But, whatever the details, both would have been broadly similar, crude and cumbrous to later eyes, but visibly from the same distinctive Trevithick stable. At all events, it was so destructive to the cast-iron plate rails that its days as a locomotive were short. Trevithick followed it up with a handful of other experiments which were equally short-lived but none the less proved the point that steam traction on railways was a mechanical possibility.

Over the next fifteen years several engineers continued the quest for a locomotive design of adequate power and reliability.[187] Being well documented elsewhere, it is not the purpose of this book to rehearse their successes and failures. But it is relevant to look at the problems all faced and the varying solutions they came up with, to appreciate the judgments which William James made when he went in search of the best motive power, the 'thoroughbred', to turn his railway dreams into practical and profitable reality.

Many compromises had to be accommodated. To generate and store a worthwhile reservoir of steam, the boiler and firebox had to be as large, and the boiler plates as thick, as possible; but, to prevent the travelling engine breaking the rails which it rode on, its weight had to be restricted. Theoretically, the higher the steam pressure the better; in reality, however, a combination of uncertain metallurgy, the inherent nature of riveted joints and the (justifiable) fear of explosion meant that pressures were restricted to not much more than 40 pounds per square inch.[188] To heat the water, the simplest method – and the one adopted by all the pioneers – was to incorporate a circular flue-tube within and along the bottom of the boiler, one end having a grate and a fire-hole through which to stoke the fuel, the other end being connected to an upturned chimney. The heating area in contact with the water was restricted to the surface area of the tube. To increase this, a number of early builders incorporated a return flue, virtually doubling the heating surface and putting the firing hole at the same end as the chimney – and at the same time separating the driver from the fireman.

Another problem was getting an adequate draught for the fire. Access of air at the grate end was limited to the fire-hole, and a pioneer in France, Marc Seguin, tackled the difficulty with a rotary fan. But the real answer lay in the blast-pipe, which directed used steam from the cylinders up the funnel to create a forced draught. The bad-tempered Victorian controversy over who first thought this up was a futile one, for we now know that it had been present in Trevithick's Penydarren locomotive. It was later to be ascribed by his supporters to George Stephenson, whereas in fact he deliberately eliminated blast-pipes from many of his engines because they made the coal burn too quickly. Certainly an over-effective blast pipe could create the subsidiary hazard of ejecting burning cinders from the funnel top. It was another design feature for which a compromise had to be found, and the threat of locomotives setting fire to the countryside or to buildings was one which would be raised time and again in Parliament. Such concerns would frustrate James's own ambitions of using steam locomotives on his railway from Stratford to Moreton, and it is a neat irony that the last parliamentary select committee that he attended as an expert witness – in 1836 – should revert to this topic.

How about the cylinders, where the high-pressure steam drove the pistons? Each of Trevithick's known engines had a single cylinder, which required a large flywheel as well, but all the next generation of engineers used two cylinders. There was a divergence of opinion on where they should be situated. One school of thought, that of Murray, Chapman and Stephenson, buried them on the top centre-line of the boiler; the other, followed by William Hedley, Timothy Hackworth and John Rastrick, positioned them on either side of the boiler, attached by separate mountings. In both cases, the motion of the piston rods was vertical, and, with the exception of Hackworth (who built his first locomotive after 1820 anyway), that meant vertically upwards. Both groups were then faced with the problem of taking this drive to the wheels, involving the complicated rods and linkages which gave contemporary locomotives the appearance of spider-crabs. The former design school had the advantage that the cylinders were kept hot, steam passages were short and the whole assembly was immensely rigid. There was a further, rather subtle advantage: it was much easier to adjust the drive linkages to accommodate different gauges of track – of which early railways had a great variety – and with this came the opportunity to standardise production to some extent. The latter school claimed the advantages of simple access and easier maintenance, but had to overcome problems of lagging the cylinders and making extremely robust brackets for mounting them on the boiler, at spacings dependent on the track gauge.

There were differing design philosophies about the final drive too – how to convert the reciprocating action of the piston into rotary motion at the axles. Because slide bars could not yet be accurately machined, engineers used ungainly parallel-motion linkages. Stephenson favoured a direct drive to an external crank on each wheel and chain linkage between the axles, but all other builders in the period 1815 to 1820 used an intermediate jack-shaft carrying, under the boiler, a gear wheel which meshed with others on the axles. This was more precise, but involved complete dismantling to replace broken gears. Stephenson's chain, in contrast, being easily serviced, did tend to stretch with use, introducing slack, which caused timing problems with the valve gear.

What about springs? The answer is that none of the early locomotives had any metal ones at all. It was recognised that they would reduce the damage inflicted on the track by a locomotive weighing several tons, particularly at the rail joints, but the metallurgical technology was simply not available. Before 1820, steel leaf springs, which might suspend a relatively light road carriage and provide some relief for its passengers, were incapable of being upgraded sufficiently, and it would take another few years before they were widely adopted. It is not quite true that no

locomotives had springs, because in 1816 Losh and Stephenson took out a patent for steam springs, which they applied to a few of their engines. The concept was ingenious. On each axle were mounted two vertical pistons which fitted into cylinders incorporated in the bottom of the boiler, so that when the boiler was under pressure it would rise a few inches and sit on cushions of steam – not unlike the Hydrogas suspension found on latterday Citroen cars. As long as driving pistons operated in a vertical plane, springing was always going to be a problem.

It is certain that in the years up to 1820 James kept a very close watching brief on the stuttering evolution of the iron horse. He would probably have chortled at one particular evolutionary backwater which arose from a preconceived idea in some engineers' minds about the adhesion – or lack of it – between an iron wheel and an iron rail. Prior to 1813, despite Trevithick's brief but successful experiment at Penydarren, it was seriously doubted whether any iron-wheeled engine could pull more than its own weight without slipping. In that year, William Hedley, the viewer at Wylam colliery, performed an ingenious experiment to prove the doubters wrong, but not before three engineers had come up with machines to overcome the imagined bogeyman.

First was John Blenkinsop, the viewer at Middleton Colliery just south of Leeds. His patented solution of 1811 was to incorporate a toothed rack into the side of the cast-iron edge rails and engage this with a pinion driven by the motion – also patented – from the cylinders of steam locomotives built by his partner Matthew Murray. The principle certainly worked and was adopted on a number of colliery lines, but to James it was an unnecessary and expensive complication, and totally impractical for 'fast' trains.

The second solution was proposed by William Chapman in 1812, involving a chain fixed at both ends of the railway, wrapped around a steam-driven capstan on the (free-wheeling) locomotive frame. It was a non-starter. Most bizarre was the third solution, proposed by William Brunton of the Butterley Ironworks in 1813, whereby two horizontal cylinders at the rear of a free-wheeling engine would act on cranked and jointed legs which literally pushed the engine and its load along the track. Amazingly, and despite being incapable of reversing, it worked sufficiently well for a replacement boiler to be ordered the following year, with tragic consequences that will be mentioned later. James very quickly concluded that his thoroughbred would have to come from quite another stable.

TEN

Choosing the Thoroughbred – and a New Partner (1821)

OF ONE thing James was very well aware. A locomotive, however thoroughbred, powerful, or reliable, was of little use if the rails beneath it kept on breaking. When in the early summer of 1821 – probably in May – he journeyed north to visit the Tyneside coalfield, his first priority was to see for himself a new type of rail. Cast-iron rails had for the past thirty years been supplanting the age-old wooden ones, and for horse-operated lines they had many benefits. The best design at the time was generally reckoned to be that patented in 1816 by George Stephenson and William Losh of Walker Ironworks. But cast iron is brittle. Rails broke even under loaded waggons, and as soon as steam locomotives were placed on them, heavy and pounding the track at every stroke of their pistons, this tendency to break became yet more deplorable. And because each rail was necessarily short, three or at most four feet in length, the jolting caused by the frequent joints did no good to a locomotive's mechanism. The greater the speed, the worse the jolting and the worse the damage both to track – particularly at the joints – and to engine. It is no exaggeration to say that, as long as rails were of cast iron, the locomotive had no practical future.

But the solution was at hand. For fifteen years or so, rails of a different material had been tried at a handful of collieries in Scotland and the North. Wrought iron, or malleable iron as it was then called, is flexible, not brittle, and the new rolling mill could make it in bars of much greater length and, weight for weight, much greater strength. These early experiments, small-scale and out of the public eye, were not wholly satisfactory. They used light bars so narrow that they wore the wheels running on them, and it was a long time before they became common knowledge. But then they came to the notice of a Scottish engineer named Robert Stevenson, not to be confused with the Northumbrian Stephensons (he was Robert Louis Stevenson's grandfather), who saw their

wider potential. He had made his name as builder of the Bell Rock lighthouse, was much in demand for surveying new railways north of the border, and had a great if unsung influence on early railway development. In 1819 he published a report on a proposed line near Edinburgh in which he extolled the virtues of wrought-iron rail.[189]

Stevenson sent a copy to George Stephenson, who passed it to Michael Longridge, owner of Bedlington Ironworks near Morpeth, Northumberland, who was about to build a waggonway to the works from a nearby colliery. His employee John Birkinshaw was inspired to improve the design and overcome the problem of wheel-wear by rolling the iron in a T section, with a broad running surface and a narrow vertical web below for strength. The new waggonway was laid with the resulting rail, which Birkinshaw patented (23 October 1820). The published specification brought the idea to the general attention of engineers.[190] Weight for weight, these wrought-iron rails cost about twice as much as cast-iron ones but, because of their strength, for a given weight of traffic need weigh only half as much. Thus the initial cost was much the same. On top of that, the wrought-iron lasted very much longer and, being rolled in lengths of 15 or 18ft, had many fewer joints. It was a development just as epoch-making as any that involved locomotives, and between them they made the Railway Age possible.

James, his finger on the pulse, would certainly have read the 1820 specification and perhaps even Stevenson's 1819 report. On that first visit of 1821 he inspected the new Bedlington waggonway and found that the rails fully matched his best expectations. Here at last was the single most important piece of hardware for his railway projects.

One can easily understand why he went to Tyneside to tap practical experience. It had a spider's web of waggonways totalling well over 200 miles in length, 22 miles of which were operated with steam locomotives. He had a short-list of three or four engineers with whom he wished to discuss his grand schemes. Having made three visits to Middleton, he would already have dismissed Murray and Blenkinsop at Leeds. Their rack rail was irrelevant and one of their engines had suffered a fatal boiler explosion. Brunton's mechanical horse was clearly an evolutionary dead-end, as well as blowing itself to pieces, killing or maiming 47 people. For loco-motives as for rails, it was on Tyneside that all the expertise and all the potential was to be found.

James knew, however, that the slow, inefficient lumbering monsters of the collieries were still hopelessly inadequate for his high-speed inter-city lines. What he needed to do was to assess which engineer had the best basic concepts, capable of future development and improve-ment. His first meeting, of which we have no detail at all, was with William Hedley at Wylam. He then went to Killingworth, though on this first visit George Stephenson himself was away from home. But he did meet William Losh, Stephenson's partner and financier in some of his patents and co-manufacturer of a few of his engines, which James had the opportunity to inspect and see at work. He was impressed, and one of the features that probably impressed him most was the patented use of steam springs. He was also delighted to discover that Losh was a fellow mason.

On his way back south, James called in at Manchester and Liverpool to drum up support for the idea he had nursed since 1802 for a railway between the two cities. At Liverpool he was introduced to a corn merchant and underwriter, Joseph Sandars, a meeting which would have far reaching results and was in its way as earth-breaking as his encounter with the Stephensons. Sandars listened attentively to James's ideas and suggested that he make a preliminary survey later in the year, while he himself would canvass support among the local business community.

Once home, James wrote to Losh on 22 June, fulsome in his praise for the skills of the people he had met in the north-east.[191] He cited his qualifications for pronouncing on the subject: on his journey back south he had visited other railways which sadly he does not name ('it can answer no other purpose than to amuse'); he had 'as a Miner at Wednesbury in Staffordshire and in Cheshire employed Rail Roads for the last 20 Years'; he had also seen and used them in Somerset, Shropshire, Wales, Lancashire and Yorkshire. All this gave him 'some Confidence in my Conclusions'. And these conclusions were

enthusiastic. The first is tinged with terminology appropriate for a fellow mason.

'I confess *Light* has at length *shone* from the *North*, and I pronounce as my Candid Opinion that the *Malleable Iron Rail Road* at Bleddington [*sic*] Works, is by far the best I have ever seen.' He is especially impressed by its unexpected resistance to rusting. He is tactful enough to give good credit to the product of his host and correspondent. 'I certainly approved very highly of the rail of Losh & Co, it is by far the best Cast Iron Rail I ever saw, but the malleable Iron is so superior to it, that I shall advise our Company to adopt it;' on, that is, the Stratford & Moreton section of his railway to link the Midlands to London and the south coast, the completion of which 'will be the Business of my future Life.' Then he moves on to the engines he has seen.

> The Locomotive Engine of Mr Stephenson is superior beyond all comparison to all the other Engines I have ever seen—Next to the immortal Watt I consider Mr Stephenson's Merit [to lie] in the Invention of this Engine.

> Although my letter is to you & Mr Pees [Pease] & his friends of a private Nature, I feel it due to the Character and Talents of the Northumbrians to declare that in the sciences of Mining & Mechanics we can in the South in no respect be compared with them, and with such great and nobleminded Men as Mr Blackett and Mr Buddle and such Abilities as Mr Stephenson's and Mr Chapman's, I cannot conceive my Observation deserving of any other Notice than to show how sensible I am of the Value of these Gentlemen, and of the Esteem in which I hold the plans and Characters of yourself and your Friends in Durham.[192]

> My respects to E. Pees [*sic*]. I lament I did not see him.

This is a generous letter, brimming with genuine respect for his hosts, and it will be worth recalling in the light of George Stephenson's subsequent treatment of James. The reference to Edward Pease is also interesting. This remarkable and fair-minded man, a Quaker businessman from Darlington, had since 1810 been the driving force behind improvements to transport in Durham. Unlike their counterparts just to the north who had easy access to the river Tyne, the coal-masters of South Durham were situated a long way from their nearest river, the Tees, and were being priced out of the market. In 1815 a scheme for a canal from the coalfield to Darlington and on to Stockton-on-Tees was rejected on grounds of cost. A new faction arose, headed by Pease, which favoured a railway instead, and commissioned a survey from the Scotsman Robert Stevenson. At much the same time yet another was made by the Welshman George Overton, who had engineered the Merthyr Tramroad in South Wales, and on his survey, despite some unsatisfactory aspects, the first Stockton & Darlington Railway Bill was based.

It was on the actual day when it received Royal Assent, 19 April 1821, that Edward Pease first met George Stephenson. He was immediately struck by his blunt, down-to-earth approach and particularly appreciated his suggestions for cost savings, involving shortening the route at the expense of some steep gradients. A few days later Stephenson was asked to organise a completely new survey. It has been suggested that this first meeting was arranged by Robert Stevenson. If so, Stephenson had cause to be grateful; but he held Stevenson in low esteem. Writing confidentially to James in November 1822, he says of him that 'knowledge of machinery has not yet entered his head at least I have not seen any marks of it when in his company and if not now its unlikely it ever will. I have heard him make some remarks on Railways which I hardly could have expected from a child.'[193]

James returned to Killingworth probably in July, this time taking his eldest son, William Henry James, now aged 25 and a trained engineer, having been a pupil under Benjamin Bevan the canal surveyor.[194] This first meeting between the James and Stephenson families was to be a defining landmark in the history of world transport. James was 50 years old, his host ten years younger (plate 7a). By all accounts they got on rather well, despite the fact that their backgrounds and personalities could not have been more different. George Stephenson was born at Wylam just west of Newcastle, the second of six children of an engine-minder on a salary of 15s a month, and the whole family of eight lived in a single room. None of the children went to school and George taught himself to read and write at the age of eighteen, by which time he was himself an engine-wright and showing an instinctive talent for all forms of machinery. He invented a successful mining safety lamp and became a skilled clock repairer in his spare time. He had built his first travelling engine in 1814.

At the time of their meeting, George Stephenson was superintendent of all colliery machinery at Killingworth, an acknowledged expert in his field and highly respected in his community. He had a number of consultancy roles with other colliery groups and had just agreed to survey the Stockton & Darlington. He was now by his own lights wealthy, and supremely self-confident, if naturally taciturn and known as a man of few words (delivered in the thickest Geordie accent). One can imagine their conversations as being somewhat one-sided, as James held forth on his list of influential clients, all hungry for better transport links, and poured out his great visions of railways carrying not only goods but passengers all over the country. If Stephenson felt he was being somewhat patronised by the rich, upper-middle-class southerner, he did not at this stage show it, but probably basked in his guest's verbose flattery.

Another crucial meeting took place that was to broaden the connections between the two families. George Stephenson introduced his only son, Robert, then aged seventeen. His father, recognising his own shortcomings, had paid for him to have a sound education in Newcastle, including private tuition in mathematics. Robert, at the time he first met James, was apprenticed to Nicholas Wood, the managing engineer at Killingworth colliery, and was learning the skills of surveying from John Dixon on the intended route of the Stockton & Darlington. He listened to James in awe as the older man expounded his visions, stitching his dreams into a tapestry of words and painting the future on a canvas that stretched far over the horizon. Years later he would say of James that 'his fluency of conversation I never heard equalled'.[195] He was intoxicated by James's aura of wealth, sophistication and worldliness, and indicated, probably well out of his father's hearing, that if ever James wanted an assistant, he would like to be considered. A year later his wish would be granted.

One matter they certainly discussed was the question of rails. In James's eyes, the patented Losh and Stephenson design was the best cast-iron rail in the country, but even it was not good enough compared to Birkinshaw's wrought-iron rail. George Stephenson was in somewhat of a dilemma. He had a vested interest in the cast-iron patent, but he too saw all the virtues of Birkinshaw's. At exactly this time (28 June 1821) he wrote to Robert Stevenson enclosing Birkinshaw's specification and adding that these rails were 'so much liked in this neighbourhood, that I think in a short time they will do away with the cast iron railways. They make a fine line for our engines, as there are so few joints compared with the other.'[196] He was honest enough to recommend that the

Stockton & Darlington be laid two-thirds with wrought-iron rails and a third with cast; which led to a fatal rupture in his relationship with Losh.

The four men undoubtedly also discussed how the steam locomotive could be improved, and in Robert Stephenson the Jameses found a most receptive mind. To George, the idea of high-speed passenger-carrying railways was a rich man's folly, but to Robert, already responsible for a number of engineering innovations on his father's machines, increased power and lower weight were exciting and essential goals. The key to higher and sustained power lay in generating more steam and at a faster rate, which meant increasing the heating surface. William Henry James must have mentioned that he was about to apply for a patent to cover his proposed solution and may have sketched his designs, which undoubtedly involved some sort of tubes. It is probable that his concept focussed on containing the water and steam *within* the tubes, with the furnace gases heating them from the outside. Theoretically, this arrangement – the water-tube boiler – allowed very high steam pressures to be generated, with less risk of explosion than if the whole boiler was pressurised. This would be a central theme of William Henry's inventions over the next ten years.

James now proposed a revolutionary partnership: he would exclusively promote the Losh/ Stephenson locomotive to his clients and recommend them as sole suppliers for all his future schemes. In return, the two Northumbrians agreed to grant James a quarter share in the profits from any locomotive sales in 'his' territory. This document, often forgotten or ignored, is a buried treasure of transport history.[197]

Know all men by these presents, that we, William Losh, of the town and county of Newcastle-upon-Tyne, iron-founder, and George Stephenson, of Killingworth in the county of Northumberland, engineer, in consideration of £5 of lawful money of Great Britain, to us paid . . . and in consideration of William James, of West Bromwich, in the county of Stafford, miner and engineer, giving his recommendation and best assistance for the using and employing the locomotive engines, for which we, William Losh and George Stephenson, have obtained two letters patent, on such terms as we shall direct and appoint, we, the said Losh & Stephenson, have granted and assigned . . . unto the said William James, his heirs, administrators and assigns, one fourth part or share of our

rights and patents in the exclusive use of the locomotive engine for working on railroads, secured to us in and by certain letters patent of his Late Majesty, and of the profits arising from the granting the use thereof to any other party or persons whomsoever – such fourth part or share of the use, right, interest and profits to be confined to engines made, used or sold in that part of England and Wales lying south of a line drawn from the town of Liverpool to the town of Hull, to have and to hold such fourth-part or share of the said patent, right and profits from the date hereof unto the said William James, during the term of the said letters patent, given under our hands and seals, this first day of September, 1821.

William Losh
George Stephenson

More controversially, because it is not mentioned by any subsequent commentator except Warren,[198] there was also a vitally important second part to the agreement.

And in consideration of such grant of one fourth share in their patent, William James hereby agrees to allow the said William Losh and George Stephenson to adopt any improvements and the introductions of tubes to their boilers, as contained in the letters patent of William Henry James, son of the said William James, as granted to him in the reign of his present Majesty.

William Henry James
William James

Losh returned this agreement, duly executed, to James on 10 September with a covering letter expressing his belief that 'this connection will prove to the advantage of all the parties' and (acknowledging the potential significance of William Henry's input) 'to the prospects of some of your family.'[199] In the light of subsequent arguments about who really invented the tubular locomotive boiler, it is strange that William Henry's water-tube patent, which was such a pivotal consideration in the partnership, was not obtained until 1825 (see Appendix A). Perhaps he was persuaded not to rush into early application until he had some practical models and had thoroughly checked earlier patents, including Richard Trevithick's multi-water-tubed boiler patent of 1815 (No. 3922).[200]

James had returned to the Midlands convinced that he had now linked his destiny with a genius,

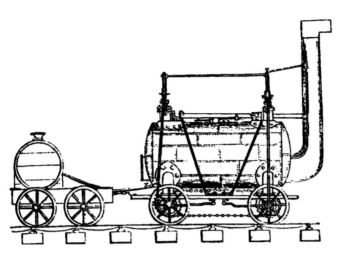

Fig.7: **William James's 'Land-Agent' locomotive,
as depicted on the cover of his 'Essay' of 1823. (see chapter 13).
This is the earliest printed image of a Stephenson locomotive,
clearly showing the patented steam springs.**

a man he felt he could trust not only as a business colleague but also as a solid, blunt-speaking friend. He was also much impressed by young Robert, in whom he spotted a rare talent. Now he had the best locomotive engineers as partners and he could (and did) extol their virtues across the country, putting the name of George Stephenson securely on the map, expressing his opinion that he had seen 'the greatest wonder of the age, and the forerunner, as I firmly believe, of the most important changes in the internal communication of the kingdom'.[201]

There was one intriguing follow-up to the James's visit to Killingworth in the summer of 1821. Perhaps at his specific invitation, perhaps as a result of the young man pestering his father to be allowed to see more of the world, Robert Stephenson paid a visit to London in the autumn, which 'greatly excited him'.[202] In an ill-fitting suit he toured the city sights of St Paul's Cathedral, Somerset House, the Customs House and, at his own insistence, the London Water Works.[203]

The opportunity for James to sell his first Stephenson locomotive – 'branded' by James as the 'Land-Agent' – had already arisen, at the opening shareholders' meeting of the Stratford & Moreton Railway on 13 July 1821. His report is a well-argued document, logical and comprehensive, agreeably compact.[204] He quoted his wide-ranging experience of existing railways in the north of England and elsewhere, and then tackled the two major issues – the type of rails to be used and the means of traction. On the former, he admitted the excellence of Losh and Stephenson's cast-iron version but made a strong case for the alternative.

> I am bound to state that I prefer the malleable to the cast iron . . . on account of its strength, facility and cheapness of construction, security from accidents and the necessity of repairs, and that by welding the pieces together the railway may be laid even for miles together without a joint.[205]

His analysis of the technical deficiencies of cast-iron rails was absolutely correct. The heavier the load, the greater the danger of fractures at the joints, leading to derailments unless the track was subject to constant and expensive inspection and replacement. When one remembers that he already had in mind trains travelling at thirty miles an hour or more, short straight cast-iron rails were out of the question. The initial cost of long wrought-iron rails with many fewer joints was no higher, and in terms of maintenance over a number of years they won hands down.

Next he turned his attention to the means of traction, harking back to his concept of the General Railroad Company of 1808.

> The employment of locomotive engines on this railway is a subject of vital importance

as it respects the prospect of profit to the Company, and of benefit to the public . . . My sentiments upon the excellence of communications by railroad worked by steam engines have been long known to many Gentlemen present, as well as my principal plan, conceived and in some degree acted upon above 12 years, of a line of communication from Birmingham to the south coast of England, of which this forms the first stage, by railroad.

Then, mindful of shareholder concerns about initial cost (he already had in his pocket a quotation for £440 per engine), he went on:

Of course the Capital for the engine trade will not be borne by this Company, but I have authority to say that another company will be found willing to make proposals for a lease of the tolls and powers of this Company, with a view to the employment of locomotive engines thereon.

James, therefore, was already working on leasing arrangements, allowing the railway to use locomotives from the start but without having to bear the initial capital cost.[206] He went on to tell his listeners that he had inspected 'all the kinds of locomotive engines now in use, but the most perfect one in all its properties is the invention of Mr George Stephenson.' He gave some figures about its ability to haul loads up various inclines, anticipating obvious questions from people instilled with the 'canal' concept of tackling gradients by means of levels linked by locks. Interestingly, he suggested that even where the combination of slope and load might become too great, the locomotive could be taken to the top of the incline and used as a stationary steam winch to haul the train up with cables. Back on economics, he extolled the cost advantages of steam versus horse. With the locomotive capable of moving at least 50 miles per day, it would work at a quarter of the expense of horses. It would cost nothing when not working. Without going into details, he claimed that the initial cost of earthworks would be less, because moderate gradients would allow a more direct route. Finally, for the benefit of the 'canal' lobby, he stated with typical confidence,

as a general principle not to be contraverted [sic], that the moving of articles on railroads by steam engines can be done cheaper, more certain, and twice as expeditiously as by boats on navigable canals, and neither the repairs of locks and banks, the want of

water, the summer's heat or the winter's frost, will retard the operation.

He concluded equally robustly, predicting that the adoption of his proposals would 'produce the greatest advantages to the agricultural, commercial, and mineral interests of the country.'

On every significant point, James was entirely right. The problem was that he was addressing the wrong audience. The incentive for urgent action just was not there. Whatever advantages the broader vision of Lord Redesdale and a few others might see in the scheme, the local communities along the route were too sparse and too agricultural to provide either the traffic or the need for a quantum improvement in communications. Moreton-in-Marsh had a population of well under 1,000, Stratford of about 4,200. Here there were no thrusting industrialists such as the mill-owners of Manchester or the coalmasters of Durham, who required cheap and reliable transport for bulk goods and were frustrated by the shortcomings of canals. Later, when expounding his almost messianic message in Lancashire, James struck a responsive chord. Not so with the cautious and conservative county investors of Middle England, many of whom had already burnt their fingers in the Canal Mania.

In retrospect, one can argue that historians have been cruelly dismissive of the importance of the Stratford & Moreton Railway, dwelling only on its latter days as a primitive, rustic anachronism. In 1821, James's proposals were at the cutting edge of transport development and he was totally justified in believing that, in the right context, his business plan was sound and practical. It is also amazing how few historians of early railways even mention his ground-breaking agreement with Stephenson, let alone give him credit for promoting across the country the interests of his new friend and partner. No one could have asked for a better public-relations advocate. With their agreement in mind, James invited Stephenson to come south to meet his survey team and discuss certain aspects of his railway which he envisaged would terminate initially in London. No railway on this vast scale had ever been seriously contemplated before, and it was already the talk of Northumberland. William Stobart of Pelaw colliery wrote to a colleague in August 1821 that George Stephenson 'was going into Warwickshire next week . . . his business is upon a long railway of about 100 miles and engines to suit it.'[207] But whatever else Stephenson thought of the project following this visit, he was obviously not impressed by Thomas Baylis, the contractor who had costed the construction of the Stratford to Moreton section, and he wrote to James warning him to 'look closely after Baylis, as it is possible he may be disposed to deceive you in laying down the section.'[208]

James now put on his salesman's hat again. The partnership agreement in his pocket, he threw himself into implementing his side of the bargain by proposing trials and, hopefully, achieving sales of Stephenson locomotives in the south. One approach was to a company which he already envisaged as an important link to his Central Junction scheme because it would provide access to the Bristol Channel. The Gloucester & Cheltenham Railway, opened back in 1810, ran from the city quay at Gloucester to the outskirts of the 'highly celebrated and improving town of Cheltenham'.[209] It was a horse-operated plateway with a length of 8¾ miles, much of it running along the turnpike road. In October 1821 James wrote to George Stephenson asking for a locomotive to try on it, but received a typically cautious response. Stephenson, understandably, wanted to know about the strength of the track, the weight of the waggons, and whether there were any gradients. He had no engines to spare anyway.

> We are expecting to commence making 3 Locomotive Engines in a fortnight's time for a neighbouring Colliery. If the Cheltenham way was found suitable we might commence making one for you at the same time but I am afraid it will not. I should be unwilling to recommend an Engine on any Line unless I was confident of it giving satisfaction.[210]

James's reply clearly did not provide satisfactory answers and no locomotive was forthcoming. It was not until 1831 that a steam engine was given a trial here, the *Royal William* from Neath Abbey Ironworks. It smashed the track.[211]

Down in Westminster, debates on the management of the economy were still largely polarised between the agriculturalists and the free traders, the bullionists against the paper-sympathisers. MPs struggled to grasp the links between production, competition and consumption, and the consequences of an unregulated money supply on the exchange rate. Each side had its protagonists, prominent among those warning of the dangers of restoring convertibility being James's friend Thomas Attwood, the Birmingham MP. His economic philosophy was influenced by arguments formulated in the Treasury by, among others, James's brother Henry, who earned

himself the nickname of 'My Lord Little Shilling'. This was 1821, and the following year James would lose a key link with government when Nicholas Vansittart, still Lord Liverpool's loyal minister, was removed from the Chancellorship of the Exchequer. Vansittart had been 'technically sound, but an inept and tactless debater' and 'though possessing no special qualifications'[212] had held the office for an unprecedented 22 years. But now the supporters of William Canning had to be appeased. At least Vansittart made certain that William Huskisson did not succeed him (he went to the Board of Trade), but there was now no hope of Peel's Banking Act being repealed, and the return to a gold standard was inevitable. Lenders would want their loans redeemed in cash, not more paper. If James did hear alarm bells ringing, he was too preoccupied to try and protect his own position. A crisis was in the making.

James was not content to let the extension of his railway beyond Moreton towards Oxford and London die through lack of financial backing in Warwickshire. During the autumn of 1821 he made plans to solicit new investors in Gloucestershire, posting an advertisement at the Shire Hall in Gloucester[213] for an enlarged version of the Central Junction, to be called, he suggested, the Thames & Avon Junction Railroad, extending still further west to the Forest of Dean.[214] At least the management committee of the Stratford Canal could see the potential benefits to them; their minute book records in October 'that a survey was being taken . . . from Moreton to Eynsham for a railway to connect the Thames and Avon under the direction of Mr James,' and it was 'resolved that Mr Kershaw be directed to subscribe £25 for the company towards the expenses of this survey.'[215]

Meanwhile, at the headquarters of the railway company at Moreton-in-Marsh, very little was happening. The next move, on 4 December, was a request by the management board that two of its members, John Greaves and Thomas Brewin, plus an 'able engineer' (elsewhere described as 'Lord Dudley's Engineer'), should visit railways in Yorkshire, Durham and Northumberland and submit an independent report.[216] Brewin and the engineer eventually left in the first week of February 1822, and found themselves sharing the coach from Darlington to Newcastle with a local man. They enquired if he knew the engineer George Stephenson and, when the stranger replied that he did, asked about his character and what he knew about railroads. In a letter to James dated 14 February 1822, George Stephenson recounted this coincidental meeting with great amusement;

he had strung them along until they were almost in Newcastle before revealing his identity.[217] 'I soon found their knowledge of Railways was very limited; it would take a volume to hold all our conversation on Railways, Locomotive Engines & Stephenson before I was known to them.'

Later in this letter he copied the table he had given his visitors, showing the maximum gradients that he felt his engines were capable of working with different loads. In practice, for ascending loads, this amounted to a gradient no steeper than about 1 in 200, though he implied that this was a deliberately conservative estimate, more so than those he had previously given to James in person. This incident, minor perhaps in itself, typifies the gulf between the characters of the two men and their attitude to risk; Stephenson so anxious to protect his reputation from any possibility of failure, so averse to risking anything that might bring him blame; James prepared to venture into the realm of uncertainties, anxious to try out a prototype even if it did not succeed at once, but confident that testing and development would lead to future success.

Brewin's recommendation resulting from his visit favoured malleable iron rails; but Greaves seems to have made a separate visit on his own and came away from his encounters with Stephenson and his colleagues with very different and somewhat confused impressions. On 28 February 1822, Greaves submitted his report.[218] His conclusions were to contradict James on virtually every point, as well as to encourage the board to postpone any definitive decisions at all.

I have been introduced to some of the most eminent engineers and proprietors of railroads, who have in the most candid and liberal manner given me their opinion and advice. From these sources of information, aided by the portion of mechanical knowledge I possess,[219] I am enabled confidently to recommend that the railroad from *Stratford-on-Avon* to *Moreton-in-Marsh* and *Shipston* be constructed on a plan calculated for the use of horses generally, and that the line be formed as *nearly horizontally* as possible ... Where an ascent is unavoidable I recommend that an inclined plane be constructed on the summit of which a fixed steam engine be erected to draw up the loads.

On the matter of the track, he came down in favour of Losh and Stephenson cast-iron rails. This conclusion is staggering because he had

been led to believe – and this is quoted in his report – that the 'patent *malleable*-iron rails of Burtenshaw and Co [sic] are cheapest in the first instance.' He seems to have been swayed by his impression that cast-iron rails were 'not so liable to oxidate [rust] and are on that account more durable' and by his complete misinterpretation of Stephenson's recommendation that the Stratford rails should be to the Darlington specification. He went on to list six objections to steam locomotive traction.

a) the weight of the engines

b) their inability to haul loads up gradients

c) resistance between wheels and the rails

d) slipping on the rails in snow or rain

e) their disruptive appearance

f) they were liable to explode

I trust this objection, combined with the others ... will induce the Committee to abandon, for the present, the locomotive engine plan, and construct a railroad upon the plan I have proposed, with as much economy as possible consistently with substantiality.

He added a procrastinating addendum, drawing the committee's attention to two recent patents for alternatives to locomotives. The first, that of Benjamin Thompson at Ayton colliery, involved a succession of stationary steam engines up to a mile apart, hauling vehicles by relays of long ropes. The second, that of Henry Robinson Palmer, Greaves described as 'very ingenious'. This retrograde scheme was for a wooden monorail and had been endorsed by Thomas Telford, who was himself not only retained by the board of the Moreton Railway as a consultant but was also Palmer's employer.[220] On 12 April 1822 the Committee resolved that 'no further contracts for the completion of the railway should be entered into until estimates had been received from Mr Palmer.'[221]

One can image James's frustrations as he sat in these committee meetings. Gone was his demonstration railway, scuppered, as he saw it, by cautious country bumpkins unable to share his vision or take the calculated risks that might make them historic pioneers. He must have been saddened by what he saw as disloyalty from his friend and cousin John Greaves, with whom he shared the business interest in the Wilmcote Quarry. Angry and disillusioned, he turned his back on his fellow-directors at Moreton-in-Marsh and headed north again, to Liverpool.

ELEVEN

Liverpool and Manchester (1822)

LIVERPOOL and Manchester are separated by about 30 miles as the crow flies. For transporting freight between them there was a choice, at the start of the 19th century, between the Mersey & Irwell River Navigation and the Duke of Bridgewater's canal, both of which were severely overloaded. Instead of competing with one another they had formed a mutually convenient price-fixing cartel, and tolls were high. Raw cotton, for example – by 1820 a trade amounting to nearly 300,000 bales a year – could take longer to get to the Manchester mills than it had taken to cross the Atlantic. Stocks of all kinds of raw materials and finished goods were overflowing from the warehouses and onto the quays, and some could not even be unloaded from the ships. The prosperity of the Liverpool docks was being throttled as they tried to handle as many as 7,000 vessels a year.

In terms of social culture and commercial attitudes, the distance between the two towns was far greater than the geographical mileage might suggest. Liverpool was cosmopolitan and extrovert. For centuries the focal point of contact with Ireland, its increasing links with the New World were now giving it a unique vision of pioneering growth derived from international trade both in goods and, increasingly, in people. Manchester was different, very different. Sitting damply under the western slopes of the Pennines, year-round uninterrupted water power from its rivers and streams was turning the new spinning and weaving machinery in the multitude of small cotton mills that had sprung up. Furthermore, the high humidity was ideal for handling and transforming the raw cotton fibres. Displaced agricultural workers flooded in from the surrounding countryside, on the one hand creating a pool of cheap labour, but on the other hand spawning the largest and most unhygienic slums in the whole country. In the years between 1790 and 1821, the population of Manchester (with Salford) increased from 57,000 to 190,000, making it by far the most populous conurbation outside London.

Liverpool was not far behind with 120,000. (These statistics make a stark contrast with those for Moreton-in-Marsh, at around 1,000 inhabitants.)

The growth of neither Liverpool nor Manchester was restrained by lack of money, nor by the inability of the evolving but still primitive banking system to provide short-term investment funding. Both business communities were profitable and, in modern parlance, cash generative. A few people the 'new money', were becoming extremely rich. Capital projects, expanded docks and wharfage in Liverpool and bigger, more mechanised mills in Manchester, could theoretically be paid for out of self-generated funds. The main problem restricting further growth lay elsewhere, in the bottleneck imposed by the totally inadequate inland transport system. The prime requirement was for the movement of goods; raw materials inland (whether it was cotton fibre or the bricks and iron to equip new factories) and finished goods for export to London, the Continent and the rest of the world. But the wealth-generating process had also created a demand for personal travel within the middle classes. Mill-owners needed to see lawyers, purchasers to discuss terms with suppliers, brokers to meet their clients. The day of the regular business meeting was dawning.

James first considered some form of railway between the two towns during his visits to investigate the Bridgewater Canal in 1802. By 1820, the region was high on his ever-expanding list of locations which would benefit from his concept of advanced locomotion, and the catalyst for turning the dream into reality had been his introduction to Joseph Sandars in July 1821. James was certainly not the only person to envisage some sort of railway in the area. Benjamin Outram and William Jessop, for example, had both proposed separate routes for horse-drawn tramroads in the late 1790s, but the wily Duke of Bridgewater played one off against the other and neither scheme came to anything. Thomas Gray, a proponent of Blenkinsop's cogged rail system,

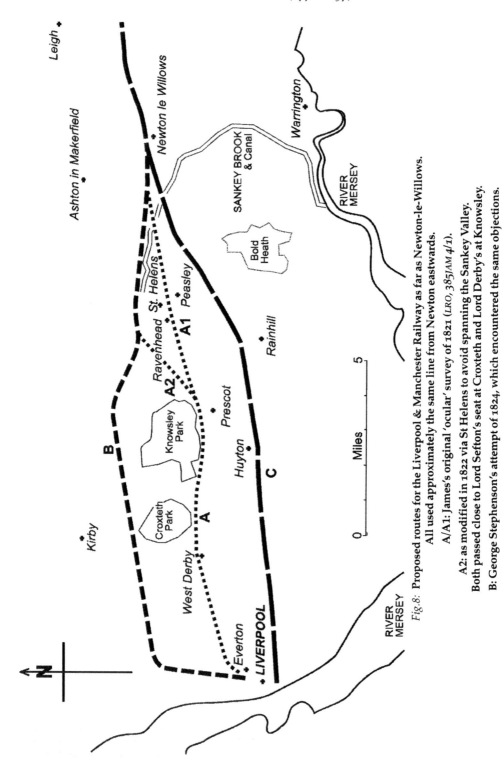

Fig.8: Proposed routes for the Liverpool & Manchester Railway as far as Newton-le-Willows. All used approximately the same line from Newton eastwards.

A/A1: James's original 'ocular' survey of 1821 (*LRO*, 385JAM 4/1).

A2: as modified in 1822 via St Helens to avoid spanning the Sankey Valley. Both passed close to Lord Sefton's seat at Croxteth and Lord Derby's at Knowsley.

B: George Stephenson's attempt of 1824, which encountered the same objections.

C: Line first surveyed by Charles Vignoles and finally adopted by Stephenson.

also advocated such a line in 1820.[222] At that time, the financial climate was not favourable; the economy had been through a period of deep depression, reaching a nadir in 1819. By 1821, however, the need was pressing and the money was doubtless available and, 'cometh the hour', two men of conviction and stature were talking and beginning to plan the greatest transport project that the world had ever seen.

Joseph Sandars was not only wealthy and an influential member of the Liverpool business community, but was active in Whig politics. He was a very successful exponent of the power of the press. Like Edward Pease, he was also a Quaker. Respected among his peers for his business ethics, combining moderation with a high degree of motivation, it is easy to understand why he was captivated by James's eloquence and enthusiasm, and why they immediately recognised in each other the qualities necessary for a working partnership. Like James, he had an impetuous streak, once being described as 'a man of rather untidy but acquisitive mind . . . he was undaunted by obstacles because he did not clearly see them.'[223] There was much to be done. The two crucial targets were a detailed survey and then an Act to authorise the raising of the necessary capital, compulsory purchase of the land required, and the terms and conditions under which the railway could operate. The first would hopefully present the least problems, though it would be imperative to quantify the engineering costs and all the ancillary expenses of setting up the enterprise. The second was bound to be contentious, needing supreme powers of advocacy and diplomacy. These qualities would also have to be marshalled for the third objective, for James – and he hoped to persuade Sandars and others to concur – was bent on employing steam locomotives as the prime means of traction.

The initial task at Liverpool was to do the survey, and early in 1822 James assembled his team. Already, the previous year, he had made an 'ocular' survey and had indicated that the railway might be built in eighteen months at a rough cost of about £100,000.[224] In this preliminary report, he highlighted a major problem.

I have employed much time to obviate the usual impediments to public works, arising, in most instances, from prejudice, ignorance and the contracted views of self interest. The residences, domains, and as far as practical, the preserves of the nobility and gentry have been avoided.[225]

By approaching Liverpool from the north, via Everton, and taking his line through St Helens, he avoided making the direct, expensive crossing of the Sankey valley which he had shown on his first sketches. But if he thought that his line was far enough away from the seats of Lords Sefton and Derby he would soon be disabused (fig.8).

Meanwhile, Sandars brought together a provisional committee of interested parties and likely subscribers. Drawn from all shades of the political, financial and commercial spectrum of both communities, this first committee had 21 representatives from Liverpool and 10 from Manchester. Only three, Dr Thomas Traill (founder of the Mechanics' Institute), Charles Tayleur (later to establish the Vulcan Foundry locomotive building business) and John Kennedy (inventor and friend of James Watt) could lay claim to any knowledge of engineering at all, and the committee was apparently happy, on Sandars's recommendation, to delegate every practical aspect of the project to James. It looked as if he was about to realise his great ambition, to control a project that would bring vast benefits to all sections of the community, act as a precedent for countless others, and ensure his place in history. Two years before, the Stratford & Moreton Railway had been a huge challenge, but it was dwarfed by what he was now taking on. He doubtless told Sandars that he was confident of one aspect at least – the supply of sound locomotives from his friend and partner George Stephenson.

James, clearly underestimating the problems of the survey, rather unwisely accepted the payment Sandars offered of only £10 per mile. But the potential rewards were great. Soon he would be the natural choice for the remunerative role of General Manager, possibly combined with Chief Engineer. If he could not find a route to avoid the estates of the most vociferous opponents, he would need to charm away their objections. Steering the final Bill through Parliament, particularly the House of Lords, was no more intimidating to him. Clear presentation of the facts, wrapped in lucid oratory, would surely persuade doubters and dispel irrational fears. The Bill to authorise the Stockton and Darlington Railway had eventually been approved at the second attempt, after a three-year campaign, and much could be learnt from that exercise, though it was inherently more straightforward. True, it aimed to be a public concern, but this merely meant that its track would be available for the use of general carriers to transport their goods, mainly coal, against the payment of a toll. In this respect it would be no different from a turnpike.[226] Carrying passengers was not even to be considered, and on the subject of motive power the company was keeping rather quiet. A warning shot had been fired when it obtained the passage of its first Bill only on the condition that horses would be the sole means of traction; the use of steam locomotives would have to wait for a later amending Act.

James wrote to Sandars, somewhat melodramatically, about the likely opposition, and also including a very rash promise.[227]

> The canal companies are aware of their danger; I have been the object of their persecution and hate . . . but if I can die the death of Samson, by pulling away the pillars, I am content to die with these Philistines. Be assured, my dear Sir, that not a moment will be lost, nor shall my attention be diverted from this concern, which increases in importance every hour, as well as in the certainty of its ultimate success.

His survey team for the route from Liverpool to Manchester was largely a family affair. The chief surveyor was his brother-in-law, Paul Padley – a skilful field operator and a fine draughtsman. Earlier differences with James, when Padley had wooed his sister Anne, were forgiven and forgotten, and the two men appeared to establish an understanding of mutual trust and confidence. His eldest son, William Henry, was on the team, as was his third son, George Walter. George Hamilton and Hugh Greenshields were two other assistants, but the last member is the most intriguing, George Stephenson's son Robert, then eighteen, who had spent the previous autumn on the Stockton & Darlington survey under John Dixon, when he was not making improvements to his father's locomotives. The months he spent working for James were to instill in him a respect and devotion, far beyond the parameters of employee and employer. James opened the eyes of this intelligent young mind to the world outside his father's narrow horizons, encouraged his further education and latent interests in finance and politics, and introduced him to his some of his own sophisticated friends.[228] In the Stephenson family there was little true warmth and affection between son and father, and it is fair to conclude that young Robert, while respecting his father, viewed William James very much as a charismatic mentor. This led, in the father, to a festering resentment which would be neither forgiven nor forgotten.

One way of avoiding sensitive estates was to take the line over unenclosed land and two such areas, Parr Moss and Chat Moss, lay directly on the eastern half of the shortest line. But against

them lay the very reason why they had never been taken into cultivation. Both were areas of boggy marsh, Chat Moss covering an area of roughly 6,000 acres and stretching for about four miles east to west. Beneath a surface of rough scrub and coarse grass lay up to 30ft of unstable, water-logged earth, which in patches behaved like quicksand. But James was interested to notice that a few squatters were already digging drainage ditches and harvesting the peat. Moreover, to increase their productivity, a few horse-drawn tramways had already been laid, supported on rafts of wattle and heather. Some of these tramways were constructed by a Robert Stannard, agent to William Roscoe.[229]

James took this to be an encouraging precedent – he recalled the temporary railroad that had been laid over waterlogged ground for building the Stratford Canal – and he led his surveying team onto the bog. One day, probing with a long rod to try to measure the depth to a solid bottom, he fell into the mire and would probably have drowned, had he not been pulled out at the last minute by his younger and certainly much lighter assistant, Hugh Greenshields. Now aged 51, following this trauma and its intimations of mortality, James wrote a will in which he left £50,000 to his eldest son, £10,000 each to his other children and several other minor bequests. This document no longer survives and we have to accept his daughter's account for its accuracy.[230] She mentions it not only to show that subsequent events deprived her of a reasonable inheritance, but also that her father was no longer quite as wealthy as she claimed he once had been.

Elsewhere the survey was encountering other problems, though James gave the impression to Sandars that everything was going well and that the complete survey would be filed in the early autumn. Encouraged that the key element would be in place to meet the 1823 parliamentary time-table, Sandars replaced the provisional committee with a more permanent one. John Moss, the respected Liverpool banker, was appointed as chairman. Such an appointment could not escape the notice of the press and the first details of the proposed 'iron-road', and its 'steam carriages', appeared in the *Manchester Guardian* on 22 July 1822. Sandars, the shrewd political operator, had meanwhile obtained another trump card to persuade Parliament of the necessity to build the railway. The committee petitioned the Bridge-water Canal for reduced tolls and, when this was summarily dismissed, the railway lobby had an unanswerable case on grounds of competitive-ness against an unreasonable monopoly.

TWELVE

Distractions and Diversions
(1822)

THE year 1822 would prove to be the crucial watershed in James's life. Prospects for achieving his ultimate ambitions had never looked brighter, but, equally, some baggage from the past was pressing its way into the foreground. And instead of concentrating his attention on this one great project, he was spreading his efforts over several other fronts. His confidence boosted by his new partnership, he began plotting yet more railways. Two of them involved companies which already had parliamentary authorisation.

James had for a while been nurturing a sales opportunity in East Anglia. In 1820 he had picked up on an abortive canal scheme of 1812 – the London & Cambridge Junction Canal – to link the river Stort Navigation at Bishop's Stortford with the Cam at Clayhithe just outside Cambridge. The promoters had obtained two Acts of Parliament, but the scheme had stalled for lack of money.[231] For them, in April 1822, James prepared a long report. He first outlines the inherent disadvantages of canals, including the cost of excavations, the supply and retention of water, slow speeds, etc.[232] He then explains that while horse-operated tramroads were in many respects an improvement, the use of steam locomotives enhanced the economics dramatically, and at the same time removed the social problem of having men – of a notorious reputation – perpetually trudging along the route. He makes the point that the amount of land needed will be much less than for a canal with its towpath, a single line of railway being little wider than a common footpath.

In comparison with navigable canals, generally speaking, articles may be moved by this improved engine system three times as fast, at one-third the expense, and with the advance of only one-seventh the capital in the construction; and in comparison with horse-labour, the engine will work at one-fifth the cost, and twice as fast; and two men

and the engine will work to more advantage than twelve men and twenty horses on the old road or tramroad system.

He then hits the shareholders with detailed comparative costs. He calculates that the canal would cost £567,000, whereas his railway could be built for only £70,789. The original canal Act had authorised a share capital of 5,700 shares at £100 each, the work to start when 4,252 shares had been subscribed, which had been the problem. The railway company would also be financed by the issue of 4,252 shares, but now with a nominal value of only £15, together with borrowings of £7,000 on a first mortgage, giving gross capital of £70,780. He estimates that the railway would take just over two years to build and, most important, that it would yield a dividend of 20 per cent, based on the canal company's own projections of 160,000 tons of freight per annum at 3d per ton/mile, the toll rate approved in the canal Act.

I calculate that the [additional carriage of] short freight, the profits of weighing machines and warehouses, and the conveyance of passengers and cattle, will pay the necessary expenses, and all the permanent charges.

He projects that his Patent Land-Agent Engines – the brand-name he adopted for the Stephenson locomotive he was now promoting – will be capable of moving more than fifty tons per day over a distance of 64 miles, at a cost of ½d per ton/mile. He then suggests that the line from Bishop's Stortford to Cambridge is only the first step; already he has his sights on extensions to King's Lynn, Norwich and Lincoln.

The situation and level of this line is most convenient for a principal, and several branch, extensions of great moment, of which surveys will be immediately undertaken, to be prepared for application for bills at the next sessions of Parliament.

Surely the promoters of the canal scheme would be persuaded by his logic? Were not the economic advantages, and the lure of substantial dividends, sufficient inducement to go ahead immediately? The proprietors had already done the most difficult part, getting a route approved by Parliament, together with compulsory purchase powers for the land. They had already received subscriptions of £121,300 and all that was needed was a small amendment to change the mode of transport. James had done his homework. The Act of 1812 actually included the words 'the company may also construct railways and inclined planes, should the same appear more advantageous, in any part of the line.' He must have felt particularly frustrated when he received the following letter from Lord Hardwicke, the chief protagonist of the canal scheme, in August 1822.[233]

> Though I am very sensible of the advantages of iron railways, yet I should certainly prefer the execution of the canal, for which the Act was obtained with so much difficulty ... and I am very doubtful how far the powers given by the above Act would be applicable to the substitution of a 'railway'.
>
> I will not at present enter upon the other important suggestions contained in your letter of the 21st ult., although, undoubtedly, the communication between Lynn and Norwich, and also with Lincoln, as well as the application of part of the fen country to the growth of the objects which you enumerate, are well deserving of the attentive and serious consideration of all who are connected with those districts.

This was to prove the scheme's death knell. Vested interests of the river navigation owners meant they would not welcome trans-shipment of goods from one form of transport to another. In James's proposal they saw a competitive threat rather than an opportunity. The chance to give a much-needed boost to the economy of East Anglia was allowed to slip by. It would take 23 years before Bishop's Stortford, Cambridge and Norwich had a rail link, and yet another year before King's Lynn joined the network.

Down in Surrey, James had two cards up his sleeve in 1822. He wrote to the directors of the Grand Surrey Canal suggesting a railway to complete their authorised link to Mitcham – and then go far beyond.[234]

> Having been employed in 1808–9 to survey and report on the estates of the Archbishop, Lord Holland, Lord Thurlow, and other

principal proprietors on the line, as land-agent and engineer, from my local knowledge, &c, I feel great confidence in being able to negotiate successfully with the landed interest, and, from my experience as an engineer, in railroads especially, already perceive the advantages likely to result to the company from its immediate adoption. As patentee of the last improved rail ... I am ready to undertake to make a survey, estimate, and report upon that part of the line from the wharf at Camberwell to Kingston and Epsom, with an explanatory plan ... The said railroads, and all person or persons, and their servants, carriages, and cattle passing thereon, shall be under the control and management of the said Wm. James and his co-partners.

The directors declined the offer and concentrated their resources into expanding their docks on the Thames.

James also turned his attention back to the Surrey Iron Railway, still the only one in the London area. It had promised so much when opened to Croydon in 1806, but had produced no return for the shareholders, of whom James was one, and he was determined to improve the prospects for his investment. By 1822 traffic had not expanded and what there was, mainly lime, was hauled by plodding mules. His request to Stephenson the previous year for a locomotive for the Gloucester & Cheltenham had failed, but now he asked again, for a locomotive for the Surrey Iron Railway. He met with the same negative response. But whereas he had not pressed the case for Cheltenham, in the Croydon venture he had a personal stake, and here he persisted, to the extent of bypassing Stephenson and going straight to William Losh. In June 1822 James wrote to him pleading for a locomotive to be sent down for a trial, and even offered to pay for it himself.[235]

> I can appreciate Mr Stephenson's objections to use his engine on this defective road; but years will elapse, and the patent may expire, before we can get a new road in the South for his engine if this plan is not embraced.[236]

No one in the south had ever seen a travelling engine, at least since Trevithick's London show of 1808. How could they begin to see its potential if they did not actually stand beside one and sense the power of the machine? Even if a short section of the 'right' sort of track had to be built, a practical demonstration was surely worth thousands of words. Edward Pease had just such an experience when he visited Stephenson at Killingworth in October 1821. He wrote to his cousin extolling the same virtues which James had recognised in their host,[237] 'He is altogether a self taught genius, a man thee would be remarkably pleased with, there is such a scale of sound ability without anything assuming.' Pease then launches into the excitement he felt at witnessing his first travelling engine.

> Previous to seeing this Loco motive Engine I was at a loss to conceive how the Engine could draw such a weight . . . don't be surprised if I should tell thee, there seems to us after careful examination no difficulty in laying a rail road from London & to Edinburgh on which waggons would travel & take the mail at the rate of 20 miles per hour.

His conclusion is the same as James's, the only difference being that James had reached it thirteen years before, when he propounded his General Railroad Company after seeing Trevithick's *Catch-me-who-can*.

In the summer of 1822 James had also to attend to pressing matters at Stratford-upon-Avon. After the Stratford Canal had linked up with the Avon, barge traffic on the Upper Avon had increased, but not to the extent James had expected. There were two reasons. The first was the additional tolls which George Perrott, owner of the Lower Avon, was entitled to levy on coal traffic from the north that was landed between Bidford and Evesham. The second was the poor state of the locks which by 1822 were described as being in a very dilapidated condition.[238] James now took the doubly expensive decision to borrow £6,000 and to close the entire Upper Avon navigation for several months while the locks were upgraded and repaired, but not lengthened. This, in preventing standard 70ft narrow-boats from trading down the river and necessitating trans-shipment of all cargoes at Stratford, was a false economy. Typically, James began to talk about introducing onto the Avon a new form of barge with stern paddle-wheels driven by steam engines designed by his son, William Henry. Indeed James wrote to him on 2 November that 'I cannot help reflecting upon your hydrogen-engine plan. It is most ingenious, and will do well, I have no doubt, if you will give serious attention to it.'[239] Nothing more is known of this tantalising will-o'-the-wisp. Several inventors of the 1820s were preoccupied with gas engines, the first of which, a hydrogen engine, was built and described in 1820 by Revd William Cecil. Nothing, sadly, came of the steam paddle-tugs either; James's financial strictures

prevented the river from witnessing sights that were to become familiar from the Mississippi to the Irrawaddy.

Yet another scheme was afoot on the Welsh border. James was familiar with the region around Oswestry, Ellesmere and Chirk where in 1805, as we saw in chapter 5, he had advised on a railway from quarries at Llanymynech to the Ellesmere Canal. This waterway was originally intended to cut northwards from west Shropshire, through the Denbighshire coalfield, and past Chester to the Mersey. But the section from the coalfield to the Dee was never built, which forced traffic from the collieries around Wrexham, Ruabon and Chirk to take an enormously roundabout route south, east, and finally northwest to Chester and the industrial markets of Lancashire. Between June and November 1822, James was in almost weekly correspondence with John Copner Williams, agent of Robert Myddelton Biddulph of Chirk Castle, about valuing farms, draining marshes and quantifying minerals on the Castle estate. The subject expanded to the transport problems suffered by the Castle's colliery at Black Park at Chirk, and James, identifying a close parallel with Clutton, deplored that 'so fine a mineral property [was] producing with inadequate means'. He offered to survey the route of an 'engine railway' from Chirk via Ruabon and Wrexham to Chester and thence the Mersey, a much more direct route than the canal. On 6 June he asked for plans of the estate, but on 26 June had to write that a bout of illness had not allowed him to 'explore the Mines and pedestrianate the Country.'[240] He continued,

> I have no doubt of great Success attending my Journey and Views at Chirk, if I am favoured with your Assistance . . . also some intelligent Guide, and pony to carry a body weighing 18 Stone, with a head bouyent [sic] with Crotchetts.

Small wonder that he had nearly been claimed by Chat Moss.

He spent a week in August riding between Chirk and Chester, from where on the 24th he wrote to Williams that he was confident of plotting a route that could 'bring the Mines into full Income'.[241] Before he returned to Chirk, he would visit Lord Grosvenor and a number of other interested parties; mindful of his problems in Lancashire, he was planning to bypass gentry's estates; and he hints that his line was to run up one side of the Dee almost to Llangollen and back on the other side, perhaps to avoid crossing the valley by a structure as tall as Pontcysyllte aqueduct or the later Cefn viaduct. Back in Manchester on the 29th, he could report that the survey of the Liverpool & Manchester was nearly finished. 'It will be a very complete line, and the measure, I have no doubt, will receive the sanction of Parliament.'[242]

The weather at the beginning of September was dreadful. On the 3rd, Robert Stephenson wrote to him,[243]

Hugh and I set off last night to see you, but were so unfortunate as to lose our guide . . . I am sorry we cannot meet your expectations in arriving at Manchester with the survey – it is impossible – had the weather been favourable to us, we might have accomplished it . . . let me assure you that no effort has been spared by Mr Padley or myself. We even by ourselves surveyed the greater part of Sunday – for God's sake!

Later he wrote to James asking for another assistant to speed up the work on his section, because George Walter was leaving to become a medical student. 'Walter and Frederick are here. I am sorry to learn that Master Walter is doomed to London'.[244] Then he asked for a new theodolite as his had been smashed in a brawl with a gang of 'heavies' recruited by a hostile landowner. One inevitable hazard was that surveyors, if they were to provide the accurate plans demanded by a parliamentary committee, had perforce to trespass on land where they could not obtain permission. There are many tales about the abuses the early railway surveyors were subjected to, from furious attacks by stone-throwing women to assaults by pitchfork-wielding farmers. Sometimes they had to work by moonlight, with assistants creating diversions with flares.[245] But in spite of these setbacks, James was bubbling with confidence and enthusiasm when he wrote to Williams on 9 September.[246]

Our business in these parts has so greatly increased in importance and the Engine Road begins to be so generally understood that I am solicited in two different quarters to survey lines of communication. I will make great exertions to get the plans ready for public inspection on the Chester line.

There was no way that James could get away to attend the General Meeting of the Moreton Railway convened for 17 September. He had written to Lord Redesdale on the 14th asking for some recompense for the time he had spent on that project, but the reply he received was not encouraging.[247] 'I shall suggest that some attention ought to be paid to the advantage derived from your labours, but I doubt whether I shall find much disposition in others to be favourable to you.'

There was, however, one item of positive news. The meeting was going to endorse the appointment as engineer of John Urpeth Rastrick, who had been involved in the building of Trevithick's Catch-me-who-can in 1808 and became his partner in the abortive Thames tunnel project the following year. He had perhaps, as we saw, already inspected railways of the North-east on behalf of the Stratford & Moreton. In the same letter, Redesdale confirmed that Rastrick endorsed James's conclusions in his original report, not only about the use of malleable iron rails, but also about the economic advantages promised by the use of steam locomotives, 'which would be improved'.[248]

But James was to suffer a major blow to the progress of the Lancashire survey when he received a blunt letter from George Stephenson on 18 September demanding Robert's return. 'I am very much in want of Robert, you will send him off as soon as possible as I want him to go to Knaresburgh and also to do business on the Darlington Railway.'[249] Robert did not in fact leave until two weeks later, writing to James from Newcastle on 5 October, the day after he arrived, to say how sorry he was not to see him before he left Liverpool.[250] 'I hope Walter and Fred are well' – Robert, an only son, was already missing the company of the young friends he now looked upon as surrogate brothers. His letter includes a paragraph that opens up another window on James's inventive thinking. 'I hope you are still convinced of the superiority of your Rail, which certainly will make a complete revolution in railways.' What was this revolutionary invention? If Robert Stephenson was impressed, it was surely something to take seriously. There are two strands to this puzzling question.

Firstly, it is possible, though proof eludes us, that James returned from the north in 1821 with a second agreement in his pocket, distinct from the Losh and Stephenson agreement. There are two hints to this effect, both mentioned earlier in this chapter. His report on the proposed railway from Bishop's Stortford to Cambridge claims that railways have been perfected 'by the invention of the Land-Agent steam-engine, and the malleable iron plate rails, secured to the present company by letters patent.' And in his proposal for a railway extension of the Grand Surrey Canal he describes himself as 'patentee of the last improved rail'. In both cases the phrasing, though curious, implies that he had an interest in Birkinshaw's rail patent as well as in Losh and Stephenson's locomotive one. Certainly he advocated both with equal enthusiasm. Equally certainly he had, by this date, taken out no patent for rails of his own. But by no stretch of the imagination could Robert Stephenson, in a letter to James, describe Birkinshaw's rail as 'your Rail'.

What then was James's rail? He or his son did indeed, in 1824–5, patent two types of rail, both of them bizarre (see Appendix A). The first was cast-iron and tubular in section. It was claimed, very dubiously, that the section gave it high strength, while at the same time allowing water (or even gas) to pass through it from end to end. This could be used to provide in-built drainage or the power to run waterwheels at intervals along the track, which might activate chains to haul trucks up an incline. The second patent addressed the problem of wheel-skidding on curves, where the outer wheel had to travel further than the inner one. This, at the least, generated friction and wear, and at the worst, especially on high-speed lines, serious deterioration of the rail surface (gauge cracking). Wheels with a slightly coned profile to the tread, which became the standard solution, were already in limited use. The Jameses suggested a more radical solution with a stepped profile both to the wheel tread and to the wrought-iron rail. On curves, the largest diameter of the wheel ran on the highest step of the outer rail, thus utilising the concept of superelevation which had been known, if little practiced, for over twenty years. The result was not only highly complicated but, surely, extremely expensive. Neither of these strange designs, needless to say, ever saw practical use. Nor, assuredly, could so level-headed an engineer as Robert Stephenson have had them in mind when speaking so enthusiastically to James about 'his' rail.

The only remaining candidate for James's rail is enigmatically mentioned in 1820. For an intended branch from his Central Junction Railway at Cassington near Oxford to the Duke of Marlborough's Blenheim estate, James proposed using 'wrought iron skeleton-edged rails of his own invention, a sketch of which is given in one of his memorandum books'.[251] 'Skeleton-edged rails' may be a misreading of 'skeleton edge rails', but the memorandum books, sadly, no longer exist. Only one other use of the term is known, by the Scottish Robert Stevenson in 1824. Deploring the usual practice of building up earth between the rails as a horse-path, which impeded both drainage and the passage of the wheel-flanges, he recommended laying the rails 'wholly above the level of the horse-track. Such a construction gives additional facilities for drainage; and may be termed a Skeleton-railway, from the whole

structure being exposed to view. This description of railway has been applied to practice with much advantage in several situations, particularly at Lord Elgin's extensive coal and lime works in Fifeshire.'[252] It is entirely possible, even likely, that James and Stevenson were in correspondence around this time; but, if there was a borrowing of the term 'skeleton railway', we do not know in which direction. Nor, unfortunately, can any more be said about James's version.

After this digression, we must return to the labour-pains of the Liverpool & Manchester. Robert Stephenson did not stay long with his father, because later in October, surely encouraged by James, he took up a place at Edinburgh University. He would stay there for six months, obtaining an academic grounding in natural philosophy, including chemistry, metallurgy and mathematics. In his parting letter to James, sent on 14 October,[253] he hopes that James had done some experiments on his rail, adding that his father was now convinced that the malleable rail from Bedlington was 'perfection itself'. He asks to be remembered to 'my friend Padley . . . let him know I often think on pleasures past'. He wants to know about progress with the surveys: 'I hope you are all right with the plans and also in a forward state with the Bolton ones'.

This refers to yet another of James's projects – a railway to carry coal from Bolton to Liverpool by a much more direct route than the existing waterways allowed. Based on his visit in 1802 (see plate 8b), he started fieldwork on a railway route which would provide an interim link to the Leeds & Liverpool Canal at Leigh and would doubtless, later on, be extended to become a branch off *his* Liverpool & Manchester Railway. And here things were still on track; James could write to Williams that his own confidence was fully shared by the proprietors and their friends. 'Great Sums have been offered as Premiums for the Scrip of the Liverpool & Manchester Rail Road shares, for a finer line never was formed than this.'[254]

George Hamilton had lodged his section of the Liverpool survey on 23 September, and he assured James that he and the new assistant, a Mr Evans, would use their 'utmost exertions to complete the survey on Wednesday morning.'[255] In the middle of October James sent a copy of the completed levels to George Stephenson, asking for his comments and his specifications to supply locomotive engines for different anticipated loads, together with stationary winding-engines for the Everton Bank, assuming that the railway would terminate near there.[256] Stephenson replied with his 'performance certificate' on 28 October, warranting an average speed of 4 mph with a 40-ton load and 13 mph with an 'express' load of only 10 tons – on a railway 'properly constructed'. He was aware that these figures would disappoint James and included a caveat that he had 'no doubt that the engines may be made to do considerably more than I have mentioned here.'[257] James must indeed have felt let down and frustrated by Stephenson's self-protecting caution; as far as he could judge, these figures showed no improvement on those given to Brewin and Greaves. Had there been no enhancements in the last twelve months? Worse still, they would not support the kind of performance figures he had expounded to the committee. He must have written to Stephenson to express these sentiments, because a few days later he received another letter from Killingworth: 'You try my conscience; I assure you I am quite inclined to do you all the good I possibly can, but you will excuse me saying more than I can perform.'[258]

When the Liverpool & Manchester committee finally got down to reviewing James's plan in October, they demanded major alterations, including a quite different terminus at the Manchester end, a Liverpool terminus in the docks ('at whatever extra cost') and complete avoidance of any part of Lord Derby's estates. James, meanwhile, was not only working on his private survey of the railway from Bolton to Leigh, but also made time to visit Robert Stephenson in Edinburgh.[259] Now he was recalled urgently and another survey at the Manchester end – more expenses – was started in the bitter weather of early November. James had to send his apologies to Williams that he had been unable to complete his report on the Chirk minerals and the Chester railway because of 'extreme difficulties' he was now encountering in Lancashire, but most of the problems were, he believed, overcome. 'We *will* establish this line which, when done, will be such a precedent as the proprietors in your neighbourhood must eagerly follow.'[260]

One problem not settled was the route's incursion into Lord Derby's estates, and James decided to tackle this issue by appealing to his son, to whom he wrote on 13 November 1822:[261]

The plans and sections of the proposed Liverpool and Manchester railroad being completed, I have applied to your noble father to allow me to submit the same to his Lordship's consideration tomorrow morning . . .

The line is set out across the valuable coal mines of the Earl of Derby, near Whiston,

and cannot fail greatly to enhance their value, as also that of his Lordship's very extensive adjacent estates; and since it secures the greatest public advantages, the promoters of the measure look with confident hope to the noble earl's and your lordship's powerful support. I shall have great satisfaction in laying the plans before your lordship at any hour this day or to-morrow you will have the goodness to appoint.

Lord Derby's reply the same day, blunt and uncompromising, stated that he was 'so decidedly adverse to any plan of the sort, that it would be useless to lay this, or any other plan before him.'[262] His attitude was shared by many of the landed aristocracy, who could only see the coming of the railways as a trespassing intrusion onto their land, splitting their estates, disrupting their hunting and spoiling their views. The railways posed them a potentially devastating threat, not only visually but with the certain accompaniment of the unruly, drunken and undisciplined armies of navvies who had attended the building of the canals only a few years before.

His pride hurt and his body exhausted by overwork, James wrote a tragic letter to Sandars:[263]

The surveys and plans can't be completed, I see, till the end of the week. With illness, anguish of mind, and inexpressible distress, I perceive I must sink if I wait any longer; and, in short, I have so neglected the suit in Chancery I named to you, that if I do not put in an answer I shall be outlawed.

The worst was indeed about to happen. On 18 November 1822, James was summoned to the King's Bench in London and committed to its Southwark prison under the arcane and draconian rules of Mesne Process. To understand how even minor debts were linked to Habeas Corpus at this time is complex but, in brief, Mesne Process allowed an unsatisfied creditor to take his debtor into 'bondage' for debts as small as £15.[264] The debtor not only lost his liberty with the full sanction of the law; he also had to remain incarcerated until both the debt was paid and the court authorised his release, the one not automatically following immediately on from the other. James's arrest arose from a minor suit in Chancery that summer, for which a certain Edward Hinton stood bail for a mere £15. When Hinton suddenly withdrew his surety, the law took its course and James was to chalk up the first of what he saw as a succession of treacherous acts by so-called friends.

THIRTEEN

Prison, Canterbury and a Family Vendetta (1823)

IFE in the King's Bench prison in South-wark, south London, would not have been pleasant, though far removed from the total degradation and squalor of the other two debtors' prisons, the Fleet and the Marshalsea. The regime depended on the corruptibility of the governor. Inmates, while they had to pay for their food and accommodation and provide their own furniture, might bring their own servants, and visitors could come and go as they pleased. For persons of James's standing, short sojourns in these establish-ments were not unusual and some of his fellow 'guests' would certainly have been known to him. Creditors knew that their targets could not escape overseas, while friends, relations and clerks could raise the wind to settle the defendant's liability; but it was up to the court and the person having the writ of Habeas Corpus to say when the prisoner could be released.

Typically, James took his enforced confinement as an opportunity to find new clients. On 20 January 1823 such a one joined him in prison. Edmund John Glynn (1764–1840) had inherited substantial properties from his father, a prominent supporter of the radical MP John Wilkes, but had led a dissipated life as an absentee landlord. When in 1821 the North Cornwall Bank, in which he was a leading partner, crashed, he found himself unable to match his liabilities – even after selling his properties outside Cornwall – and was imprisoned on the charge of his erstwhile partner, Edward (Stackhouse) Pendarves.[265] To add to his misfortunes, in 1819 his great house near Bodmin had burnt down. James and Glynn struck a deal. Glynn would appoint James as agent to sell his Cornish estates to repay his creditors; James, recalling that the Glynn land adjoined that of his former client Charles Agar, would, once released, re-establish contact with Agar's widow. Surely she was a natural buyer for adjacent properties.

It seems that George Stephenson was unaware of James's incarceration, because on 25 November 1822 he addressed a letter to him at the inn in Newton-le-Willows, Lancashire, where James had set up his surveying headquarters.[266] Stephenson had been dangerously ill with a fever caught from travelling too long in wet clothes. 'I am *not* falling off in the power of my engines, but, Sir, I want to run safe both for your credit and my own. I assure you it is my wish to do you all the good I can and hope your intention's the same to me.' A few years later these repeated expressions of committed friendship and support would ring very hollow. A long letter from young Robert the following week included warm family matters. 'I wrote a day or two after you left Edinburgh to my friend Walter, and have never received a reply . . . I should very much like to hear from him. Give my kind regards to Frederick and Mr Padley and Hugh Greenshields.'[267]

Another letter from George Stephenson, dated 18 December, was forwarded to James from Sandars's office.[268] It asked for 'the return of the Darlington Railway Act of Parliament with your alterations and remarks upon it . . . as the Darlington people wishes [sic] to see it.'

Perhaps Edward Pease had sent it for James's comments, which would certainly have stressed the importance of including approval both for carrying passengers and the specific use of steam locomotives. The next paragraph in Stephenson's letter must have been particularly hurtful: 'I hope you are prospering with your projects. I expect I shall see you in London on the meeting of Parliament when we shall have some time to enlarge upon Railways.' In the New Year, James wrote back requesting details of progress on the Stockton & Darlington, particularly wage rates for the navvies and how the company was tackling the problems of fencing against animals. Stephenson replied on 16 January.[269] 'We are getting on with our work exceedingly well; the earth work will be done at less than my estimate – it is going on at from 4d to 6d per cubic yard.' Some men had been earning as much as 30d a week. He gave news of the capability of the winding engines installed on the Hetton Railway incline and discussed a new type of bearing he had devised for reducing the rolling resistance of waggons, which it was too late to employ on the Stockton & Darlington because the castings had already been ordered. 'I was thinking to inform the Stratford Railway company of it as it could be used there, but I should not divulge it unless they would pay me well for it.' Then he made a rather sly dig at Rastrick's appointment to build that line. 'If *I* had been the Engineer, I would have adopted it without any remuneration.' This invention, which promised to 'diminish the friction considerably when passing curves', would re-emerge at Stratford the following year, but out of the pocket of someone else.

At least James now had ample time for writing, and he used his incarceration to good effect. He had invested time and money in the years up to 1821 doing an 'ocular' survey for his great scheme for a railway in the south-east of England, linking London with the naval dockyards at Chatham and Portsmouth. As mentioned earlier, the idea had initially forced itself upon him as a result of the shambles of the remobilisation in 1815. Now he wrote up the whole scheme in his *Report, or Essay, to illustrate the advantages of direct inland communication through Kent, Surrey, Sussex and Hants, to connect the Metropolis with the ports of Shoreham, (Brighton) Rochester, (Chatham) and Portsmouth, by a line of Engine Rail-road* (Figs 3a and 4). To give this document instant appeal to the large number of disgruntled shareholders who were nursing losses in various associated enterprises, the title continued . . . *and to render the Grand Surrey Canal, Wandsworth and Merstham Rail-road, Shoreham Harbour, and Waterloo Bridge shares, productive property*. It was intended to be the first of no less than twelve essays on James's schemes for developing the railway system, on land reclamation, harbour improvements, sources of minerals and specifications for improvements to locomotive engines, particularly those of 'the author's greatly esteemed and scientific friend, Mr George Stephenson.' Even from prison he was proving to be a worthy advocate for his partner.[270]

The *Essay* ran to 31 pages. Nothing like it had ever been published before and the breadth of its scope, covering social, industrial and agricultural issues, was remarkable. The preface, intensely and probably tactlessly political, was a tirade against the government's handling of the currency which had led to the downfall of entrepreneurs like himself. He suggested that Government might 'relieve these suffering individuals, by granting to them lands in the colonies proportionate to their several losses, and in furnishing them with the means of emigration . . . this principle of compensation being admitted in the case of the American loyalists.' The main text gave precise details of the route of his proposed railway, with chapters on 'public advantages', 'private advantages' and 'prospects of income' for investors in his scheme. Among the many advantages he quantified, 'a saving of at least £60,000 a year will be made to government; in the cheap, speedy and secure removal of stores and troops; in the diminution of the *permanent* stock of stores at the different arsenals and docks etc. etc.' Here he is anticipating the concept of 'just-in-time' deliveries. It is a strange mixture of very precise costings and a rambling analysis of the need to improve transport links throughout the region. 'The inferior quality and great exhaustion of the cultivated land; the wretched state in point of morals and comforts of the poorer inhabitants (owing, principally, to bad roads and barbarous habits) must point out the necessity and utility of cheaper and better communications through this neglected but highly interesting and beautiful country.' He concluded, 'the present state of public affairs . . . renders the present period particularly auspicious for the prosecution of this great national work.'

He sent it off to be printed, at the same time writing to his survey team in Lancashire asking them to stand by to join him down south when he started surveying the line in more detail.[271] Then, on 4 February 1823, a fortnight before his release, James wrote a long letter to Joseph Sandars recapitulating his achievements to the committee so far.[272] He confirmed that, despite the delays caused by his illness and the atrocious weather, plans had been completed and the necessary notices had been deposited with the Justices and pinned up in public places. These legal preliminaries being in place, there was no theoretical reason why the Bill should not be prepared for the present session of Parliament, although he understood that several members of the committee wanted a postponement until the following year. He stated that he had already spent £500 out of his own pocket on paying his survey team, for which he had had only £290 refunded. In addition, he had expended seven months of his own time on the project, including soliciting new subscribers in Manchester and sounding out the likely degree of opposition in Parliament. To confirm his total commitment, he pointed out that he had also taken a long lease on an office near Liverpool. He concluded that, on balance, he too would recommend a postponement to the 1824 parliamentary session, not because he had any doubts about the validity of his survey and estimates, but because by then a number of other lines with 'travelling engines' might be in operation, optimistically alluding to Warwickshire (his Stratford to Moreton line) as well as Lancashire, Cheshire and Surrey. Opponents could then see for themselves how powerful and beneficial they were. He implored Sandars to encourage his colleagues to have as much faith and commitment as he had.

> I need not tell you that my life has been spent hitherto in what the world has called impossibilities, and that the remainder of my life shall be employed in this and similar concerns. My character for perseverance in this country is fixed. No one knows my labours and privations in the progress of this work; but if my friends are firm in their intentions, they will find that, against another session, many of our present difficulties will be removed by progressive measures which have not yet met the public eye.

Here he was probably alluding to the patents that he and his son had been working on, the filing of which had been seriously delayed by lack of funds – each patent cost £200 for registration alone, on top of the expenses of having drawings lithographed etc. Their numerous inventions for improving the locomotive in power, efficiency and weight, and for reducing the cost of permanent way, were indeed extraordinary, but either so utterly impractical or so farsighted that in the short term they had no influence on our story. They are important to understanding the scope of James's vision and the extent to which he analysed problems of future railway operation, some of which are only being confronted and solved in the 21st century. They are described in Appendix A, but in the early 1820s their only impact was accumulated costs of a few thousand pounds.

All in all, James could believe that the Liverpool project was still 'on track', even if they did have to wait until the parliamentary session in the following spring. This would allow him time to refine his survey which, despite his assurances to Sandars, he knew was not sufficiently detailed to satisfy the requirements of a Bill. He could also make more accurate cost estimates, helped by the friendly input from his partner at Killingworth. His brief sojourn in prison was no more than an inconvenience. He could also get back to some of his other projects while waiting for new instructions from Liverpool.

James was released from the King's Bench prison on 19 February 1823,[273] and there was a brief but joyful reunion with his wife and family in West Bromwich. He was probably back in London, however, when he received a letter dated 19 March from his assistant George Hamilton.[274]

> I have just heard from Mr Evans, who says that he has received a letter from you, in which you mention the idea of a railroad from Chatham to Portsmouth is in agitation. I hope you may bring it about, and beg to say I shall be very happy to assist you thereon . . . I intend to take away from Everton the Bolton surveys, as I dare say you will agree that they will be safer in our custody than Miss M'George's, Mr W. H. James having, I understand, left . . . We are about removing to Shrewsbury . . . at the same time beg to say, that we shall be ready to attend at your commands in any part of the country. Can I say anything for you to Mr Copner Williams? I shall see him next week.[275]

The rumours reaching James that he was losing the trust of certain members of the Liverpool & Manchester committee were well founded. They knew that he was actively involved in surveying and promoting other railways. Men of somewhat limited vision and cautious integrity, they had difficulty in coming to terms with a mercurial entrepreneur: his energy was infectious, but what if his health cracked again and he could no longer be relied upon to meet their demands, when his talents and time were spread across the country? His spell in prison had merely made things worse.

Elsewhere, away from Liverpool, people who held promissory notes from James began to feel increasingly uncomfortable, but had been encouraged by his assurances that he, and they, were soon to realise fortunes from the promised Railway Age which would make the canal boom of the pre-war years look like very small beer. The restoration of convertibility had been accompanied by a period of savage deflation: owners of capital assets were suffering from the phenomenon of negative equity and creditors were demanding the repayment of loans in bullion. One individual, however, bore a much meaner and more personal grudge against James. It had simmered for several years and was now about to explode into a ferocious family vendetta.

The roots went all the way back to 1807 and James's promise to his father on his death-bed, that he would look after his sisters and care for them financially, with the proviso that any marriage dowry would depend on his blessing on the intended union. To some extent, this was an assurance to his father that he would adopt a serious, moral role *in loco parentis*. But there was perhaps another motive. James was at that time associating not only with the gentry, but with those at the pinnacle of the aristocracy. How fine a thing it would be if his sisters married into the peerage! The eldest of the four, Mary, the one he adored most, did not acquire a title, but when she married a suitable gentleman James settled £20,000 on her. This would generate an income of nearly £1,000 a year, the sort of figure that characters in Jane Austen novels regarded as ensuring a very comfortable family life-style.

James's second sister, Anne, had probably spent much time, staying in London with her brother in New Boswell Court. Here she met and fell in love with Paul Padley, two years older than her and James's future chief surveyor on the Liverpool & Manchester project. He probably came from Swansea, the son of a merchant of wine, hardware and building materials.[276] The family were Quakers and played a prominent role in the commercial life of the town, but this was certainly not the sort of alliance James had hoped for. However, he blessed their marriage on 8 August 1808 at St Clement Dane's in the Strand, London, and settled another £20,000 on the couple. Following in her sister's footsteps like a twin, Susannah James wanted to marry another of her brother's employees and now James could hardly raise any objections, even if he did not positively approve. Another wedding took place and another £20,000 endowment promised. These gifts could only have been made by an extremely wealthy man, and this is exactly what, in those days, James was; at least on paper. What mattered most was his credit-worthiness, which remained high as long as his influential admirers continued to back him, his transport speculations offered exciting future rewards, and his partners kept faith and stayed true. The Stratford Canal enterprise, while it had proved expensive, had if anything enhanced his reputation for grasping a project and driving it to a conclusion. The Upper Avon Navigation had been a bad investment, but it had not deterred him from sinking more money into a salt works near Droitwich, probably in a deal with Francis Rufford and William Furnival.[277]

Against this background, when his youngest sister Elizabeth eloped with a most undesirable character named Peter Mudie, James was extremely disappointed. After a secret marriage, the bridegroom approached his brother-in-law for 'his' settlement. James was incandescent, dug in his heels, and refused to give them a penny. The matter festered for a time and Peter Mudie tried to pursue his claim through a civil action for breach of contract, but the claim was thrown out of court on the grounds that James's promise to supply dowries was, in the judge's words, one 'given by a good and affectionate son to a dying father'; a moral, not a legal, obligation.[278] Here, however, had been sown the seeds of revenge.

In early April 1823, unaware of the brewing storm, James travelled down to Kent at the invitation of a number of merchants in Canterbury, who were desperate to improve communications to their ancient cathedral city. This is situated on the river Stour, which had so silted up over the centuries that by now it was only navigable – and that for quite small craft – as far as Fordwich two miles to the east. In 1783 a bold scheme had been promoted to drive a canal northward into the Thames estuary at St Nicholas's Bay, followed, when this failed, by another to dredge the entire length of the Stour – about 22 miles – all the way down to the sea at Sandwich. This scheme did secure weighty local support, Thomas Telford was appointed as engineer, and by 1823 the first draft of a Bill to present to Parliament was being prepared. Early estimates suggested a capital outlay of about £80,000, but James was convinced he could come up with a railway scheme which would cost less than a third of that.[279]

This project was nothing like as ambitious as the Liverpool & Manchester, but had the advantage of not having to cross bogs or any large estates, and he could really make this one his own. He told his audience that he had done a preliminary survey of three possible routes between the city and Whitstable, on the Thames estuary, and, compared with Sandwich, only half as far from London. The town did not have a harbour, but a small dock by the copperas works just to the east and was the starting point for all of his three alternatives. What had to be taken into account was a substantial hill with a summit plateau at 230ft lying directly between the two destinations, and, inconveniently, a ridge of almost equal height immediately above Canterbury. The first route he proposed, looping round to the east, was most level but, at about eleven miles, the longest. The second, the one he favoured, involved moderate gradients over the bluff to the east of Tyler Hill, but, he assured his listeners, well within the capability of his Land-Agent locomotives. This route was about 7¾ miles long. The third alternative was virtually direct and parallel to the turnpike road, only a little over six miles in length but involving a very steep climb with gradients of 1 in 37 over (or rather through) Tyler's Hill.

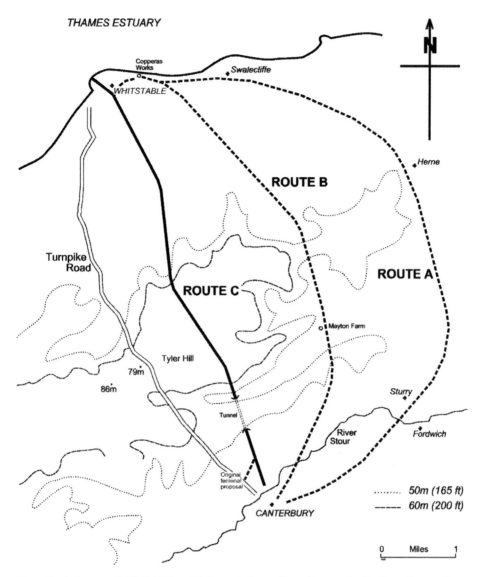

Fig.9: **Canterbury and Whitstable, with James's three alternative routes for the railway, 1824. The company eventually settled on C, the shortest but most expensive.**

No way could this be operated entirely by steam locomotives, except for the initial mile or so. The rest demanded fixed engines and rope haulage, to James's mind a most retrograde step.

Those who attended the meeting were infected by James's enthusiasm and oratory, particularly liking his first estimate that the railway might be built for no more than £25,000. They were impressed by what he told them of progress with

his scheme up in Lancashire and how he could deliver a complete package, from a precise survey to steering a Bill through Parliament. He extolled the merits of his partner, George Stephenson, who would supply all the machinery and locomotives. He left them to decide amongst themselves which of the three routes they favoured, and perhaps implied that if they got together an effective committee to raise the capital quickly, Canterbury could have the first steam-hauled passenger railway in the world. Another race was on.

Elsewhere, however, yet more impatient creditors were baying for James's blood and Peter Mudie, now determined on revenge, found willing takers when he fermented a number of creditors to press for immediate payment. On 14 May James found himself once again in prison on a writ of Habeas Corpus from the King's Bench, Mudie being one of the appellants.[280] Now there could be no more stalling, no more shuffling of his accounts to buy time. A Commission of Bankruptcy was appointed and a date for the opening of their official proceedings in Birmingham was set for July.

If the Liverpool committee felt that James had not been devoting himself sufficiently to their business, another of his ventures was much in need of a forceful hand on the tiller. The solicitor to the Stratford & Moreton Railway, Thomas Hunt, felt himself adrift on a sea of apathy. He was trying to place the initial construction contracts, noting in his expense book that a meeting of proprietors scheduled for May had failed even to produce a quorum. They needed to consider George Roe's estimate (£1,440) for building the bridge over the Avon and another from John Bradley for supplying malleable rails at £11 15s per ton.[281] In July, Hunt managed to get some of the parties round a table, but the shareholders would not pay their calls and the contractors would not start without money up front. One of the few contracts that was agreed was the supply of 66,000 stone blocks or sleepers to support the track at 3ft intervals, each block being 14in square and 8in deep, with two 1in diameter holes for wooden plugs to nail the cast-iron chairs to. For part of this contract, the successful applicant was James's quarry at Wilmcote, and over the following months the blocks were duly boated down to Stratford.[282] Payment, however, might have to wait.

Up in Liverpool, members of the railway committee were becoming restless. They were more concerned than ever that their project leader would be unable to devote the necessary time, particularly to preparing the full plans and estimates for the Bill which would have to be filed by the end of November for consideration by Parliament in the spring of 1824. At an informal meeting in June they decided to review the whole management and to ask Jesse Hartley, the chief engineer at the Liverpool Docks, to review James's surveys. But where were they? James knew that they were his key bargaining tool,

and as far as he was aware they were still locked up in his office.

There was much more positive action taking place in Newcastle. On 23 June 1823 the locomotive building firm of Robert Stephenson & Co was incorporated with an initial capital of £4,000, divided into ten shares. George Stephenson, Michael Longridge (the banker and owner of Bedlington Ironworks) and Robert Stephenson had two shares each, while Edward Pease held four. He also lent £500 to young Robert to help him pay for his investment. Not only was the company named after the youngest shareholder but he was also appointed as chief executive. Both factors gave public recognition to the young man's talents, but there was probably a subtler motive in the mind of his father. By giving him these responsibilities, would it not keep his career tied to Northumberland and his father's apron strings? Longridge was a committed friend and admirer of Robert, and much of their correspondence survives. In one letter he wrote that he was waiting to join George Stephenson to take the mail-coach to Scotland, which 'recalls to my recollection the day when . . . I entered the self same coach and found you, your father, Mr Hill, and our friend James seated "Cheek by Jowl" – "alas how time escapes".'[283]

The Bankruptcy Commission charged with hearing James's case convened in Birmingham on 12 July 1823 and started taking evidence.[284] The chief claimant was Edward Smith, the Birmingham public notary whom James had used as his broker for buying and selling shares for himself and his clients. There were substantial calls due on some of James's shares. Smith had already in 1821 obtained a court ruling against James for over £1,200 which was still unredeemed. Miss Colmore, the heiress to Charles Colmore, also claimed that she was owed £1,200. Joseph Povey, James's loyal, long-standing and, one has to say, long-suffering book-keeper and clerk gave evidence, and was forced to admit under cross examination that 'for many years past, William James has been a great pecuniary defaulter and much embarrassed for money.' A touch of humanity, almost of levity, was provided by the evidence of one William Sheldon, who seems to have been employed as a sort of general factotum and to have spent most of his time diverting creditors from West Bromwich and telling them that James was not at home.

The commissioners ruled that James had indeed become a bankrupt and notice to this effect appeared in the London Gazette on 15 July. The following day it was widely reported in the local press as well as *The Times*. On 9 August the chief creditors – Edward Smith, Francis Rufford, Miss Colmore, Thomas Biggs and Paul Padley[285] – met at the Royal Hotel, Birmingham, to appoint two assignees (administrators in modern parlance) to sell James's property and investments and raise money to pay off the creditors. Until this was done to the satisfaction of the commissioners, James would remain incarcerated in the King's Bench prison. One of the assignees appointed (in his absence) was Archibald Kendrick, described as an iron-founder of West Bromwich, who was owed £1,305. The other, more controversially, was Edward Smith himself, who moved quickly to protect at least his own interests. He immediately had Dinah James and the daughters evicted from Hill Top, and they were forced to move in with her son, George Walter, then working as a surgeon in West Bromwich. Dinah had to surrender her own closed carriage, but her daughter recalled that she never complained at losing this convenience and this important status symbol.[286] In selling the house in Warwick and a number of other properties, Smith apparently accepted knock-down prices so that he could selfishly recover what he was owed – to James's detriment and that of the other creditors.

Also in July the Liverpool committee held a formal meeting to discuss offering Jesse Hartley a permanent appointment as chief engineer, for subsequent endorsement by a full shareholders' meeting. James was informed of these manoeuvrings to undermine his authority in a letter from his friend on the committee, David Holt, dated 16 August.[287] Holt told him that Joseph Sandars was insistent that if James could not attend the meeting himself, he must send all the plans with Paul Padley. Holt then went on to suggest that there were other, subtler reasons why James should have someone who enjoyed his full confidence to represent his interests 'and satisfy the minds of the subscribers that in thee they have every security for the due performance of what thou hast undertaken.' The last paragraph was particularly revealing, as Holt was one of the Manchester minority on the committee. 'I write this officially, and Mr Ewart [of the Liverpool faction] begged me to say that this enquiry originated with thy friend, Mr Sandars! Most sincerely wishing thee a speedy and effectual release from all the difficulties and perplexities with which thou hast to contend.'

A few weeks before, James had received a letter of considerable encouragement from his friend Thomas Bell, a partner in the ironworks of Losh, Bell and Wilson in Newcastle.[288]

I assure you that nothing would give me greater pleasure than to hear that you succeed in this very large undertaking, which would certainly be of the greatest advantage to the districts in question . . . I shall always be glad to hear of your progress in this undertaking, and if anything arises in which any of us can be of service, I hope you will not fail to inform us. Mr George Stephenson has been recently from home . . . so that I have not seen him at all. I am quite sensible of the exertions you have made in attempting to introduce the locomotive engines, and though they have hitherto proved fruitless, I am sure Mr Losh and Mr Stephenson ought to consider themselves greatly indebted to you.

James evidently replied to this letter saying that one of the main reasons for the delay in selling locomotives was the negative and obstructive attitude down in Westminster. Bell wrote back on 14 August.[289]

My partners and myself are extremely sorry to hear of your misfortunes; and we hope you will be able to defeat your enemies in so shameful an attempt upon your property. In passing through Manchester and Liverpool, I took an opportunity of talking to some of my friends about the proposed railway . . . and they were of opinion, that if the goodwill of the landed proprietors, through whose grounds you pass, could be obtained, and if it were clearly shown that you would convey goods much lower than by the navigations, it would be impossible for the Marquis to put a stop to the Act of Parliament being obtained. Manchester has a powerful assistant in Mr Peel, and Liverpool in Canning and Huskisson, regarding all parliamentary matters. We shall be very glad to see you at Newcastle; and I hope you will find your friends here . . . too liberal to allow what has taken place to alter their opinions of you.

But of all the letters he received during this traumatic period in prison, the one that would have given him the greatest pleasure came from young Robert Stephenson dated Newcastle, 29 August.[290]

It gives rise to feelings of true regret when I reflect on your situation; but yet a consolation springs up when I consider your persevering spirit will for ever bear you up in the arms of triumph, instances of which I have witnessed of too forcible a character to be easily effaced from my memory. It is these thoughts, and these alone, that could banish from my soul feelings of despair for one; the respect I have for him can be easier conceived than described. Can I ever forget the advice you have afforded me in your last letters? and what a heavenly inducement you pointed before me at the close, when you said that attention and obedience to my dear father would afford me music at midnight.

Ah, and so it has already. My father and I set off for London on Monday next . . . on our way to Cork . . . Our return will probably be about the time you wish me to be at Liverpool. If all be right, we may possibly call and see what is going on. That line is the finest project in England. Hoping to see you or Mr Padley in a few days.

Sadly, the letters from James that are referred to no longer survive. He had clearly been disturbed by a developing rift between father and son: Robert, still under twenty, rebelling against his father's authoritarian obstinacy, and George, James's crucial business partner, ambitious for his son's advancement and success, but fearful of losing his influence to someone of palpably better education and worldliness. James's sermon on the fifth commandment would work for a time, but within a year Robert was to find his divided loyalty torn to breaking point.

The summer of 1823 passed without any apparent progress at all on the Liverpool project. The parliamentary session for that year had come and gone, the survey had stagnated, and when Sandars and his colleagues carried out their 'enquiry' they had some justification in blaming James's absence for the inactivity. At least James believed he still held the trump card. The survey was his property. He had paid for it largely from his own resources. In fact he had had to ask his wife for the money to complete it, and when she handed over the last £1,000 of her own dowry she commented, 'I fear I am doing a most unwise action; but if I should never live to have this returned to me, I trust it may hereafter benefit my children.'[291] In the light of subsequent events, her remark has an awful feeling of déjà vu.

And what was happening down at Moreton-in-Marsh? On 16 September 1823, having rejected Henry Palmer's fantasy monorail, the board confirmed John Rastrick of Stourbridge as the engineer to build the railway.[292] He agreed with James on using malleable iron rails, one reason

being that this would keep open the option of locomotive haulage at some later date. Cost considerations demanded some moderate gradients (modest by the standards of only a few years later) as the line undulated approximately along the route of the Oxford turnpike road and passed right through the centre of the village of Alderminster. These factors, born out of financial stringency, would later prove to be nails in the coffin of James's ambitions for the railway which crucially involved the use of his Land-Agent locomotives (plate 7b).

In late September 1823, all his assets having been assigned to the Court of Chancery, James was discharged from prison.[293] He probably went to join Dinah and their son George Walter for a few days, but he was soon off on his travels, not to Liverpool but to Cornwall. He had re-established contact with the widow of the Hon Charles Agar, Anna-Maria, owner of the Lanhydrock estate near Bodmin and large areas elsewhere in the county.[294] Furthermore, he had persuaded her senior trustee in London, a lawyer by the name of Baugh Allen, that she needed his help. Allen wrote to her in early October saying that he had engaged James to survey all her properties and make recommendations about improved means of communication. 'James is certainly a man of talent and he is sanguine. I think he may be able to suggest good counsel, but it must be cautiously followed.'[295] He had also agreed that James should be paid a salary and all his expenses refunded.

James wrote to his new patron asking for maps and plans and she replied that, on arrival, he should make contact with Alfred Jenkin, her mining agent and chief steward, and Roger Henwood, her agent in east Cornwall. Jenkin had succeeded his father to the stewardship in 1820, and, like him, combined this role with that of purchasing and shipping agent for a number of copper refineries in South Wales – and of rival Cornish mine-owners.

On 11 October James wrote to Anna-Maria from Oliver's Hotel at Bodmin with his preliminary impressions, copied to Allen. The estates had been sadly neglected but he was certain that they contained 'inexhaustible minerals and huge potential'; he later confided that he was only sorry that he had not done more thorough surveys during his visit in 1808. He estimated that she owned 12,000 acres scattered across the county, of which 3,000 were 'waste, the rest miserably occupied' except for 3,500 acres around Mullion. He was appalled by the state of local transport: 'you may pass from Liverpool to New York for less money than from Padstow to

Fowey.' But he was particularly excited by his discovery of granite of a quality 'to match that of Aberdeen' and he quickly despatched samples to Allen in London. If a railway could be built from Padstow to Fowey, he believed that this granite could be shipped for John Rennie's proposed London Bridge, undercutting the Scottish stone by 6d per ton. He was to mull over the concept of this railway during the next two years.

This was certainly not James's first excursion into the county. In 1808–9 the Duke of Cornwall and the Hon Charles Agar had been clients, and on the latter's behalf James may well have visited the first railway enterprise in the region, in which Agar was thinking of investing.[296] During the early 1800s the economy of Cornwall had a dynamic of its own and one of the main driving forces was copper, which was extensively mined around Camborne, Redruth and Chacewater. In 1809 a five-mile plateway, the Poldice Tramway, was being built down to the north coast at Portreath where Lord de Dunstanville was creating an artificial harbour, there being no natural harbours along the whole 25-mile stretch of coast between Hayle and Newquay. The total cost of the whole operation was calculated at £20,000 and the line opened the following year.[297]

By 1823 the other mine owners around Redruth urgently needed an improved transport link to export their ores to the smelters in South Wales. But Lord de Dunstanville was not prepared to co-operate, and Portreath harbour was closed to shipping in the winter months anyway. The alternative was to find a harbour on the south coast, and the nearest possibility was at Point Quay on Restronguet Creek, an inlet off the river Fal. Thus was born the Redruth & Chasewater (sic) Railway. The line was intended to pass along the bank of the river Carnon through the community of Devoran, which lay just above the proposed southern terminus. Much of Devoran, as James very quickly discovered, was owned by Anna-Maria Agar. What a golden opportunity! With sound planning and shrewd investment, this sleepy village could be turned into a great trading port, with new docks and quays, work-shops and warehouses, and all the housing needed by an expanded population. The first problem was to secure possession of those areas not owned by his patron and acquire freehold rights from her tenants. Anna-Maria was currently 'asset rich but cash poor' and not susceptible to expensive investment schemes; James would have to wait a while to make his big pitch.

Positive that the new railway would be in her best interests, he urged her not to oppose its route where it crossed her land. He was doubtless jealous that it had not been one of his own initiatives, but might there not be opportunities to promote the adoption of his Land-Agent locomotives?[298] When he returned to London in November. he delivered a second report to Baugh Allen, urging that Anna-Maria should improve the fertility of her land and invest in mine adventures and his railway proposals. Allen relayed the substance of this report back to Anna-Maria, but tempered his review with the suggestion that she should encourage others to take the initial risks and only come in as a 'piggy-back' investor. He was clearly bemused by James's enthusiasm for the steam locomotive, which he described as being 'a large machine something in the shape of a tea kettle.'

James had also used this visit to see the Glynn estates which he had agreed to sell, and he had started to talk to Jenkin about those that bordered Lanhydrock, as the steward related to Anna-Maria on 1 December 1823,

> I presume William James may have by this time reported to thee the results of his late visit to the county. I was particularly engaged in the accounts so I could not be with him as much as I wished. I pointed out to his attention Mullion Cove as a desirable situation for a roadstead for vessels, which would be very beneficial to the property thereabouts, of which thou hast a large proportion. He seems to think the place very capable of improvement – his principal attention, however, appeared to be directed to the property around Lanhydrock. He promised to let me know his plans for the improvement thereof when sufficiently matured, which could be very gratifying to me.[299]

On this score he was to be disappointed, in 1824 James had more urgent matters to attend to; but, like many other entrepreneurs from London, James was captivated by what he saw as the 'new frontier' investment potential in Cornwall.

In the last weeks of 1824 there was one surprising development for the provisional committee of the Liverpool & Manchester. The railway was no nearer to being started, but the Trustees of the Bridgewater Canal realised that the potential threat had to be taken seriously and they needed to gain some friends. They announced, along with the Mersey & Irwell Navigation, that from 22 December their freight rates were to be cut by 25 per cent.[300] It would, however, prove to be a case of too little, too late.

FOURTEEN

Betrayal
(1824–1825)

*'Those who carry on great public schemes must be proof against the worst delays,
the most mortifying disappointments, the most shocking of insults and, what is worse,
the presumptuous judgments of the ignorant upon their designs.'*

Edmund Burke

THE YEAR 1824 started with rumblings of discontent among a number of James's creditors, including Paul Padley and Joseph Povey, who were becoming increasingly alarmed that Edward Smith was selling items from James's estate so cheaply that there might be nothing left for them. In February they successfully petitioned the Lord Chancellor to appoint new assignees, on the grounds that Archibald Kendrick had never accepted his appointment in the first place and that Edward Smith was abusing his monopoly position. This intervention might slow things down, but at least it would prevent 'distressed' sales. The replacement assignees appointed by the commissioners in March were William Hawkes and Samuel Bill, James's site manager at Bexhill and a signatory of the Distress Memorial of 1816. He was to prove a true friend.

James still had a role on the Stratford & Moreton Railway and in April was back at Moreton-in-Marsh, where he found a fascinating letter awaiting him. It came from Robert Stephenson, not the young son but George's youngest brother (1788–1837), who was angling for a job.[301]

I beg leave to inform you that I have for some time back been in treaty with one of the Mexico Mining Compy as Engineer and the Superintendence of a Railway, having had perhaps more general practice than any other person in that line in the Kingdom, but in consequence of the great disapprobation of my Wife and large family, which must ever be my chief care I am obliged to relinquish the very liberal offer

which has been made me . . . Should you be in want of an assistant, I flatter myself, I could be very useful and should be glad to engage with you.

He offered 'the strongest testimonial proofs of my assertions', and here he could speak with some justification. He had been responsible for implementing his brother's plans for the eight-mile Hetton Railway to Sunderland, once described as 'the most perfect having locomotive engines'.[302] James, keen to maintain his friendship with the whole Stephenson family, invited him to come down for a meeting in June.

April also saw some interesting moves around Birmingham. In the wake of the Liverpool & Manchester proposals, the so-called Railway Fever was developing. Riding the current frenzied tide of dubious company promotions for mines, gasworks, docks and the like, it somewhat resembled the later and larger Railway Mania. The two decades between 1801 and 1821 had seen a mere 52 railway Bills put before Parliament, of which nineteen had resulted in Acts. The two years of 1824 and 1825 alone saw prospectuses published for at least 70 railway schemes.[303] Most died an instant and deserved death.

A few, like the Liverpool & Manchester, bore rapid fruit. Some had to await their time and this was one. Several years previously, James, largely motivated by a desire to by-pass the intransigent Birmingham Canal, had planned a railway from the South Staffordshire coalfield to Birmingham.[304] The idea was now embraced enthusiastically by a wider group of his fellow iron-masters, whose ambitions had grown considerably and

84

whose target was now to link Birmingham with Liverpool. On 26 April 1824 a meeting was held in Wolverhampton to launch the Birmingham, Manchester & Liverpool Rail Road Company, with William James's name prominent among the list of promoters – but not as the chief engineer. The following resolution was passed unanimously:

> That a Rail Road from the town of Birmingham through the whole of the Staffordshire collieries and ironworks, and from thence through the neighbourhoods of the Shropshire ironworks and Staffordshire potteries to the River Mersey, with branches to the towns of Manchester and Liverpool would be of the greatest advantage to the above mentioned places and districts and productive of essential benefit to the nation at large.[305]

This and a parallel scheme for a railway from London to Birmingham were perhaps the most ambitious of the Railway Fever, and the meeting opened a subscription list to raise an initial capital of £500,000. On the following Monday, *Aris's Birmingham Gazette* reported that 'a great number of shares have been subscribed for, and an early application is expected to be made to Parliament for an Act of Incorporation.' The promoters evidently spent money on a publicity campaign to draw support from a wider public, for a fine engraving was commissioned *(plate 11b)*.[306] Dedicated to the 'Proprietors of the Birmingham & Liverpool Rail Road Company', it has a number of intriguing features. The two trains consist of waggons with sundry loads, though the only passengers are a company of cramped soldiers with their baggage and artillery. Domestic animals are shown grazing contentedly, totally unconcerned by the passage of the trains – moving along unfenced track – while country folk go about their normal lives.

The committee decided to submit a Bill to Parliament the following year, and in this bold venture we can detect the seeds of the Grand Junction Railway, later to be acclaimed by George Stephenson as one of his finest achievements. By an ironic coincidence, *Aris's Gazette* for 26 April, the day of the meeting, also carried an advertisement for 'A Genteel Residence at Hill Top, West Bromwich, to be sold by Auction at the Swan Inn, West Bromwich on Wednesday 12 May, 1824, by order of the assignees of William James.' But there was no time for self-pity, and James threw himself back to work in London, though when he got hold of a draft of the Redruth & Chasewater Railway Bill, he had some serious

reservations on behalf of Anna-Maria Agar, who received a letter from her solicitor dated 15 May: 'Mr James and myself have today had an interview with Lord Falmouth and his solicitor relative to the Railway Bill and I trust the clauses will be settled consistent with your interest.'[307]

To try to get things moving on the Liverpool & Manchester Railway, Joseph Sandars headed a visit by four committee members to the north-east to gain some hands-on experience of railway operation.[308] They saw construction progress on the Stockton & Darlington under George Stephenson's management and visited Killingworth (though he was away that day and none of his travelling engines was working) before moving on to Hetton Colliery where they did get a chance to ride on one of his locomotives. They returned complete converts to this form of traction and reported accordingly to the full committee on 20 May. They also reviewed Jesse Hartley's report, which concentrated mainly on the extension of the railway into the docks, and resolved to form a joint stock company with a capital of £300,000 as soon as Parliament authorised the Bill. Sandars, now that he had experienced it for himself, might well have wished to congratulate James on his persistent championship of steam traction, but James was elsewhere and not inclined to return to Liverpool without a positive invitation to re-adopt his role as chief surveyor and engineer. He had written to Sandars on 7 May asking to see a copy of Hartley's report, but when the reply came on the 26th it proved to be a thunderbolt.[309]

> I cannot send you a copy of Hartly's report; it is very long. I think it is right to inform you that the committee have engaged your friend Mr G. Stephenson. We expect him here in a few days ... I very much regret that, by delay and promises, you have forfeited the confidence of the subscribers. I cannot help it. I fear now that you will only have the fame of being connected with the commencement of this undertaking.
> If you will send me down your plans and estimates, I will do everything for you I can; and I believe I possess as much influence as any person. I am quite certain that the appointment of Stephenson will, under all circumstances, be agreeable to you. I believe you have recommended him yourself.
> If you consent to put your plans, &c, under my control and management, your name shall be prominent in the proceedings; and this, in such a mighty affair, will be of

importance to you. You may rely upon my zeal for you in every point connected with your reputation.

The letter also said that the subscription list of £300,000 was filled and that the Manchester interests had conceded the entire management to the Liverpool faction. Sandars was still a member of the committee but no longer in a role of executive authority. Although some subsequent writers, particular Ellen Paine, have interpreted this letter as a kiss of Judas, one must feel that the committee had come to a sensible conclusion. James had indeed extolled the virtues of his partner George Stephenson, but only as a supplier of practical locomotives and a consultant on their capabilities. Sandars and his team had now seen for themselves his supervisory work on the Stockton & Darlington and had probably been misled into believing that he had not only been responsible for the survey, but also for designing the civil engineering features and preparing the cost estimates, most of which had in reality been done by others. He must have also struck them as being sound, if somewhat bluff and taciturn, and as northerners themselves they would have recognised in 'Geordie George' the solid virtue of blunt reliability. How different from the mercurial William James! Stephenson had another outstanding merit: he was available. He arrived to take up his appointment in Liverpool on 12 June, accompanied by his son Robert.

Five days later, the Redruth & Chasewater Railway obtained its Act of Parliament, but when James saw it and the attached plans – lithographed by his brother-in-law Paul Padley (plate 13) – he wrote to Baugh Allen in utter disgust; the route would not serve Anna-Maria's lands to the west and north of Redruth, his suggestions had been ignored, other landlord's mines had been given priority, and he suspected that secret deals had been done 'which do not meet the light.' [310] He had further grounds for complaint. When briefly back in Cornwall on 14 June to see one of Anna-Maria's properties in Truro, he had made an appointment to meet Alfred Jenkin, which the steward failed to keep. James took this as a personal insult and told Allen that he 'would not be sidelined'; Allen later described this letter as a typical 'Jeremiad'.[311] Once opened in 1825, the Redruth & Chasewater Railway certainly stimulated trade, carrying not only copper ore to the coast for export to South Wales but also the coal which made up the return cargoes.[312] Other areas of Cornwall needed a similar boost from better transport links, and

James returned to his plan for an even more ambitious scheme which would for the first time link the south and north coasts of the county.

We now reach a moment of high drama which historians and biographers have interpreted in a number of different ways. The fact is that within a week of arriving at Liverpool in June 1824 young Robert Stephenson had set sail for South America and would not return for three years. It is also a fact that this was not a spur-of-the-moment decision. Some months earlier, before his father had been offered the role on the Liverpool & Manchester, Robert had accepted the job of supervising the installation of mining machinery in Colombia on behalf of the Colombian Mining Association. This was one of the more ambitious schemes of the banker Thomas Richardson, founder of the great banking discount house of Overend, Gurney & Co and a cousin of Edward Pease.[313] A responsible appointment in the new El Dorado was an exciting opportunity for an ambitious young man – though Samuel Smiles would later suggest that he went for the sake of his health – and Robert may even have received encouragement from James to spread his wings and see the world. But now his father urged him to stay in England as he needed his support and, more than anything else, he needed the surveying skills that James and Dixon had taught him. There is little doubt that Robert, had he wanted to, could have rescinded his overseas contract, but he was probably aware of the sub-plot being hatched behind James's back and could not bear to think that his mentor, the man he idolised, might feel that he was involved in the next piece of treachery.

James could console himself that in the vital survey plans locked in his office he still had a bargaining tool. In June he wrote to Paul Padley setting him on a new survey, possibly in connection with the Canterbury project or perhaps in Cornwall. What he did not know was that Padley had made copies of the Liverpool & Manchester plans. When he received a reply, dated 28 June, he must have been shattered.

I am sorry it is not in my power at this time to act according to your instructions by going into the country immediately. I am much obliged by your intention of giving me employment. In the first place I could not leave town for some days until my business in hand is finished, and in the next, because, believing that you had altogether relinquished the Manchester business, I have accepted an offer kindly made me

by Mr George Stephenson (a few days
since,) of becoming one of his surveyors
on that and other business . . . I have written
to him to say I will do so at the end of this
week, and I am now awaiting his reply
to say when and where; and I know you
would not think me acting honourably to
accept another offer while this is pending
. . . As I have scarcely time to save this post,
I hope you will excuse my finishing my
letter rather abruptly.[314]

Ellen Paine professed disgust at 'the hesitating
and unmanly tone' of this letter from her own
uncle. Certainly it must have been difficult to
write. He had many reasons to be very grateful to
James, yet he did have his own career to consider
and he suspected that any continuing employment by his brother-in-law would be unpaid.
Worse than that, he might find himself being
hounded by more of James's creditors. James
himself vented his anguish in a letter to his son
William Henry at the beginning of July:[315]

The reason why you have not heard from
Padley is that he has made terms with
George Stephenson; so he is lost to us for
ever. He knows my plans, of which he and
Stephenson will now avail themselves.
I confess I did not calculate upon such
duplicity in either.

At the same time, more of James's assets were
put up for auction in Birmingham, including his
holding in the Upper Avon Navigation. He might
have appreciated the bathos in the auctioneer's
blurb, which described this lot as a 'valuable
property, presenting an opportunity for investment which seldom occurs for the Capitalist,
Merchant or Speculator . . . and which cannot fail
to prove a source of immense profit to the
proprietors.' James probably regretted that he
had not cut his losses in 1822 when he had been
offered £5,000 for the tolls. Instead, he had
insisted that the true value was nearer £18,000,
hoping to make George Perrott bid up against the
Stratford Canal Company. James's holding in the
Upper Avon was not exactly snapped up, but
eventually sold in December 1825 to a syndicate
of seven men, including James's cousin John
Greaves. The price was £5,000.

At last it seemed that the major creditors had
been satisfied and the loyal Samuel Bill put up
some sort of personal guarantee to the Court.
James was free, but he was also a pauper. All his
shares were forfeited, as well as all his many
leaseholds, which included the wharfs at New

Hall Hill in Birmingham, the wharfs and kilns
at Kings Norton, and probably most of the
coalmines. All would revert to the owners of
the freeholds, without any compensation for
the money that James had invested in extending
and improving them. As an example, he had
apparently spent over £9,000 on the New Hall
Hill site and at least £15,000 in the coalmines
leased from the Earl of Dartmouth. That left his
remaining freeholds. The assignees might have
imagined that it would be relatively easy to sort
out the one from the other, but they had not
bargained on the chaos and complexity of
James's record-keeping, or lack of it. Even with
the help of 'poor' Povey – who probably had not
had his salary paid for years – it was impossible
to work out who owned what, and who owed
how much and to whom. The whole unwinding
of James's affairs would eventually take twenty
years and, as usual, the main beneficiaries would
be the lawyers. One unwitting casualty of his lack
of discipline was his eldest son William Henry, to
whom he had gifted several properties. Sadly it
appears that his generosity had not been followed
up by the appropriate conveyancing.

The commissioners of bankruptcy cannot
have envisaged this mammoth timescale either.
According to Ellen Paine they proposed that,
while the matter was wrapped up, her father
should be allowed an annuity of £600, which, she
claimed, he was 'too proud' to accept, as if his
honour demanded that he suffer abject poverty
to atone for his own failure.[316] Certainly he felt
humiliated and mortified by the shame and social
disgrace he had brought on his family, and in a
letter to one of the Liverpool directors, probably
David Holt, he poured out his pent-up resentment that he had been dropped from any further
involvement in that enterprise.[317] As he saw it, he
had completed his surveys, he had lodged them
with the clerk to the justices, and he had even
incorporated a last-minute adjustment to the line
to take it through Everton. It was not his fault that
he had been ill as a result of his 'exertions in the
most dreadful weather', nor that he had been
arrested on 'an illegal demand' for which he had
'suffered the horrors of a prison.'

I must be insensible to the value of the
approbation of good and liberal men, if
I were not much hurt at the loss of your
estimable connection. Great and unmerited
as have been the persecutions to which
I have fallen a victim, this has been a more
severe pang of anguish … I never had
abandoned the hope of prosecuting this

measure of my own creation . . . I do not quarrel with Mr Stephenson's good fortune, although, through his fraud, I have lately lost the Birmingham [to Liverpool] appointment.

This is a harsh indictment. But he had been stabbed in the back by a man he had gone out of his way to applaud and whose interests he had sought to promote at every opportunity. To James's character, this was the ultimate disloyalty. Was this the way to repay friendship? And it would not be the first or last time that George Stephenson prosecuted his own career at the expense of others.[318]

But James was at least comforted by the fact that he still had a role to play not only at Canterbury but at Moreton-in-Marsh where he was confident he could rely on the continuing support of his friend Lord Redesdale. And how about the approach from Robert Stephenson Snr.? We know that his intended visit to Moreton in June had had to be postponed because 'my wife and two of my children lie ill of the fever . . . and the Doctor says that I must not leave as they are not yet considered out of danger'.[319] Norris in his definitive history of the Moreton railway makes no mention whatsoever of Robert Stephenson Snr., but it appears that he was taken on in a consultancy role under John Rastrick, probably heading up the mechanical department. There is clear evidence that he was living in Stratford by December 1824.[320]

In the first week of September James received a somewhat enigmatic letter from his cousin John Greaves about the hesitant progress on the Moreton railway.[321] James must have proposed some rather contentious step to use the company's already stretched resources, perhaps even involving some retrospective salary.

I really cannot reconcile myself to deviate from the instructions of the General Meeting, viz. to distribute £800 among the contractors, &c, and thereby keep on the works until the next meeting, on Monday week, when, I have no doubt, a bill of indemnity will be passed for any measure which you, in the zeal which you have to promote the concern, and save it from impending ruin, may think fit to adopt; but I beg you will let it emanate from yourself alone . . . Do see Lord Redesdale soon.

Three days before the General Meeting on 20 September, Lord Redesdale wrote to James asking him, among other things, to get in proxies from Moreton to ensure they had the minimum quorum of 200 votes, thus avoiding the embarrassments of earlier meetings.[322] He also stated that Mr Dudley – as distinct from the Earl of Dudley – was prepared to advance up to £15,000, but with a number of strings attached, one of which was that Brewin, who acted as his agent, should take over the accounts. While James doubtless bridled at this suggestion, he was persuasive with the reluctant shareholders – 304 votes were represented, the highest 'attendance' in the company's history. The main business was to receive a financial report from James, minuted as the company's 'Manager and Engineer'. Out of the original capital of 670 £50 shares, only 400 had been sold, on which calls worth £5,466 were still unpaid. The earthworks were progressing, but there had been no money for the mechanical department to buy waggons or machinery to bore holes in the stone sleeper-blocks. James estimated that it would take another £17,657 just to complete the trackbed and proposed that the shortfall be made up from two sources: firstly by accepting Dudley's offer of a loan (but only to the extent of £10,000) and secondly – recalling the success of his Memorial of 1816 – by applying to the Commissioners of the Exchequer Bill Loan for another £10,000 at 4 per cent, plus an annual repayment of 5 per cent. In his opinion, the other terms of this loan (preference over all other charges and the commissioners' right to inspect the line) had to be accepted; once operational, revenue should be at least £2,870 per annum, enough to cover the interest and give a satisfactory dividend. Then it would be much easier to sell the unissued shares and redeem the loans. The motion was carried.

Meanwhile, George Stephenson, struggling with a new survey for the first section of the Liverpool & Manchester Railway, was encountering James's problems with the estates at Croxteth and Knowsley. James, increasingly disillusioned by his partner's behaviour, might even have relished the discomforts he was suffering, which Stephenson outlined in a letter to Joseph Pease, Edward Pease's son, dated 19 October.[323]

We have sad work with Lord Derby, Lord Sefton, and Bradshaw, the great canal proprietor . . . Their ground is blockaded on every side to prevent us getting on with the survey. Bradshaw fires guns through his grounds in the course of the night, to prevent the surveyor coming on in the dark.

Sandars had informed James in his last letter that the initial subscription list had been filled by allocations to the committee and their friends, but now it was time to find a wider market for the shares and the first public prospectus of the railway was published on 29 October 1824.[324] A few weeks later Charles Sylvester, a respected civil engineer, wrote a well-informed report for the committee on the future potential of loco-motives. He concluded that, in theory, there was no limit to the speeds they could attain. He tempered this by warning that high speeds would 'be attended by proportionate danger' in the event of an accident. 'This new application of locomotive power is of infinite importance to the country and I should regret to see it abused'. In summarising this report Charles Lawrence, the then chairman, concluded that the advantages of steam locomotion were 'so striking that it is a matter of surprise that this mode of conveyance has not been resorted to earlier. Its adoption is now inevitable.'[325] Had James been privy to this report, he might have been tempted to say 'I told you so'.

More encouraging for James was news from Canterbury, where his project had made some progress during the autumn. A committee had been formed and the Canterbury Rail Road Company was officially launched at a meeting on 5 November. A notice to that effect was inserted in the local newspapers, the first clause stating 'that a Rail Road from the City of Canterbury to communicate with the Port of Whitstable would be of the greatest advantage . . . and productive of essential benefit to the county at large.' The capital would be £25,000 divided into 500 shares of £50 each. James, probably unbeknown to his creditors, managed to acquire ten of them.[326]

The prospectus outlined the potential advan-tages to be gained. 20,000 tons of goods were currently transported every year between Canter-bury and Whitstable which at 5s per ton – more competitive than existing carriers – could yield a potential income of £5,000. 'An eminent engineer' had already done preliminary surveys, con-cluding that that the length would not exceed eight miles and that the country presented 'extraordinary facilities for laying the rails'. For fear, perhaps, that the stigma of his bankruptcy would not help in promoting the share issue, James was not specifically named. Nor, clearly, had the committee yet made up its mind on which of his three routes to adopt. This indecision is repeated in the advertisement published on 16 November, stating that a Bill would be presented to Parliament the following spring. The railroad would 'pass through or into' several named parishes and townships, including some which lay on the longer routes as well as those only on the direct line. A decision had to be made by 30 November, and it was James's plan and section for that short but 'alpine' route which was deposited with the Clerk of the Peace for Kent. But his estimated construction cost of £24,000 could not take into account the long tunnel necessary through Tyler's Hill. So why did the committee choose this route? There is a nice bit of local folk-lore that the 'intermediate' route, with its modest gradients and easier earthworks, was indeed their first choice, but that there had been uproar when people heard they might be denied the thrill of travelling through a tunnel.[327]

Once the details appeared in the press, the correspondence columns filled with letters from the cynical and the satirical. The carriage rate of 5s per ton did not allow for moving goods to and from the stations; the estimated income assumed that every ton of freight would desert the turnpike; the construction costs were ridiculously under-estimated and average speeds could never reach the 8 mph quoted in the prospectus. And in answer to the correspondent who wished to know the site of the proposed lunatic asylum, the *Kent Herald* surmised that 'it will be built somewhere about Blean Common and command a full view of the projected Whitstable Railroad.'[328]

On the very last day of 1824 there was another significant development up in Newcastle: the formation of George Stephenson & Co. Its pro-prietors were the same as for Robert Stephenson & Co but, in contrast to the engine-building operations of that firm, the new one was devised as a railway construction consultancy. With young Robert abroad, George Stephenson could control the recruitment of staff, and virtually all the eighteen employees, with the exception of John Dixon, were young apprentices with little or no practical experience. They included Thomas Richardson's son Joshua and the fourteen-year-old John Cass Birkinshaw. None of George's brothers was invited.

This cost-cutting approach to recruitment would be a bone of contention between Robert and his father for years to come, and the lack of expertise in the team is a criticism voiced by others.[329] 'The most obvious omission was William James, who could have contributed much to the railway-building endeavour, based on his lifelong experience'.[330] Had he been included, it might have saved the Liverpool & Manchester directors much time and money – and the acute embarrassments of early 1825.

FIFTEEN

The Witch's Broomstick, Moreton and a Burst Bubble (1825–1826)

JANUARY 1825 found Robert Stephenson Snr settling down to his new assignment at Stratford. He was as anxious as James to persuade Rastrick and the board, particularly the sceptical John Greaves, to adopt steam locomotive traction on the railway sooner rather than later. If George Stephenson's engines were not up to the job, how about trying a different supplier? Overtures were made to Robert Wilson, who owned a small engineering works in Forth Street, Newcastle, just down the road from Robert Stephenson & Co.[331] Wilson had been around a long time; he is thought by most historians to be the author of a 'Memorandum' on the Gateshead locomotive of 1805 designed, though not built, by Richard Trevithick for John Whinfield. James, now justifiably resentful against his erstwhile friend George Stephenson, was not averse to encouraging a potential competitor and, though Robert Stephenson Snr's position must have been a touch more delicate, he too resented his brother's dismissive attitude towards him. His first task was to convince Greaves that he was an expert on all matters to do with steam-powered machinery, to which end, on 21 December 1824, he gave him a long 'Report of Steam Engines'.[332]

It is a confused, rambling document which focusses on stationary winding engines and engines for marine applications, all based on Watt-type low-pressure condensing technology. It does not mention high-pressure locomotives. One wonders whether Greaves was any the wiser, or indeed whether he was any more confident about the writer's expertise, particularly as Stephenson introduced his bizarre theory that 'when steam is rarified to a high degree, it is very inflamible [sic] . . . which no doubt is the cause of so many serious accidents.' At least he was addressing one of Greaves's main objections to the use of locomotives.

While Greaves tried to absorb the implications of all this, Robert Stephenson Snr received a delightfully mis-spelt letter from Robert Wilson, addressed to him at the Rail Road office, Stratford-on-Avon and dated 14 January 1825.[333] Described as 'a clever engineer',[334] Robert Wilson had just completed his first – and only – railway locomotive, which he called the *Traveller*

> I have this day set my men to paint and finish of the Travler & I mean to clead it in so as to make it look as well as pasible. I have had an application from an engineer in London for it to go on the Birmingham Rail road[335] when it is done but I think you had better set it to work on your road first.

The letter contains many other fascinating details. 'I am happy to hear that you are getting on so well and that you are not likely to be stopt for want of mony in completing your railroad.' There is local Newcastle gossip. 'Poor Willy Gray has made an invention upon the Travling Engine and had the misfortune to show it to Mr Longridge before your worthy brother George saw it, and he has taken such high umbrage as to discharge poor Willy'. Returning to the *Traveller* he says, 'I wish you had her and I had the money, an article I am very much in want of at Preasent'. He offers Robert Stephenson a commission if he can effect a sale for him, and ends, 'Give my love to Mr James, and tell him I should like to see him and his son here in their Patent Travling Carriage.'

Since 1822, William Henry James had been concentrating his inventiveness on steam carriages for use on common roads. He was one of several pioneers in this field, along with Joseph Reynolds, John Dumbell, David Gordon, Julius Griffiths and Timothy Burstall. He was still obsessed with water-tube boilers and intent on solving (as was necessary with road vehicles) the problem of differential drag when turning sharply. His patented solution of 1824 involved four cylinders each driving its own wheel, and his first road carriage built on this principle in the same year much impressed the contemporary commentator, Luke Hebert, who stated in his

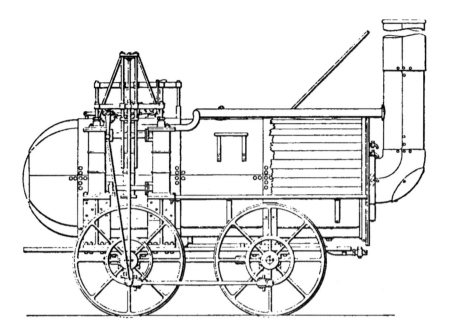

Fig.10: **Conceptual drawing by E. Forward** (*The Engineer*), **of Wilson's 'Traveller',
later known as 'Chittapratt'. The wheels are certainly wrong,
and would have been to Wilson's plug design.**

Register of Arts that it was 'so efficient that the carriage could be made to describe every variety of curve; he has seen it repeatedly make turns of less than 10ft radius'.[336] Little more is known about this vehicle – it certainly never went to Newcastle – but William Henry James persevered and we will hear more about the outcome in a later chapter.

Nor did Wilson's *Traveller* ever come south. We next hear of it later in 1825, when it was offered to the directors of the Stockton & Darlington at a deeply discounted price of £380 and a month's free trial. It was not a great success. It did, however, include some very advanced features, which probably contributed to its unreliability. For one thing, it had (like young James's road steamer, but coincidentally) four cylinders rather than two, mounted in vertical pairs on either side of the boiler. For another, steam was distributed to them by means of piston valves rather than the conventional slide or plug valves. The composite construction of the four driving wheels was also unique, with an inner disc keyed into an outer toroidal disc that included the tyre. This technique allowed larger

wheels to be made and with greater strength and accuracy. The concept was adopted successfully by Timothy Hackworth, and many commentators have attributed this invention to him rather than the impoverished Wilson.

One consequence of the four-cylinder arrangement was that the locomotive had a strangely staccato exhaust beat when moving, earning it the nickname of the *Chittapratt*. The Stockton & Darlington directors did buy it in the end, but only because they wanted the boiler, which may have been used as the basis for Hackworth's very successful *Royal George*.

In March 1825 Parliament considered Bills for three railways which had been initiated by James. First was the Birmingham & Liverpool, but 'the canal proprietors and landowners opposed the bill and it was thrown out.'[337] Second was the Liverpool & Manchester, which also came up against vehement opposition, not only from the Earl of Derby and his allies but from a lobby organised by Robert Bradshaw and the trustees of the Bridgewater Canal. The Liverpool Corporation had also turned against the project in its current form. This Bill too was lost, to a large extent because of the unconvincing and hesitant performance of the chief engineer, George Stephenson. The committee rooms of Westminster were an alien environment to him and he crumpled under acerbic cross-examination. He was forced to admit that the detailed design of the Sankey viaduct had not been considered and therefore could not be costed. Possessing no personal surveying skills himself, Stephenson had allowed his assistants Elijah Galloway and Hugh Steel to make gross errors which were easily exposed. He even tried to suggest that they had been planted on him by Bradshaw. As Smiles put it, 'he wished for a hole to creep out of the witness-box, and felt he could not find words to satisfy either the committee or himself.' William James, in contrast, would have been in his element, but it was too late. Perhaps regretting that they had dropped their champion too soon, the directors started looking for a replacement for Stephenson. Another year had been wasted. The public shares, however, were booming. Mrs Arbuthnot, a confidante of the Duke of Wellington, wrote in her diary for 16 March 1825, 'We have ten shares in the railway for which we paid £3 apiece and which are now worth £58 each'.[338]

By contrast, the third of the Bills, for the Bolton & Leigh Railway, was passed and received the royal assent on 31 March. This short railway in the middle of Lancashire (the 'Witch's Broomstick', for reasons that will emerge later) has received little attention from historians, yet it has a significance that far outweighs its modest length and may, indirectly, be considered as one of James's more successful achievements.[339] It was not only the first public railway in Lancashire, but also the culmination of James's endeavours to improve the transport links for the coalfield where he had done preliminary work as far back as 1802. We know that he had spent time on surveying various routes over the hilly terrain south of Bolton while his main team was struggling with the Liverpool survey in 1822 – his absence in October caused Sandars concern – and he had settled on a line to Leigh on the Leeds & Liverpool Canal, a distance of 7½ miles. This was good politics. A route to the Bridgewater Canal, while shorter, would be ruthlessly opposed, whereas the rival canal company was positively in favour, though only if the line terminated at their wharf. Any question of crossing the canal and heading towards a direct junction with the Liverpool & Manchester railway would have to wait. A year before the Act, James's assistant, George Hamilton, had removed the Bolton plans away from their Liverpool office as a security

precaution, but Paul Padley had copies and thus they too found their way into Stephenson's hands. They joined those for the Birmingham & Liverpool in the portfolio of surveys which Stephenson would now adopt as his own, and were soon to be joined by those for the Canterbury & Whitstable.

The successful plans and books of reference for the Bolton & Leigh were lodged with the Clerk of the Peace at Preston on 30 November 1824, and although they were signed off by George Stephenson (and the unreliable Hugh Steel, who was to commit suicide in 1827) it seems most likely that they were, in reality, James's plans with a different signature.[340] Stephenson had presented himself to the directors of the Bolton & Leigh in the summer of 1824, and they, impressed by his reputation from the Stockton & Darlington and by the fact that he had James's plans in his pocket, appointed him as their chief engineer. His estimate for completing the line totalled £43,143 1s, including £14,231 2s 4d for the earthworks, £8,360 for the rails and £5,400 for buying the land. Within the balance, £3,000 was allocated for two stationary engines to work the inclines at Chequerbent and Daubhill, while two locomotives (to be supplied, naturally, by Robert Stephenson & Co) were priced at £600 each.[341] The on-site surveyor was to be Hugh Steel and construction started in 1826 under Robert Daglish of Orwell colliery. But Stephenson also wanted his brother Robert involved, and ordered him to leave Stratford and help look after his interests at Bolton. At no stage, it seems, did he invite James to add the weight of his experience to the project and now, to underline the slight, he was poaching a man who had an important role on the Stratford & Moreton Railway.

Returning to 1825, we need to re-introduce Nicholas Wood, one of Stephenson's most successful associates at Killingworth and his companion at that first meeting with Edward Pease. Wood acquired considerable status later in life – a fellow of the Royal Society and president of the Institution of Mining Engineers – but in February 1825 he was in a quandary about the publication of the results of experiments he had been conducting on the locomotives under his charge at Killingworth. Without the modifications that Wood had introduced, the performance of Stephenson's machines was not impressive. Would this disclosure be harmful to the reputation of his boss? He unburdened his predicament in a letter to Edward Pease.[342] 'Of course if the publishing them [the experiments] to the world should injure Mr Stephenson I should, notwithstanding,

Fig.11:
Wilson's plug design for locomotive driving wheels.

with-hold them, but after mature consideration I do not think they will.' Wood was hoping to make money from publication and added a sentence which James would empathise with: because 'I am several pounds the worse for all my experience with Rail Roads I trust you will not blame me for endeavouring to reimburse myself.'

Wood's *Practical Treatise on Rail Roads*, published later that year, became something of a classic, more for its almost unique status in that era than for the actual results it contained. His tests, though meticulously conducted, were not extrapolated into what might be feasible in the future. His conclusions about future power and speeds were as cautious as Stephenson's – he toed the party line – but his book, because it was the only work of reference available, would often be quoted by critics of the locomotive and act as a damper on the acceptance of 'advanced locomotion'.

Royal assent was given to two further Acts of Parliament in June 1825. Like those in March, both related to schemes on which James's future depended. One looked to James like a triumph, the other a major disappointment. The first authorised the Canterbury & Whitstable Railway, giving it powers to raise £31,000 in shares, of which £25,000 had already been pledged. James, having learnt tough lessons from parliamentary restrictions on raising additional funds, had drafted it very carefully and this Act gave the company 'unlimited power . . . for borrowing any additional sum on mortgage of the under-taking.'[343] The route finally selected by the local

committee was the shortest – just over six miles long – but equally the one that James favoured least and certainly not the one on which he had based his costs. Furthermore, the terminus would be some way from the centre of Canterbury. But James's name was on the deposited plans and beneath his signature was the proud title 'Chief Engineer'.[344]

Confirmation that the railway could now be built was heralded in glowing terms by the *Kentish Gazette* on 14 June. With competitive pride, the editor noted that a railway from Liverpool to Manchester was 'anxiously desired . . . but the Bill for that purpose has been, it appears, unaccountably lost in Committee.' James's second horse might yet win, for the Canterbury railway, in contrast, 'will be completed with all possible celerity . . . and will afford a safe, a rapid, a certain and regular communication from the sea to Canterbury. It will then place this ancient and respectable City for all purposes of trade and advantages of commerce at the mouth of the Thames, a river which is the great emporium of all the commerce and wealth of the world.' Finally, to avoid any accusation of neglecting a minority interest, the article ended, 'It is needless to say that the inhabitants and property of Whitstable will also participate in the success of the undertaking.' James must have confidently awaited the call to start the engineering work.

The second successful Act of June 1825 arose from the necessity to authorise the extra borrowings for the Stratford & Moreton Railway which

James had highlighted in September 1824 but were not catered for in the original Act. Parliament's *quid pro quo* for lending the money on Exchequer Bills would be what many committee members saw as interference in the way the railway could be run. Inspectors from the Board of Trade had visited the works, which had now progressed several miles south of Stratford, but were disturbed to find that the route ran alongside the turnpike road and through the heart of the village of Alderminster, the rails being close to several houses. This rang alarm bells with them. The threat of buildings being set alight by sparks and cinders from locomotives was an objection frequently raised by opponents of the spread of railways and, as we shall see, was an issue which ten years later would be the subject of a select committee of the House of Lords. The second Stratford & Moreton Railway Act approved not only the extra borrowing but also a branch to Shipston-on-Stour, but it specifically banned the use of steam locomotives on the six-mile stretch south of Stratford. To James, this was a shattering blow. His dream of introducing modern motive power to the Midlands lay in ruins, destroyed by remote bureaucrats. Robert Stephenson Snr must have been disappointed too. His job at Stratford was now debased, and one assumes that he was forced to write to Robert Wilson declining any further interest in his freshly-painted *Traveller (plate 8a).*

In May James received more bad news: the death of Lord Whitworth who had been a resolute ally during the Bexhill venture and remained a firm friend thereafter. He had agreed to be godfather to the James's fourth son, born on 25 March 1808 and christened Frederick Whitworth Tarleton James – the 'little Fred' about whom Robert Stephenson enquired so earnestly in letters to James during 1821. James, lodging in Stratford at the time, poured out his grief to Earl Spencer at Althorp in a letter dated 17 May, which may also imply that Whitworth had been giving him some sort of allowance.[345]

The papers of this morning announce the death of my old and esteemed friend Lord Whitworth . . . To me this event is an irretrievable loss, as his friendship was my principal consolation in my altered circumstances. His cordial approval cheered my exertions, and his place, as regards my future destiny, can never be supplied . . . His qualities and virtues as a man were of an exalted nature; but as a warm friend, which no change of fortune could change,

he was the glowing ornament of the species; if there are angels in heaven, he is one.

When a few weeks later Whitworth's widow, the redoubtable Arabella Duchess of Dorset, died of a broken heart, James had lost yet another patron and a valuable link with the past.

Perhaps James had not yet given up all hope of returning to the Liverpool & Manchester project and, in his impoverished circumstances, he may have put his Christian charity to one side and positively exulted in George Stephenson's discomfort and exclusion. He must have written to John Moss offering his services again, should the committee be considering a new Bill for 1826, for Moss replied on 13 July 1825,[346]

It certainly is the intention of the Rail Road committee to apply again to Parliament next session, and with great hopes of success. What line we take is not decided upon. Should you visit Liverpool, I shall be glad to see you, but you have so often talked of coming that I shall not calculate upon it until I see you.

This was hardly a positive invitation to return and pick up the reins. Doubtless pricked by the overt reference to his unreliability, James buried himself in more practical matters near Moreton-in-Marsh. He had persuaded the shareholders that it was vital to secure some land adjoining the Stratford Canal basins and arranged an option to purchase, payment to be made two years after the railway opened. The building of the line was making headway, despite having to save every possible penny. Construction standards were pared to the bone and cuttings and embankments were made with sides too steep, which later led to destructive earth slippages. These were the concerns of Rastrick and Robert Stephenson Snr. James, still determined that the extension towards London should not be neglected, concentrated on more visionary matters. He occupied himself with a detailed survey of a new line heading southeast from Moreton to Shipton-under-Wychwood, where he envisaged a junction to Cheltenham, and full parliamentary plans for this ten-mile section were completed and deposited later in 1825.[347]

Yet another of James's ambitious initiatives had already been published. We saw in Chapter 13 how during his visit to Cornwall in June 1823 he had postulated the idea of a railway from Padstow to Fowey, and over the following months he must have taken soundings from landowners along the route. At the northern end, this would involve the Prideaux-Brune family and William Molesworth of Pencarrow, whilst around Lostwithiel the line would have to pass through property owned by the Hext family, Lady Grenville of Boconnoc and the Earl of Mount Edgcumbe. He was perhaps more confident of the route round Bodmin itself, which was mainly Agar and Glynn territory. The line would cross Halgavor Moor (spelt Algavoar by Ellen Paine). James would probably have had most difficulty with William Rashleigh, who had already objected to a railway proposal by his neighbour J. T. Austen in the region of Fowey itself. Nevertheless, inspired by the speculative boom of 1825 and anxious to cash in, James had the following advertisement printed in the *Royal Cornwall Gazette* of 4 June 1825.

ENGINE RAIL-ROAD from PADSTOW TO FOWEY. Notice is hereby given that under instructions from the principal Land-Owners and persons interested therein, (the Surveys of Investigation having ascertained the practicability of the measure) application will be made to Parliament in the ensuing Session to obtain an Act for making and maintaining a RAIL-ROAD adapted to Locomotion of Carriages by Engine Power, between the ports of PADSTOW and FOWEY, with several collateral Branches therefrom, and also an Act for making an harbour with proper Wharfs, Bridges, Piers and Breakwaters, at MULLION in Padannec, in Mounts Bay, with several lines of ENGINE RAILWAY connected therewith.

The Prospectus of the Committee will be immediately published with the Plans annexed, and then proposals for Shares will be received at the Banks in the principal Towns, also at Plymouth, Bristol, Swansea and in London.

W. JAMES Land Agent and Engineer Thavies Inn, London 4 June 1825

The same journal carried another advertisement from James on 9 July, offering the 'manors, advowsons, mines and several thousand acres of land' of the Glynn estates for speedy sale by auction. The properties around Bodmin were to be 'intersected by the proposed railway from Padstow to Fowey, by which, when completed, the carriage of shell, sand and lime, and the valuable granite, copper, lead, tin (lodes of which have been proved), coal and other minerals and produce will be effected at a very reduced rate'.

His timing was unfortunate because the great crash of 1825 was about to happen. As already remarked, the previous eighteen months had already witnessed an unprecedented number of speculative schemes. The total amount of capital sought from the public was £280 million, and under the increasing weight of fantasy paper the structure imploded. Country banks collapsed like skittles.

William Rashleigh certainly did see James's advertisement, and suggested to his steward that a further notice should be posted to the effect that he and other landowners would object to it.[348] He need not have bothered; the scheme was dead before it had a chance to go anywhere. For the time being; but there is every likelihood that William Molesworth (later Sir William) based his own Bodmin & Wadebridge railway of 1832 on James's original proposal,[349] and in this he would prove to be more successful than he had been in affairs of the heart. Molesworth had been the first love of the heiress Juliana Pole-Carew, but his political views were far too radical for her father, who forbade an engagement. Later she would make a good dynastic marriage into another great Cornish family, by becoming the wife of Thomas James Agar-Robartes, the heir to Anna-Maria Agar.

SIXTEEN

Kidnap in Kent and an Ox-roast in the Cotswolds (1825–1826)

THERE was still no summons from Canterbury. What James did not know was that George Stephenson had done here exactly as he had done with the promoters of the Birmingham & Liverpool and the directors of the Bolton & Leigh. He had had himself appointed as the line's engineer. The Canterbury directors wrote to him on 10 July 1825, requesting his attendance at their meeting on 1 August to 'receive instructions for your surveys etc', but Stephenson was now far too busy completing the Stockton & Darlington to make the journey. Prodded by a further letter from the directors on 19 July – 'it is very important to commence work without delay' – he delegated to John Dixon the post of resident engineer, and would never himself play more than a consultancy role with the railway in Kent. Dixon did not arrive on schedule either, which led to more terse letters in August. 'We have received a letter from Mr Richardson requesting us to forward the Railway plans to you [so] that Mr Stephenson may explain what is necessary to be done upon your survey. We herewith send the Plan and Section made by Mr James . . . and we trust you will not lose any time in coming.' [350] Yet again, the products of James's self-financed efforts were being given to Stephenson for free.

A Special General Meeting of the Moreton company was held on 31 August at the George Inn, Shipston-on-Stour. The ten proprietors who turned up discussed the perennial problems of shortage of cash and of shareholders not paying their calls – in some cases because the individual had died – and charged James with two tasks: to persuade backsliding members, or their executors, to pay up within a month under threat of legal redress, and to find 'persons whom he may think likely to advance money on credit of the works, upon such terms as the company can grant.' It was agreed to review the situation at a further meeting on 4 October. One interesting feature of the minutes is that James now appears, for the

first time, not only as an executive officer of the company but also as a shareholder. Somehow he had acquired three shares.[351]

Around this time James called in at Birmingham to see the demonstration of a half-size model made by his inventive son, William Henry. It was in effect the prototype multiple-unit train, embodying the ideas that formed the basis of his patent No 5117.[352] The model, hand cranked, was exhibited in the timber yard of a Mr. Crowther, near the Cresent, and the track had a level section including a sharp curve and two gradients, the second having an inclination of 1:12.

* * * * *

IN County Durham, on 27 September 1825, an event of epic proportions took place. This is an overworked phrase, but the opening of the Stockton & Darlington Railway is recognised as one of the quintessential milestones in the history of world transport.[353] For the very first time, a public railway with steam locomotive traction was operational. James, though he was not present, could not avoid reading the acres of newsprint devoted to the occasion. It was hailed as a great success. Tens of thousands of people witnessed Stephenson's *Locomotion* or *Travelling Engine No.1* hauling a train consisting of ten waggons loaded with coal and one with flour, a specially-built passenger carriage named *Experiment*, and twenty-one waggons fitted with temporary seats. Tickets had been issued to 300 guests, but joy-riders who clung to the sides of the waggons lifted the total of passengers to perhaps double that number. Despite this increased load (and one of the waggons derailing) the first 8½ miles were covered in just over one hour's running time. George Stephenson, at the controls of the locomotive, had reason to be pleased with himself and to feel that he had brought the whole project to a satisfactory conclusion. But it was not of national or strategic importance, nor did it really break any new ground – it was merely a logical extension of the traditional local colliery railway which included rope-hauled inclines and fixed steam engines. The only real innovations on *Locomotion* were the outside coupling rods between the driving wheels, made possible by progressive accuracy in machining tolerances, and the built-up wheels of Robert Wilson's plug design. It was still very much a first-generation machine. The whole enterprise could claim to be a 'first', but in evolutionary terms it was a dead-end.

There was one notable absentee from the celebrations: the man who had dreamt up the scheme, masterminded the funding, and entrusted George Stephenson with guiding the project. Edward Pease was at home on the day which should have been the crowning glory of his wise and patient stewardship, grieving over the body of his son Isaac who had died the night before.

* * * * *

ON 4 October 1825 Lord Redesdale chaired another Special General Meeting of the Moreton railway. The proceedings were brief. It seems that James had not asked Mr Dudley to deliver all the money he had promised to lend, hoping, one suspects, that he would not then press the case for Brewin to take over the accounts. The meeting demanded more urgent action and ordered that 'Mr James do apply to Mr Dudley for a further loan, and also to any other person whom he may think likely to advance money on Credit of the Works.'[354]

Not only was James now in danger of losing control of the finances at Moreton, but his connection with the Canterbury & Whitstable was also being wound up. In the middle of October he received a letter from the company's solicitors informing him that they were making a final settlement of his claim for expenses, offsetting it against the money he still owed for the first tranche of calls due on his ten shares, £7 on each. Would he please pay the balance of £4 12s 4d?[355] This coincided with George Stephenson's first and only visit to the Kent project, and we may suspect that it was he who insisted on the railway severing any lasting commitment it had with James. The minutes of a meeting on 21 October reported that 'Mr Stephenson, the Engineer, is now upon the line, stumping out the land and preparing for an immediate commencement of the works.' It was also decided that application should be made to Parliament for a new Bill allowing a different terminus near the

centre of Canterbury, and that a turf-cutting ceremony should be held before their distinguished guest headed back north, leaving the works under the control of John Dixon. On 31 October the directors and several interested locals assembled below the site of the proposed tunnel through Tyler's Hill. They had been promised that the line would be completed in eighteen months, with Whitstable Harbour in operation shortly afterwards, and loud cheers rang out as the chairman, John Brent, cut the first symbolic sod and dumped it into a wheelbarrow.[356] Dixon would start excavating the earthworks in December, but was somehow unaware that a vital bit of land outside Canterbury had not been secured. The disgruntled owner would make life very difficult indeed for the railway committee throughout the following year.

As the New Year unfolded, James's personal situation was looking increasingly bleak. He was, understandably, hurt and resentful that all his pioneering work in Lancashire, Kent and Staffordshire had been usurped by Stephenson. At least he was still notionally in some control at Moreton, but his dream was being so diluted by financial stringency and the narrow-mindedness of the Board of Trade inspectors that he was losing heart over this project as well. Dudley wanted more clout in return for his loan and, as far as James was concerned, was determined to extract his pound of flesh as well. Depressed and bankrupt, James wrote to his eldest son, William Henry, on 26 January 1826.[357]

> I have not heard from Canterbury, therefore I conclude Stephenson's intrigues still are predominant there . . . I expect I must give up this [the Moreton] concern finally on the 10th of February, as a general meeting is to be called on that day. Lord Redesdale will not attend, and I then expect my foes will outnumber my friends, as they state they will be there to vote me out of office, and are in high spirits at the prospect they have of getting the concern into their own hands.

Redesdale owned 62 shares – just under 10 per cent – a block which might have been crucial to the outcome. It is not known why he decided to abandon his friend at this moment; even if he could not attend in person, he could have left proxy votes in James's support. James continued his letter, 'I will not either pertinaciously hold, or insultingly abandon it, but will adhere to my friends as long as they think my services valuable.'

James maintained a correspondence with Edward Pease. He had read in the papers about the specially-built coach which had conveyed the most important guests at the opening of the Stockton & Darlington and was curious to know whether it was now in regular traffic. Was his vision of trains of passenger carriages, hauled by steam locomotives, being realised on this alien railway? Pease replied on 4 February 1826, four months after the opening, that they 'run a daily coach, carrying twenty to thirty passengers, drawn by one horse.' He was by now rather sceptical about employing steam traction at all, feeling that the directors had 'placed locomotive engines on the line for the haulage of coals (only), before it is either creditable to them, or of advantage to the company.'[358]

James was now aged 53. He had spent his fortune on pursuing and promoting his railway visions and from them he had had no reward whatsoever. He was largely responsible for the reputation on which George Stephenson was now riding so high, while his friend and protégé, young Robert Stephenson, was several thousand miles away in South America. He felt guilty about the way his family were having to suffer from his ill-fortune and his own mistakes. No wonder he wanted to wipe the slate clean. He confided to his son, in the letter just quoted,

It is quite indispensable that I shall take up some pursuit in which I can have some compensation for my labour, and I shall make land-agency and other objects my principal pursuit in future.

He did make one last effort to get back on the Canterbury & Whitstable. He travelled down there some time in early 1826 and certainly met up with John Dixon, who confided to him all the difficulties he was having with incomplete land purchases, overpriced local tradesmen, shortages of materials and lack of support from Newcastle. Worst of all, in the financial crisis that hit the whole country at the end of 1825, the company's bankers had failed, leaving Dixon with no money to pay the wages. James was sympathetic and offered, rather ambitiously one has to say, to solve Dixon's problems. We know about this because, soon after his visit, Dixon wrote to his 'esteemed friend' Timothy Hackworth and, apart from pouring out his woes in great detail, included the following words.[359]

Just at that very time, Mr James came forward with wholesale proposals to do all manner of work and quit the Company of all trouble, but they wished to give us a fair trial, and when we got a few waggons to

work and three or four hundred yards of way laid down, the change of sentiment was very great in our favour.

James had suffered yet another rebuff, and in April the final curtain was to be brought down on his involvement with the Moreton line. Lord Redesdale was back in the chair when the proprietors met in General Assembly at the Bell Inn, Halford, on the 12th. Most of the meeting was taken up with finance, confirming Mr Dudley's loans – now matched with equivalent amounts from Lord Redesdale – and how the money should be allocated to various contractors. The remaining earthworks were to be finished as quickly as possible, with a view to opening the line in time for the harvest. Some appointments to the General Committee and the Committee of Works were ordered, including Dudley. He had won his power struggle. Some salaries were confirmed: John Rastrick to be paid four guineas a day and his assistant, Mr Oakley, three guineas a week. Robert Stephenson Snr's position was to continue temporarily at £150 a year,[360] while Joseph Hanson was proposed as the new company clerk on a salary of £200 a year. The meeting ordered that James should hand over all the books of accounts and be paid the balance of £163 11s 10d due to him. Redesdale stayed true in the end, as the following minute recorded:

The Company in parting with Mr James have done so in compliance with the wishes of some of the proprietors and not from any disapprobation of his conduct, and it is ordered that the sum of £200 be paid to him instead [of the above-mentioned sum] and for that purpose Lord Redesdale has agreed to advance a further £200.

As things turned out though, this was not quite the end of the story. Another meeting was convened for 20 July. Redesdale had asked James to prepare yet another report on 'the circumstances of the subscriptions, shares and defaulters' which was duly read to the proprietors. He had also had to tidy up some problems with tenants on the company's property. These had kept James in office until 15 May and he had put in a claim for £52 16s 0d for himself and his assistant, which was approved.[361]

* * * * *

APRIL 1826 also witnessed the passing of the revised Liverpool & Manchester Railway Bill. The directors had appointed Charles Vignoles, a skilled operator with a military training, to prepare a new survey under the joint management of George and John Rennie. At one stage, Sandars had thought of trying to prise Rastrick away from Moreton-in-Marsh and had even gone down to interview him.[362] Heeding the lessons of the previous year, they had planned their approach to Parliament much more thoroughly. And in this, the key player behind the scenes was a man whose name would be linked forever with that of this great railway.

William Huskisson had been elected to the House of Commons as a Tory in 1806, having previously been a conscientious but unremarkable civil servant in the Departments of War and the Colonies. While neither a charismatic orator nor an impressive figure, he was thought to be sound on the key issues and initially supported the 1815 Corn Laws. Gradually, though, as he rose to ranks of greater significance, his philosophy changed to a more liberal one, absorbing and adopting the ideas of economists like David Ricardo. He became a staunch advocate of Free Trade, linked with the concept of a stable currency backed by gold, and found a ready ally in the young, ambitious Liverpool MP, George Canning. Together they became crusaders of Catholic emancipation and political reform in the party and, under a benign premiership, Huskisson was appointed to high office as President of the Board of Trade. Nowhere in the country were the opportunities, but also problems, of rapidly expanding trade felt more acutely than in Liverpool, and in 1823 he was persuaded, on the retirement of John Gladstone (father of the future prime minister), to exchange his seat at Chichester for the second of those representing the northern port. Soon he found himself being lobbied both by the local canal interests and by supporters of the new railway proposals. It was a tricky political balancing act, in which he succeeded by putting his weight behind any schemes that promised to improve local transport links. Because of his Liverpool connection, he could not sit on the committees reviewing the second railway Bill, but he could and did use his influence with the Tory chief whip, William Holmes. Holmes was persuaded, and told Huskisson 'your Liverpool friends need not be alarmed, for I pledge myself that they shall have 18 to 25 peers in the Committee, and I really do not believe that there will be found 5 peers to vote against them.'[363] And so it was. The company directors could celebrate that at last they were able to proceed. One of their first moves, to the acute annoyance of Charles Vignoles and the Rennie brothers, was to recall George Stephenson to the post of chief engineer.

WHILE one of William James's initiatives could now start to crystallise, another was almost ready for public traffic. The Stratford & Moreton Railway was opened on Tuesday, 5 September 1826, in conjunction with a Great Market at Moreton-in-Marsh.[364] It was a thoroughly jolly affair. People flocked into town from the surrounding countryside in such numbers that the Oxford Journal reported that 'the innkeepers had more mouths to feed than bread and meat to fill them with. In saying that a fat ox was roasted entire . . . it need hardly be added that its bones were picked clean.' To the accompaniment of the statutory brass band, the members of the railway committee arrived down the line in a horse-drawn waggon, followed by several other trucks bearing coal and coke, wood and grindstones, and 'other articles of merchandise required in the neighbourhood'. Someone had composed a celebratory song, the second verse of which applauded one of the main benefits that James had foreseen when he first approached Lord Redesdale six years earlier.

> To see our iron railway,
> It makes one's heart content
> To know what's saved in firing
> Will nearly pay our rent.

Reporting the opening in its issue of 9 September, the Warwick Advertiser claimed, 'The ease and expedition with which passengers can be conveyed upon this rail-road has induced some spirited individuals to propose a daily coach.'[365]

James's pride in sharing the festivities was tempered with acute disappointment that the final manifestation of 'his' railway was a poor shadow of what he had originally planned (plate 7b). Admittedly the rails were robust and modern, but there were no Land-Agent locomotives to thrill the crowd. Rails apart, it looked all too similar to the primitive Surrey Iron Railway which was about to celebrate its twenty-fifth plodding anniversary. Was this progress? Instead of being the first leg of his high-speed inter-city link between London and the Midlands, he saw a bucolic affair which certainly did not fill the column inches in the national press.

Perhaps he was even relieved that he would no longer be involved in the boardroom politics of a railway company, nor have to spend his time cajoling reluctant shareholders into paying their dues, nor try to extract loans from fractious lenders. In these sentiments he was not alone. Edward Pease had masterminded the Stockton & Darlington to its triumphant opening, but only after he had had to finance much of the completion phase with his own money. In 1827 he 'retired with a resolution never to enter a railway meeting again!'[366] James himself had to contemplate his own penurious retirement, but first he had to tidy up a small matter in Kent. The secretary of the Canterbury & Whitstable Railway had written to a banker in Liverpool in January 1827 seeking a loan of £10,000 to expedite the completion of the line, which was suffering from a massive cost overrun as a result of problems with the tunnel.[367] The writer pointed out that there were still 36 shares unsold, but they were holding their par value and he believed they would be taken up shortly. There was only one known seller, 'Mr James of Moreton-in-Marsh, our former Engineer,' who was anxious to sell some of his holding to pay the outstanding calls on the remainder.

It was probably during this period of enforced retirement that James seriously considered emigrating with his whole family to Canada, and Ellen Paine would later quote from a 'Memorial' in her father's handwriting, composed for submission to Parliament, pleading for some recompense for his public services.[368] It covered several pages. It made reference to his service with the Warwick Volunteer Cavalry: 'I had the promise of an appointment from the late Lord Melville in 1800, in consequence of having in those disturbed times . . . spent a large sum of money in raising two corps of volunteers.' It listed the achievements of his prosperous years – the coal-mines, the Stratford Canal, the Upper Avon Navigation etc – and how he had given a livelihood to several hundred employees. He calculated all the man-years that he had spent on devising and promoting railway schemes for the public good. Indirectly, he implied that his financial collapse was really to be blamed on government policy, on the Bank Restriction Act and the way that the Treasury had handled, or mishandled, the restoration of convertibility in 1819. His great capital investments had 'sustained a depreciation of at least £70,000 in value by the diminution of the circulation of the currency.' All his projects had been undertaken as much to benefit the public as himself and his own reputation. 'I have done some service to my fellow subjects.' The Memorial was to end as follows:

> Therefore, whilst my facilities remain unimpaired, and my body is capable of labour, I have resolved to emigrate with my family to some of His Majesty's colonies, where the talents and labours of myself and [my] five sons may procure a subsistence, and my family may be spared the misery of insult and persecution.

Perhaps he could not find a sponsor; perhaps his confidence had been too much undermined to allow him to carry it through; perhaps he felt his guarded jibe at the government's financial policy was too near the knuckle; perhaps he was just utterly exhausted. He dropped it into his desk and closed the drawer.

SEVENTEEN

Cornwall – Act 2, a Death and a New Life (1827–1829)

'The late and present distress is regarded as one of those periodic visitations inseparable from the progress of manufactures, which has been indeed aggravated by over-trading, by wild speculation in shares, and by indiscreet and unreasonable legislation, but which could not be altogether evaded.'

Royal Cornwall Gazette, 12 August 1826

BY EARLY 1827 the economy was recovering and James's health and self-confidence were also restored. Now he really was determined to relocate his family to a new home, not overseas, nor to the continent as so many fellow-bankrupts had done before him, but to the remote county of Cornwall. He set about his unfinished business there.

Anna-Maria Agar was the owner, not only of the great estate of Lanhydrock, but also of extensive property in Truro and the rest of the county (*plate 14a*). Her 'outer estates' comprised 24 manors across 82 parishes from the far south-west to Tintagel in the north, making her the seventh largest landowner in the county.[369] Unfortunately for her, this inheritance had not been accompanied by any of her great-uncle's fortune. An absentee landlord, she had been content to leave the administration of her estates to her stewards, the Jenkin family, provided that the modest rental income covered the maintenance costs. She was a formidable and well-informed lady, not averse to standing up to her neighbours; 'I am well aware,' she said, 'these people think a woman may be easily imposed upon – it consequently becomes necessary for me to be both steady and severe.' Her instincts were very risk-averse, but two events in 1825 had allowed her to adopt a more extrovert view of her circumstances.

The first was the imminent completion of the Redruth & Chasewater Railway through Devoran, and the second was the death of her mother. Anna-Maria was left £55,742, and with this new financial freedom she realised that she needed new independent advice. She asked Baugh Allen, her senior trustee, to give William James a new contract. Over the next three years he would blow somewhat hot and cold in his opinion of James's approach to his role, and would spend much time pouring balm over disgruntled sensitivities as James pursued his mission. Alfred Jenkin had taken over the stewardship from his father in 1820. His family were Quakers, steeped in Cornish traditions and entrenched in their roles as guardians by proxy of Anna-Maria's estates and mines, and he did not appreciate the introduction of a new broom, particularly as he had a hidden agenda and was running another business on the side.

James returned to Cornwall in 1827 to take on what he saw as the starring role in reorganising Anna-Maria's estates, in making them far more productive, and in instigating a revolution in the county's transport system. And if he could get good prices for the Glynn properties, still unsold, his reputation might be fully restored. He began to draw up plans for the development of Devoran as a major new port, trading centre and residential area. There was talk of a new turnpike road to Truro, only three miles away, and James could see exciting scope for enhancing the value of Anna-Maria's properties at both locations. First, however, he had to tackle exactly the same problems that had beset his ambitions for the Earl of Warwick. There were no maps, title deeds were vague, and the terms of existing tenancies were uncertain. His requests to Jenkin for information about these matters were largely ignored.

James submitted his outline plan to Baugh Allen in March 1827. His prime objective was to secure Anna-Maria's claims to the waterfront land at Devoran, followed by negotiations with T. Daniell (a wealthy merchant with interests in mines and copper smelting) about his road developments, with the aim of changing the routes to pass closer to Anna-Maria's property. As well as plotting a new railway from Truro to St Agnes Bay on the north coast, he suggested that Anna-Maria ought to buy those parts of the Glynn estate which bordered Lanhydrock. In his assessment to Anna-Maria, Baugh Allen was basically supportive and advised that James should be given quite a wide brief; but with reservations. 'James speaks highly of the improvements likely to take place in the neighbourhood of Truro . . . I hope he may be a true prophet . . . I have a very good impression of his knowledge and, when he uses it, his judgement, but he so often speaks without consulting his brains that I have always a considerable mistrust of what he says.' He is more cautious about the Glynn purchases, detecting that on this matter James could hardly be impartial: 'I think I should prefer Mr Jenkin's opinion.'

Throughout the summer of 1827 James made good progress on the road issue and the prospects for enhancing the value of Anna-Maria's property in Truro, if only he could confirm what it actually consisted of. He also became convinced that money should be spent on improving Truro harbour. The Devoran leases were even more of a problem; the boundaries of each tenement were ill-defined, especially along the crucial bank of the creek, and there had been incursions from one to the other. The Agar plots were not contiguous and James had to play a subtle game of Monopoly to buy out the leases of all those along the waterfront in order to realise his plan for a trading estate and a floating dock. He had to deal with the powerful Fox family, the Lemons and Lord de Dunstanville, the sitting tenants Hugo and Plummer, and the mining firm of Magor & Co. None must be aware of his dealings with the other. The knot would take him another three years to untangle.

He was also alarmed by what he saw as 'squatter's rights' being established by Alfred Jenkin for his shipping activities, which he was progressively transferring from Penryn to Devoran. James was having to play a cat-and-mouse game and, as far as he was concerned, Jenkin was running with the mice. This distrust was not lost on Allen, who gave Anna-Maria a favourable review of James's first report but added that he feared that James and Jenkin were 'by nature formed to dislike each other'.

It is a matter of very considerable delicacy to say whether or no a man in whom you have confided for so many years has acted fairly by you or not; Mr James certainly suspects him . . . if Mr Jenkin has been a dealer in copper on his own account, he may have an interest in opposition to yours.

On 13 December 1827 James put the Glynn properties up for auction again – with high reserves – and two of the very few lots that did sell were indeed bought by Anna-Maria, who acquired the properties at Hill and Tawna for £2,200. There was still much more to do. Crucially, he had made a favourable impression on Allen, who conceded in his last report of the year to Anna-Maria that James was a good negotiator, despite having to overcome many prejudices and a traditional disregard for the law – smuggling and wrecking were well-established Cornish pastimes.

There is everything in your county combining to ruin the moral character of men of the law . . . I feel it may be necessary for you to make a choice of evils at some future time . . . your property is too inviting to your neighbours for them not to attempt at plunder, especially if it should be weakly guarded.

But it would be wrong to assume that James was now concentrating only on Cornwall. While awaiting a renewal of his contract from Anna-Maria, he reactivated his association with the Warwick family and his long-standing interest in the Earl's coal-bearing land at Clutton in Somerset, but now with an even more fantastic and visionary twist. Clutton needed a direct link with Bristol while Cornwall needed better inland communications out of the county, so why not kill two birds with one stone? Why not promote a railway from Bristol to Truro – via Clutton? Subsidised by the new Earl, he had spent some time doing an ocular survey of the route, which would pass on its most direct line through the estates of Lord Waldegrave at Chewton in Mendip. On 11 March 1828 James wrote to the Earl from Bristol, where he was spending Easter as a guest of the Bishop.[370]

I thank your Lordship for the £30. Your Lordship will in no shape be responsible beyond the £20 to make up the £140 at which I estimated the out of pocket expenses for this section and prospectus. Although these expenses will greatly exceed that sum because of the peculiar difficulties of the line, I look for the discharge thereof, and for the compensation for my trouble, to the measure being taken up by subscribers as a beneficial public measure. As I shall remain with the Bishop and some other kind friends for some time at Easter, I shall be able to introduce the measure to the notice of many principal persons in these parts. The coalminers at Clutton are proceeding very slowly with their level-driving, so that the Railroad to the canal is not very urgent as they have no coals yet to supply the trade with.

I have sold some considerable estates in Cornwall at what are considered to be high prices and I hope next week to sell others. I have about 8,000 acres to sell in lots, with two Advowsons and five large and valuable Manors, which I hope to sell in the course of this year. This, and other business will so occupy my time (for about 1½ years) that I have an idea of removing my residence, clerks and Establishment to this place, or Bath, at my return, which will enable me to promote the Railroad by personal agency. I have many good friends, who solicit my assistance in Somerset, Devon and Cornwall, but I hope still to reside in my native county as soon as I can realise a small Competency and pay all just demands. Till then, I cannot do otherwise than labour without ceasing.

One of James's past labours was about to bear fruit, though without his presence. The Bolton & Leigh Railway, while not finished, had reached the mines of the chairman, William Hulton, and the official opening took place on 1 August 1828. The elaborate instructions for the ceremony have fortunately survived and include the following items:[371]

The Directors, proprietors and other gentlemen to whom tickets for the waggons have been given, to assemble at the extremity of the completed line at Fletcher's Fold soon after 11 o'clock ... At 12 o'clock, the locomotive engine to proceed from Fletcher's with the coals and twelve waggons, two of which will contain the band ... On their arrival, the naming of the locomotive will take place.

This ceremony was performed by Mrs Hulton. She stepped on to the engine, a garland of flowers

was attached to the chimney and she addressed the crowd. 'No one can observe, without admiration, this beautiful engine. I therefore beg leave to name it after an object universally attractive – "The Lancashire Witch".'[372]

The church bells rang out, the band played and the directors, proprietors and their ladies adjourned for a cold collation at the Commercial Inn; a dull affair compared to the rumbustious festival at Moreton-in-Marsh two years earlier. Here at last was James's prototype 'modern' railway on which the new generation of loco-motives could be tested, and the *Lancashire Witch* was indeed a revolutionary design.

Originally ordered – prematurely – for the Liverpool & Manchester, it incorporated many of the new features which young Robert Stephenson had devised since his return from South America the previous year. For one thing, it had direct drive from inclined cylinders, which allowed all four wheels to be sprung. The valve gear allowed the steam to be cut off at half-stroke, a key feature for economical use of steam. And the fuel was coke, necessitated by a clause in the Act which required the locomotive to produce no smoke, against a fine of £50. But the crux lay in its ability to generate steam, not from a single flue within the boiler, but from a pair of parallel tubes (originally planned as three), each with its own grate and stoke hole. Here is the precursor of the multiple fire-tube boiler, the concept which, thirteen months later, would do more than anything else to win the Stephensons a £500 prize and worldwide renown. The scene would be an undistinguished corner of Lancashire, seventeen miles to the west of Leigh, but its name would soon be a household word – Rainhill.

In October 1828 James was given his new contract, based on his plans 'for raising a great Possession and Large Income' for Anna-Maria. He concluded his letter of thanks:

I beg you will have the goodness to notify Messrs. Jenkin and Henwood, directing them to cooperate with me, to promote the objects we all ought to have at Heart, the interest of yourself and Mr Robartes in improving this noble estate.

He was to be paid £200 for the next twelve months, but his role fell short of the overall land agency, Jenkin and Henwood being merely asked to accept his advice 'on those points where his skills are much beyond theirs.' Underlying frustrations remained. Jenkin complains to Anna-Maria that he cannot understand why the management of Devoran has been given to James 'whose conduct has all along been marked with great conceal-ment towards me.' In his turn, James complains to her about the slow pace at which Cornish people work.

> In Cornwall there is no value attached to Time, which is mainly attributable in rural affairs to the Lifehold Tenures, in public matters to the influence of Borough Politics, and the clergy, to whom six days in the week are disengaged.

But he finally managed to buy out most of the crucial leases at Devoran for £4,400 and Baugh Allen came down for the concluding assignments. James took him (and the young Thomas Agar-Robartes) on a tour of all the other areas where he wanted Anna-Maria to make further invest-ments; they inspected progress with the Liskeard Canal, where James suspected nefarious practice over the supply of water to one of the Agar mills; they looked at the new roads being built around Truro; and James outlined his ambitious plans for rebuilding Truro harbour. He also tried to solicit backing for his railway from Truro to Bristol. Allen was impressed and reported back to Anna-Maria that the value of her lands had already benefited considerably from James's efforts; he believed that Devoran alone would be worth £22,000 in seven years. But she, increas-ingly nervous of any further commitments, put all future schemes (outside Devoran) on hold and withdrew herself to Leamington Spa for a rest.

Meanwhile, James himself had made a major personal commitment to his own future by renting a dilapidated farmhouse near Bodmin called Plasnewydd, about a mile south of the town centre on the Lostwithiel road and just north of the boundary with Lanhydrock *(plate 14b)*. 80 acres of land went with the farm and he initially took one of his sons with him.[373] There was much work to be done to make the property habitable before he could ask his wife Dinah to join him. His daughter implied that he set up this new home to get away as far as possible from 'the machinations of his enemies, being also disgusted and annoyed with his false friends.'[374] Certainly, in terms of distance, he could hardly have gone farther within the borders of England, but of course the main reason was remunerative employment – and respect. Another reason, perhaps more tenuous, takes us back to Richard Trevithick,, or rather his great supporter Davies Gilbert (Giddy), whom we first encountered in Chapter 5 and who had for many years been MP for Bodmin.

Richard Trevithick had arrived back in Cornwall from Latin America in October 1827, all his ventures in the silver mines of Peru and the gold mines of Costa Rica having ended in disaster. He was penniless. It was only as the result of a fortuitous meeting with young Robert Stephen-son, also on his way back to England after his three years in Colombia, that he had been able to take passage across the Atlantic at all. Robert had given him money for the fare. (Just before leaving New York, Robert Stephenson was received into the brotherhood of the Freemasons, as recorded in the annals of St Andrews Lodge No 7.[375] Perhaps he had a letter of introduction from William James or perhaps, anticipating being reunited with his mentor, he had thought that this action would please him, though Robert did not retain a masonic connection back in England.)

Trevithick now tried to claim money from his erstwhile partner in his boiler patents, John Williams, who reluctantly gave him £150, but only on condition that he gave up any rights to further royalties up to the time the patents expired in 1830. Direct approaches to the Cornish mine venturers, who had prospered on the back of the cost savings they had derived from Trevi-thick's inventions, were equally unproductive. But Davies Gilbert, recognising the injustice of the situation and in a position to do something practical about it, drew up a petition to be presented to Parliament. A number of inventors, who had done a public service without fair return for their efforts, had been rewarded in this way. Samuel Crompton had been awarded £5,000 in recognition of his unpatented invention of the spinning mule. The inventor of the power loom, the Revd Edmund Cartwright, had received no less than £10,000. Gilbert had himself been instrumental in getting government support for Humphry Davy to develop his safety lamp and for Charles Babbage to continue work on his analytical engine, that mass of caged cog-wheels which became the very first mechanical computer.[376] With the written backing of several Cornish mine-owners, Gilbert presented his new petition in February 1828, the main basis of the claim being that the use of Trevithick's 'strong steam' boilers had led to savings in the use of coal amounting to £500,000 in Cornwall alone. Perhaps Parliament found this sum unbelievable, perhaps it was incredulous at the other inventions cited – the iron flotation tanks and buoys, the steam carriages and locomotives – but for whatever reasons the petition was rejected.[377]

It may be that James's decision to base himself at Bodmin was influenced by hearing about

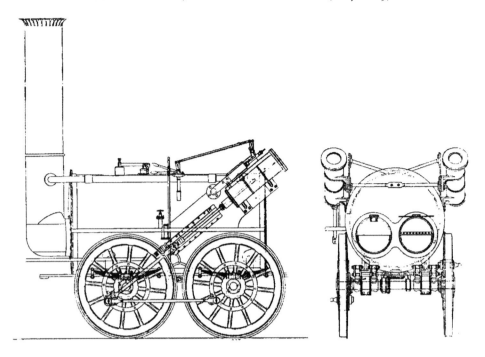

Fig.12:
Robert Stephenson's 'Lancashire Witch' 1828.

Gilbert's intended petition. Perhaps he waited to see the outcome before approaching Gilbert with his own 'Memorial'; and, when it failed, he probably put aside any thoughts of pursuing this particular road to recognition and remuneration.[378] At least for the time being.

He had yet another reason for starting a new life far from the Midlands. This was a feeling of guilt that he had not had the foresight to ring-fence some of his assets and keep them out of the clutches of his creditors. His own father had made over a major part of his own property portfolio to William during his lifetime so that, although he died a pauper, his estate was to some extent protected. James had indeed given property worth many thousand pounds to his eldest son William Henry, but the proper legal assignments had never been completed and they became forfeited to the Commissioners of Bankruptcy.[379] This omission, inexcusable in a lawyer, must have weighed heavily on James's conscience.

Surely it was his intention to move his wife down to live with him at Plasnewydd, which was now 'improved and fitted up with taste'.[380] But she had never been of a strong constitution, and during her husband's imprisonment and bankruptcy her health had evidently deteriorated. When they forfeited all their houses in Warwick and Staffordshire, she moved in to live with their son George Walter, along with some or all of their younger children including the two daughters, the sickly Marianna then aged twenty and the spirited, resentful seventeen-year-old Ellen who wrote later that her mother bore their changed financial circumstances with Christian forbearance and stoicism, and that the family managed to retain something of their standing in the neighbourhood.[381] Dinah never made the journey to join her husband in Cornwall. Subsequent events suggest that she settled at Lapworth, just north of Henley-in-Arden, either returning to her roots with Tarleton relations or given refuge by John Kershaw and his family who had moved there. It was at Lapworth that the youngest son, Alfred Percy, was buried on 16 August 1828, aged eighteen.

To console himself, James took the opportunity of Anna-Maria's absence at Leamington to take himself on a working holiday in the Isle of Wight. Here, in November, he suffered an accident while looking for fossils, falling eighteen feet down a cliff and breaking his leg, an injury which would dog him for years. He had to spend several weeks convalescing at Gatcombe, the family home of Edmund Glynn's deceased wife, although this did not prevent him from carrying on an extensive correspondence about Cornish affairs. His opinion of his fellow-professionals not having altered, he was particularly pleased to outwit the machinations of Lord de Dunstanville's agent – 'there are few minds so just as to admit error, fewer among agents.'

He was back in Cornwall by January 1829 and stayed there until April, suffering bouts of fever as a result of his accident but fearful of predatorial moves by the neighbouring landowners if he was not on site. He was right to be watchful, but despite his vigilance Anna-Maria had been persuaded – probably by Jenkin – to grant a mining lease within Devoran to a syndicate involving the Williamses, the Foxes and the man James described as 'that little Lord' de Dunstanville. This, as well as undermining James's authority, threatened his whole strategy and, quite literally, undermined the new road he was building into the community. Nor was this his only problem. He was still owed his £500 commission on the partial Glynn sale and was forced to beg for an advance of £50 from Anna-Maria. Furthermore, a Mr Solomon had tried to get title to part of the Glynn estate by fraud.

James had returned to London by May, convinced that he could there do 'more in a fortnight than a year in Cornwall'. Unable to afford a residence of his own, he stayed with his sister and brother-in-law, Anne and Paul Padley, who lived at Thavies Inn, a few hundred yards from his old office at New Boswell Court.[382] With Baugh Allen's help, the mining leases at Devoran had been revoked, precipitating an abrupt and hardly civil response from Jenkin. But at least he now provided James with some of the long-awaited information about the Agar-Robartes properties in Truro. James worked with the family solicitor, a Mr Kent, on trying to get £400 compensation for Anna-Maria from the Truro turnpike trust for their unauthorised enclosure of part of her land, but his main project at that time was to draw up a prospectus for the 'Devoran New Town and Floating Dock' venture *(Fig 16a)*.

The introduction to this ambitious development scheme stated that the completion of the Redruth & Chasewater Railway had stimulated a large increase in trade and commerce generally, quantified at 55,000 tons per annum, with a modest estimate that this would rise to at least 60,000 tons. New connecting roads to the Truro turnpike were being built. The proposed floating dock would allow vessels as large as 200–300 tons to transfer cargoes against new wharfs without any lighterage and at all tides; sites on an adjacent estate of five acres could be rented on 50-year tenancies, with special introductory terms for the first five years. A combination of gentle south-facing slopes, picturesque scenery, pure and abundant springs and excellent building stone offered scope for the construction of 'a respectable, opulent Neighbourhood . . . Few situations present such advantages for the retirement of the Wealthy or for the spirited Enterprise of Trading and Commercial Men.' James was envisaging a high-quality, 'high net worth' development; no wonder he was picky about tenants, refusing to let one plot to 'a slovenly Cornish farmer'. (By October, he was forced to admit that he still had not found a satisfactory tenant, and even envisaged taking it himself.) This was not to be a location for foundries or refineries. The special terms of the prospectus stated that 'no noxious trades or manufactories will be permitted upon the Estate.' He saw it as a Salcombe, not a Swansea.

Official publication of the prospectus had to wait at least another eighteen months. James complained to Anna-Maria that he was 'hindered and opposed in all quarters and I have not had fair play since I came to Cornwall'. Baugh Allen was forced to concur. 'I am inclined to suspect that they [Jenkin and Henwood] are too mixed up with county matters of their own to serve you with advantage.' But these were local difficulties when viewed in a national context, while in Lancashire a revolution was about to take place; not a social upheaval, but an engineering trial which would become a landmark in transport history.

EIGHTEEN

Revolution at Rainhill
and a Damp Day in Liverpool
(1829–1830)

By EARLY 1829, with the railway half completed, the Liverpool & Manchester directors still had to decide on the motive power – should it be locomotives or fixed engines with ropes, or a combination of the two? In the preceding years several collieries had given up their locomotives and reverted to horses. In 1828 George Stephenson's *Locomotion*, which had so proudly led the opening parade at Darlington, had exploded, killing its driver. Nicholas Wood, one of the few people to have published on the subject, claimed that locomotive haulage at speeds of more than ten miles per hour was neither practical nor desirable on health grounds.[383]

Robert Stephenson, however, had no doubts about the capabilities of the locomotives he had developed since his return from South America in November 1827, although his father was more cautious, still favouring a proportion of fixed engine haulage. The directors were in a quandary. Some of them were actively turning against their chief engineer anyway, seeing his management style as increasingly arrogant and autocratic. To award the haulage contract to his family firm might open themselves to a charge of nepotism at best, perhaps even of negligence. They therefore decided on a competition between rival locomotive designs to assess their capabilities of speed, sustained hauling power and economy, under realistic conditions and within restricted limits of weight and boiler pressure. So much has been written about this competition on the Rainhill level in October 1829 that it is unnecessary to repeat the details. At the end of ten days, the prize of £500 was awarded, somewhat by default, to Robert Stephenson's *Rocket*. One contender never reached the starting line and the other two (*Sans Pareil* and *Novelty*) failed to complete the assigned programme.

The Rainhill Trials caught the imagination of the public in a way that would not be equalled until the Great Exhibition of 1851 or the building, and attempted launching, of Brunel's *Great Eastern* steamship in 1858. Of the contenders, the popular favourite was undoubtedly Braithwaite and Ericsson's dashing and colourful *Novelty*, and the correspondence columns of the *Mechanics' Magazine* soon filled with letters implying that the judges had been unfair to eliminate it on a 'technicality', with darker hints that they were biased in favour of the Stephenson family from the outset. When it became known that one of the reasons for the failure of Timothy Hackworth's *Sans Pareil* was a poor cylinder casting supplied from the Stephenson foundry, suspicions ran higher still. The directors had offered to buy the two losing contenders, probably with genuinely altruistic motives of offering some sort of consolation prize, but the Braithwaite and Ericsson camp took this as yet another deception, a ruse to allow the Stephensons to dismantle their rival and understand its secrets. They withdrew their machine in a huff. Very soon, however, the *Liverpool Times* could tell its readers that 'a considerable alteration has been made in Mr Robert Stephenson's "Rocket", which has considerably increased its powers . . . drawing the enormous weight of 20 tons at the rate of from 18 to 20 miles per hour.' The judges appeared to be vindicated after all.

Now the correspondents could concentrate on the social and industrial implications of high-speed long-distance rail travel becoming a reality, not in the far distant future but in the next year or so. William James's prophesies were about to take shape, his 'fantastic delusions' were soon to be facts, and people could work out for themselves the economic benefits that he had been promoting to previously deaf ears. A leading article in the *Scotsman* spelt it out for its readers.

> The experiments at Liverpool have established principles which will give a greater impulse to civilization than it has ever received from any single cause since the [printing] press . . . The introduction of steam-carriages places us on the verge of a new era . . . when railways are made along all our great thoroughfares.

A Leeds or Manchester manufacturer may take an early breakfast in his own house, dine in London at five, transact business that night or the next morning and reach his home on the following evening, while a two-pound note will cover his whole expenses. Compared to the mail coach, savings in time will be in the ratio of 2½ to 1, the expense 4 to 1 and the comfort and convenience as 6 to 1 in favour of the steam conveyance.

Others were doing more intricate sums. In October 1829, John Herapath, the founder of the first *Railway Magazine*, wrote a letter to the prime minister, the Duke of Wellington, speculating on the benefits that would arise from the rapid substitution of all the horses used in the coaching trade. Quoting Adam Smith's figure that 'one horse consumes for food as much land as would maintain eight persons,' he suggested that if all the pasture-land used to make hay was 'thrown on the spade or the plough', it would not only provide employment for the poor, but also ensure national self-sufficiency in arable crops. Furthermore, as there were over a million horses 'engaged in staging and mailing', he contended that 'our country might be able to support, with only the land at present in occupation, double or treble, or perhaps quadruple, its present inhabitants!' Cheaper transport costs would mean lower prices, leading to an automatic increase in consumption. 'Thus will all orders of the state be doubly and trebly benefited – the merchant and the manufacturer by an augmentation of trade; the poor by an increase of employment; the Government by an additional revenue and the whole public by a diminished taxation.' James could hardly have put it better himself; his concept of 'advanced locomotion' had been tested and proved, and the Rainhill trials had apparently launched the country on a virtuous spiral of national prosperity.

To James, the outcome of the trials had been a foregone conclusion. His judgment had been completely vindicated. Eight years previously he had concluded that a practical 'travelling engine' would emerge from the combined talents of the Stephenson family, Robert's engineering flair and imagination capitalising on his father's stolid foundations. Alone among his contemporaries, James had also had the conviction that locomotives would very soon have the power to haul trains up reasonable gradients and – this was the most audacious of his visions – at express speeds.

The *Rocket's* supremacy lay in a number of features. Judicious use of the blast pipe was one, a feature which Robert tuned to maximum efficiency, although his father, always suspicious of the concept, had even removed it from most of his Killingworth machines because in his hands it was wasteful and threw the fire. The cylinders were inclined at an angle of 35 degrees, allowing the driving wheels to be sprung – as with the *Lancashire Witch* built the year before. Another winning feature, as on the *Witch,* was the direct drive from pistons to simple cranks on the driving wheels, guided by machined slide bars.

But the *Rocket's* supreme achievement lay in its boiler design, its separate firebox and its multiple fire-tubes, and James could reflect on those lively discussions that had taken place in the summer of 1821. While he and George Stephenson had drawn up the terms of their commercial partnership, their sons had debated ways of increasing the transfer of heat between the fire and the water in a boiler. As correspondence shows, the two young men certainly became very close friends at that period. As they relaxed over jugs of ale after a gruelling day with the chains and levelling instruments, the local inns became hothouses of thermodynamic debate. Narrow tubes, with their large surface areas, lay at the heart of the solution, though William Henry James argued that to his mind there were overwhelming advantages in circulating the water and the steam inside the tubes (with the heat from the fire on the outside) rather than the other way round. In his concept, steam pressures of 200 psi – and more – could be safely contained.[384] Furthermore, the steam would be automatically given 'enhanced elasticity' by being superheated, a concept that was not introduced into locomotive practice until the start of the 20th century, when it became the single greatest improvement ever introduced to the basic Stephensonian concept. With steam pressure at these levels, four times that allowed in the Rainhill regulations, how much smaller and lighter could the boiler be made, while delivering the same power output? Small compact steam generators could be installed into self-propelled road carriages, and here there was surely an enormous market, not dependent on building a separate iron railway first. As Rolt pointed out, the work of the steam road-carriage designers in London deserved to be taken into account by the railway locomotive builders of the north. 'Robert Stephenson had the good sense to realize this, with the result that the steam carriage had an important influence on locomotive development, which is too little recognized.'[385]

William Henry James remained committed to the water-tube concept and between 1825 and 1838 filed several of his own patents on this theme (see Appendix A). The lure of 'safe' high pressure steam was for him an overriding goal, a Holy Grail, but,

Fig.13
William Henry James's steam road carriage 1829, incorporating his patented water-tube boiler.
(*Mechanics Magazine* No.327, November 14, 1829)

like so many of his father's projects, his concepts were far-sighted but impractical.[386] It is probably unrealistic to suggest that the Jameses had any real influence, apart from stimulating discussion, on Robert Stephenson's engineering breakthrough.

By November 1829, the correspondence columns of the *Mechanics' Magazine* were still running a slanging match over the failure of the *Novelty*'s boiler, its defenders playing down any danger to the public while the detractors suggested that it was only a matter of luck that there had not been a catastrophic explosion. One in the latter camp was Luke Hebert, editor of the rival *Register of Arts*, who submitted a drawing and notes about a steam vehicle with, he believed, a much safer and more satisfactory boiler arrangement. This was the 'patent steam-carriage of Sir James Anderson Bart and W. H. James Esq'.[387]

The drawing was not a theoretical illustration to support a patent application, but based on a vehicle which had recently been built and subjected to preliminary trials. The weight, including fuel for 50 miles and water for 20 miles, was stated to be no more than 26 cwt. The same article quoted the observations of William Culbard, who had ridden on it 'about six o'clock in the evening, when the machine proceeded from Vauxhall Bridge to the Swan at Clapham, a distance of two and a half miles, in about ten minutes, at the extraordinary rate of fifteen miles an hour'. In a footnote, the editor of *Mechanics' Magazine* explained for his 'unscientific' readers that the 'friction or resistance to the motion of a carriage on a common road is seven times more than on a good iron railway'. He concluded that had this vehicle been at the Rainhill trials, 'it would have gone three or four times faster than the fastest of the vehicles tried' – a very interesting speculation.[388]

What else do we know about this promising machine? According to Hebert, there were four cylinders in two blocks, each measuring 1ft by 2ft and placed between and behind the rear wheels, and each pair of cylinders turned a single driving wheel by means of cranks on the stub-axle. The power delivered to each driving wheel could be varied by regulating the steam to each pair of cylinders. On a road carriage, this was an important factor in negotiating sharp curves and William Henry James suggested in his patent no. 4957 of 1824 that it could be automatically achieved by rods linked to the steering mechanism – turn the front wheels to the left and more power was delivered to the right-hand driving wheel and vice-versa.

At the heart of the machine was James's patented water-tube boiler (no. 5186 of 1825). This had a cylindrical outer casing into which was fitted 'a series of hollow rings or annular tubes – made we understand of the best iron, and three-fourths of an inch in diameter – each communicating with the other and arranged spiral-wise, so as to form a cylinder of rings. Within this, a furnace is inserted upon suitable bearings, and capable of sliding in and out.' There was no provision for a blast pipe, but one of his complementary patents alludes to a 'blowing machine' based on mechanically-driven bellows, which may have been incorporated. The water-level was designed to be kept just above half-way up the annular rings. Steam pressure was regulated at 200 psi, but the tubes had been tested to 4,000 psi. As the editor of the *Mechanics' Magazine* explained, 'the great hindrance to the use of water-tubular boilers has hitherto been that the water deposits earthy matter, which adheres to and encrusts the interior of the tubes, speedily choking them up'. The familiar problem of scaling or furring from hard water was accelerated, as in a domestic kettle, by the high rate of continuous boiling. For this, James had a solution: to place in the bottom of each ring 'a few shots, marbles or other loose objects in order to clean the interior of the boiler by friction.' Now the annular arrangement of the tubes came into play. When cleaning was necessary, as his patent explained, the furnace would be withdrawn, the water and steam pipes disconnected, and the whole coil assembly 'rotated or vibrated to break up the deposits of earthy matters' which would then be flushed away.

The editor was sceptical. 'We must confess we have but an indifferent opinion of their efficacy … the incrustations will indurate so quickly, that unless he repeats his hurdy-gurdy process every twenty-four hours at least, we suspect he will find himself literally playing at marbles.' Such cynicism was justified. After its initial run, this particular model probably never ran again, though for many years James persisted with different water-tube boiler designs in further road-carriages.

* * * * *

As 1829 came to a close, William James submitted his general bill for land agency and left Cornwall to spend Christmas with his son George Walter in West Bromwich. He was in serious pain, presumably as a lingering result of his fall twelve months earlier, and he needed the 'aid of a skilful surgeon'. Perhaps his leg had not been properly set at the time; perhaps, and this would have been typical, he had returned to work before it had completely healed. He was back in Cornwall by 27 February 1830, and dashing around Truro trying to establish the full extent of Anna-Maria's interests there. He had at last got details – incomplete – from a reluctant Jenkin. Furthermore, he had also discovered some old maps which proved that some of her property had been enclosed illegally by the Spry family. But, because there was as yet no settlement with Magor and Baynard, his Devoran prospectus was still in limbo. And there was another frustration. Anna-Maria was claiming she had no resources with which to back his improvements, so James suggested, with Baugh Allen's support, that she should sell off some of her outlying properties to concentrate her power base around Lanhydrock, Devoran and Truro. The trouble – and Allen should have known this – was that the relevant parts of the estates were held in trust for her son! James's report to her in May, therefore, was largely one of business not completed, in part because of bad weather but mainly because of 'the interruptions and backward-ness of the people I have had to deal with.' James was not yet in harmony with the locals in his adopted county and they were reluctant to adapt themselves to his thrusting urgency. Another recurring problem, moreover, was raising its head again – his expenses were being queried by Anna-Maria's solicitor, Mr Kent.

By coincidence, it was in the county of Kent that one of James's pioneering ventures would be opened to the public on Monday 3 May 1830, the Canterbury & Whitstable Railway being cheered on its way by tumultuous crowds under a cloudless sky. The local dignitaries and their guests – but without William James – seemed particularly thrilled by the experience of being hauled through the Tyler's Hill tunnel. Robert Stephenson's 'Invicta' locomotive hauled the train for the final stage into Whitstable and James's dream that 'his' Canterbury and Whitstable Railway would be the first steam-hauled passenger railway in the world, had come true. Robert Stephenson made a speech praising the operation and the directors, but in a voice 'so low that [people] could not distinctly hear what he said'.[389] Was it shyness? Or was it embarrassment that the Stephenson family was yet again basking in plaudits which should have been shared with Robert's mentor?

But in September, far away from Kent and Cornwall, another of James's earlier obsessions had at last been completed and this time he was invited to the Grand Opening. It must have been with mixed emotions as well as physical discomfort that he once again travelled the turnpike to Liverpool.

* * * * *

By contrast to the Rainhill trials, the official opening of the Liverpool & Manchester Railway in September 1830 was somewhat of an anticlimax. The day became infamous for the mutilation and lingering death of William Huskisson, the popular MP for Liverpool and industrious ally of the railway project. Not that the organisers could be blamed for that disaster. In his eagerness to contrive a rapprochement with the prime minister, the Duke of Wellington, Huskisson disobeyed clear instructions by leaving his seat when the trains stopped and shunted to re-water the locomotives near Newton-le-Willows. In gaining the Duke's attention, Huskisson was trapped in the narrow space between the two lines of track, fell, and his leg was run over by the oncoming *Rocket*.[390]

Subsequently, however, the organisation fell into chaos. Joy and jubilation at the start of the day in Liverpool deteriorated into scenes bordering on a riot by the time the trains of invited guests finally reached Manchester, over an hour late. Unaware of the cause of the delay, the crowds assumed it was somehow due to the autocratic Duke of Wellington, whom they blamed for the fact that they still had no representative in Parliament. How was it possible that the second largest metropolis in the country was politically disenfranchised, while the tiny community of Newton returned two MPs? And when they did understand that Huskisson had been mortally wounded, the man who had put his political career at risk on this very issue, their mood became even uglier. Memories of the Peterloo riots at Manchester were uncomfortably fresh in the minds of the directors who decided, probably wisely, that the prime minister should not leave the station to attend the civic reception.

The return journey became a nightmare. Sorting out the overcrowded terminus caused yet more delays. It began to pour with rain. Then several locomotives suffered breakdowns, carriages had to be roped together into longer trains, and over-loaded engines struggled to pull their loads at much more than walking pace. Some passengers opted to abandon the journey altogether, entrusting them-selves to the 'security' of horse-drawn carriages. By the time the trains approached Liverpool it was pitch dark, slowing progress even more, and it was 11 o'clock before the last guest could stagger away.

The best-known chronicler of the events leading up to the opening was the young actress Fanny Kemble, who recounted not only the activities but her reactions to the personalities involved – she was especially captivated by George Stephenson ('with whom I am most horribly in love') who gave her a trial run on the footplate of *Northumbrian*. 'I stood up, and with my bonnet off drank the air before me . . . When I closed my eyes this sensation of flying was quite delightful, and strange beyond description.' Thomas Creevey, however, one of the MPs who had been an entrenched opponent of the railway, came away from his 'private view' with a very different reaction:[391] 'The quickest motion is to me *frightful*; it is really flying, and it is impossible to divest yourself of the notion of instant death to all upon the least accident happening.' Nor was the Duke of Wellington impressed: 'I see no reason to suppose these [locomotive] machines will ever force themselves into general use.'[392]

But on the opening day there was another crucial witness. We know that William James was there because he confirmed the fact to a select committee of the House of Lords in 1836 when he appeared as an expert witness (see Chapter 19). When asked, 'Have you travelled along the Manchester & Liverpool Railroad?' he replied, 'At the time poor Mr Huskisson lost his life, I went twice.' Sadly we

have no written record of how James felt on that day. It must have been an emotional occasion as he passed the places he had last seen in 1822. For much of the eastern section, the final route closely followed the one he had surveyed with so many tribulations and at such personal risk, although Lord Derby's seat at Knowsley Park was now only a remote vista to the north. We must imagine his feelings as his carriage climbed through the Olive Mount cutting, then clawed its way up the gradient to the Rainhill level and rushed down the other side before the watering stop at Newton, where he had once set up his headquarters at the inn. Did he marvel at being drawn smoothly across the barren wasteland of Chat Moss? What were his feelings if he caught a glimpse of Lord Stanley, whose father had so obstinately refused to discuss his plans? Did he ride in the fourth train, the one under the direction of Joseph Sandars? Surely he would have made every effort to have a few words, however brief, with the Stephensons, preoccupied though they were with the driving of three of the eight locomotives involved. Robert Snr was in charge of *North Star*, his nephew of *Phoenix*. George Stephenson had the responsibility for the leading engine, *Northumbrian*, and it was therefore his painful duty to make the mercy dash to Eccles with the bleeding body of Huskisson.

James's name does not occur among those of the nobility and gentry who made up the most honoured guests, lists of whom have been published in various accounts of the opening day.[393] But among the other invited guests were 'distinguished engineers', the list of which he did head: 'Mr Wm James of Cornwall, Mr Rastrick of Manchester, Mr Wood of Killingworth, Mr George Rennie of London, Messrs Buchanan and Granger of Edinburgh etc.'[394] James did keep one souvenir – a fabric print commemorating the opening day. It would reappear, exactly a hundred years later, among a collection of his papers that were handed down via one of his grand-children.[395]

The grand banquet at the Adelphi Hotel on the opening night, at which 230 guests were expected, was attended by only 47, all of them exhausted and soaked to the skin. The 'Engineers and their Friends' had planned their own dinner in another room at the hotel, with James's friend Joseph Yates in the chair, but 'only a few gentlemen attended and a general gloom pervaded the evening'.[396] The toasts at the main banquet too must have had a somewhat hollow ring to them. Huskisson had prepared a long speech praising the directors for their achieve-ments and heralding the new dawn of safe and rapid transport. On the following morning, the text was found in his jacket pocket by the undertakers.

NINETEEN

Reform, a Wedding and a Mail-coach in the Snow (1831–1837)

A T THE end of 1830 and the start of 1831, things were not going well for James. Not only was there an epidemic of smallpox in Cornwall but, as he confided in a letter to Anna-Maria, he suffered an 'afflicting loss'. His wife Dinah, 'that sainted angel', had been laid to rest in the churchyard of St Mary's, Lapworth, on the last day of August 1830. On top of this, he himself had undergone a painful operation.

The bulk of the Glynn estates were still unsold. On the one hand, James was holding out for prices close to his valuations, while, on the other, there were rival claims as to which members of the Glynn family held title to which properties. Was Edmund Glynn (or rather his assignee) entitled to sell them at all? Sir William Molesworth was starting to rally support for his Bodmin railway, and correspondence suggests that he wanted James to do the surveys, but Thomas Agar-Robartes, who was now taking over control of his family affairs, was more in favour of a canal. James had to accept a lower salary for the year, and in 1832 it would not be renewed. Baugh Allen also withdrew his support – 'James's notions' he told Agar-Robartes, 'are something too eccentric to be retained, except on the occasional consultancy basis.' He ordered James's account to be closed.

So James urgently needed to find other clients, and when he got wind of the proposed sale of an estate on the river Fal not far from Devoran, he pitched in, as Alfred Jenkin recounted to Anna-Maria. 'Sir H. Vivian and T. Daniell had, I understand, nearly agreed terms respecting Trelissick, when the latter determined to call in the assistance of Wm James, and now I think it is doubtful whether they will ever agree.' He ended with a comment which echoed Allen's: 'Wm James's ideas are too magnificent for poor Cornwall.'[397] But James did Daniell a good turn, selling Trelissick a few months later to the Earl of Falmouth at a price within 5 per cent of his own (much higher) valuation. It was a major coup and

the substantial commission would solve James's immediate financial worries. Nor did he overlook the consequence that Sir Richard Hussey Vivian would now be in the market for somewhere else. They started negotiating over the Glynn properties, although at that stage Vivian was prepared to offer only £20,000 and James was holding out for £32,500.

*   *   *   *   *

I T IS difficult for us in the 21st century, with our increasing apathy towards elections in general, to comprehend the popular fervour engendered by the failure of the Reform Bills of 1831 and the run-up to the great Reform Bill of 1832. Nowhere did this manifest itself more vigorously than in Cornwall, though for reasons different from those in some other parts of the country. Unlike Manchester and several other growing industrial conurbations with no parliamentary representation, Cornwall, with a total population of only 300,000, returned no fewer than 62 MPs, mostly from pocket or rotten boroughs. There was a mood of serious political unrest and James had to warn Thomas Agar-Robartes not to dismount during a visit to Devoran because of 'movements of the seditious'. James, still inherently suspicious of 'democratic tendencies' which he associated with the worst excesses of the French Revolution, wrote to him in March, 'By the present measure, many wild spirits will be let loose on the country and it will require all the influence, firmness and wisdom of all persons of character and consideration to keep them in due bounds'. The forthcoming elections in Bodmin were beset by feuds and jerrymandering. James commented in June that he perceived that 'a fine illustration of the Blessing of Reform will be shown, not in the destruction, but the extension of corruption. The inhabitants are literally mad with marches and mass gatherings . . . all interest will now be consolidated by the

COLLIERIES.

Names.	Situation.	Weekly Produce.	Quality of Coal.
STAFFORDSHIRE.			
Wednesbury, Balls Hill, and Golden Hill Collieries, & Lime Works.	On the Old Branch of Upper Level of Birmingham Canal, leading from Ryder's Green to Turnpike Road at HILL TOP above WEDNESBURY, 7 miles from Birmingham, and contained in 140 Acres of Land.	TONS. 600	The same as Wednesbury Old Mine.
Pelsall Colliery.	On the Wyrley and Essington Canal, about 7 miles from LICHFIELD, and contained in Acres of Land.	500	Same quality as Brown Hills, most excellent for culinary Purposes, and the Cokes are superior for Maltsters.
Birchill Colliery, Iron Furnace, & Foundry.	On Wyrley and Essington Canal, about 1 mile from WALSALL, and contained in 85 Acres of Land.	500	Same Quality as last named Mine.
WARWICKSHIRE.			
Wykin Collery.	On Oxford Canal, about 3 miles from COVENTRY, and the nearest mine to London and the South Country, and contained in 530 Acres of Land.	600	This Coal is most pure in its Nature, and highly valuable for Bakers, Engineers, and other Uses where strong Heat is required.

N.B. *These Mines are just opened, and the Works are still extending, so that the Public may rely on a constant supply at a regular price ; and as the Proprietor, at his Iron, Lime, and Brick Works, consumes near 300 tons of inferior coal weekly, coal of a superior quality is selected for sale.*

HEATHCOTE, BOOKSELLER, WARWICK.

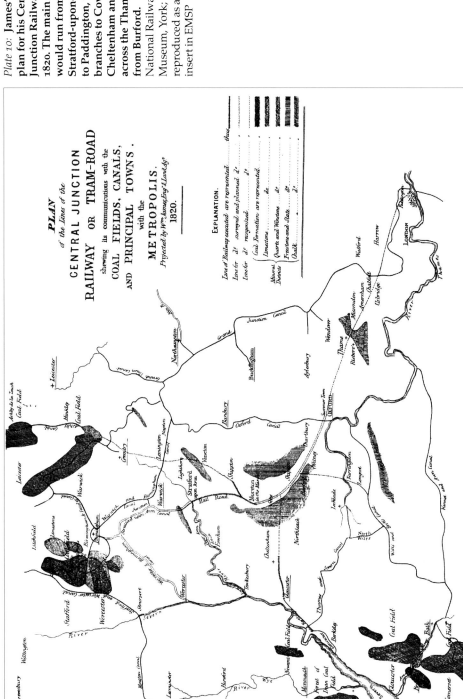

Plate 10: James's plan for his Central Junction Railway, 1820. The main line would run from Stratford-upon-Avon to Paddington, with branches to Coventry, Cheltenham and across the Thames from Burford. National Railway Museum, York; reproduced as an insert in EMSP

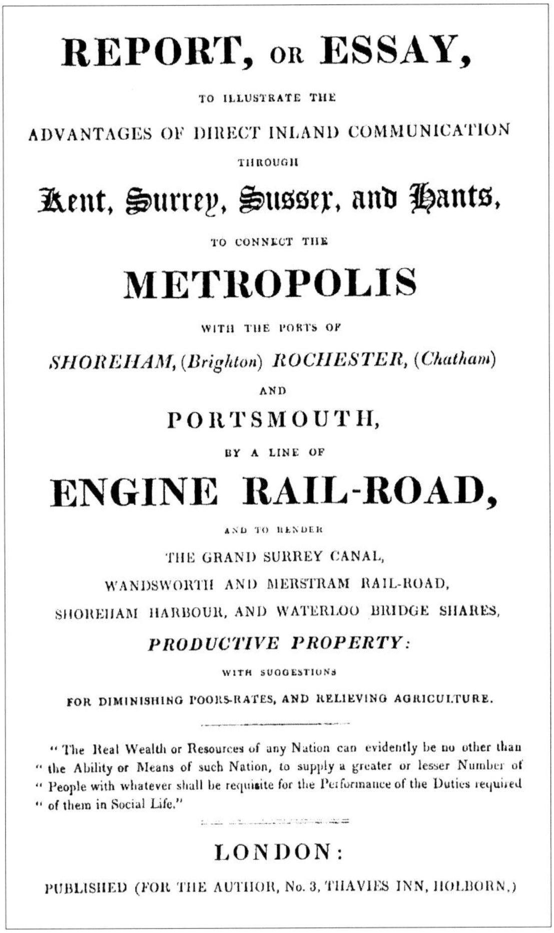

REPORT, or ESSAY,

TO ILLUSTRATE THE

ADVANTAGES OF DIRECT INLAND COMMUNICATION

THROUGH

𝕶𝖊𝖓𝖙, 𝕾𝖚𝖗𝖗𝖊𝖞, 𝕾𝖚𝖘𝖘𝖊𝖝, 𝖆𝖓𝖉 𝕳𝖆𝖓𝖙𝖘,

TO CONNECT THE

METROPOLIS

WITH THE PORTS OF

SHOREHAM, (*Brighton*) *ROCHESTER,* (*Chatham*)

AND

PORTSMOUTH,

BY A LINE OF

ENGINE RAIL-ROAD,

AND TO RENDER

THE GRAND SURREY CANAL,

WANDSWORTH AND MERSTRAM RAIL-ROAD,

SHOREHAM HARBOUR, AND WATERLOO BRIDGE SHARES,

PRODUCTIVE PROPERTY:

WITH SUGGESTIONS

FOR DIMINISHING POORS-RATES, AND RELIEVING AGRICULTURE.

"The Real Wealth or Resources of any Nation can evidently be no other than
"the Ability or Means of such Nation, to supply a greater or lesser Number of
"People with whatever shall be requisite for the Performance of the Duties required
"of them in Social Life."

LONDON:

PUBLISHED (FOR THE AUTHOR, No. 3, THAVIES INN, HOLBORN.)

Plate 11a: **Title page of James's** *Report or Essay* **on his strategic railway from Chatham to Portsmouth with links to London, 1823**

Plate 11b: **Publicity engraving of 1825 for the Birmingham & Liverpool Railway, initiated by James.** National Railway Museum, York

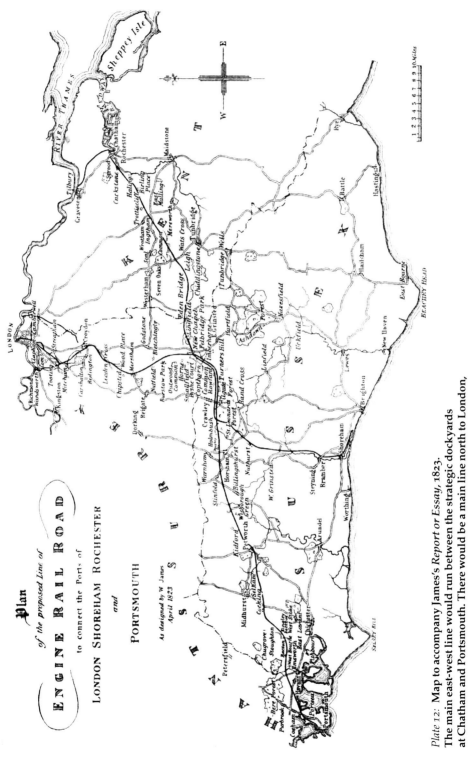

Plate 12: Map to accompany James's *Report or Essay*, 1823.
The main east-west line would run between the strategic dockyards
at Chatham and Portsmouth. There would be a main line north to London,
via Croydon, and a southern branch to Shoreham, where James had plans
for major development.

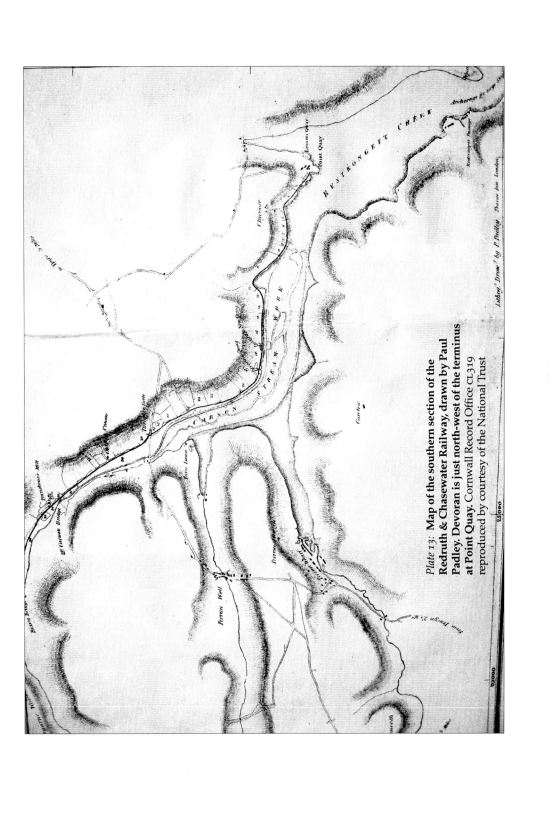

Plate 13: **Map of the southern section of the Redruth & Chasewater Railway, drawn by Paul Padley. Devoran is just north-west of the terminus at Point Quay.** Cornwall Record Office CL319 reproduced by courtesy of the National Trust

Plate 14a: **Anna-Maria Agar of Lanhydrock, William James's patron from 1824 to 1831.** Reproduced by courtesy of the National Trust. Photo by Cameracraft

Plate 14b: **Plasnewyd(d), Bodmin, William James's home in Cornwall 1827–37. The addition on the left side is modern.** Author 2003

Plate 15: **Surviving relics of the Central Junction Railway**

a) **Stone sleepers on trackbed between Armscote and Ilmington** (GR 226452). Author

b) **Underbridge ¾ mile south of Stratford.** Author

c) **Waggon preserved at National Railway Museum, York.** National Railway Museum, York

d) **Original wrought iron rail in Guildhall Garden, Henley-in-Arden.** Author

Plate 16a: **Elizabeth James (née Butt) in later life, William James's second wife and 36 years his junior.** Reproduced by courtesy of the Liverpool Record Office

Plate 16b: **Plan accompanying James's 'Prospectus' for the redevelopment of Devoran, 1830.** Cornwall Record Office CL320 reproduced by courtesy of the National Trust

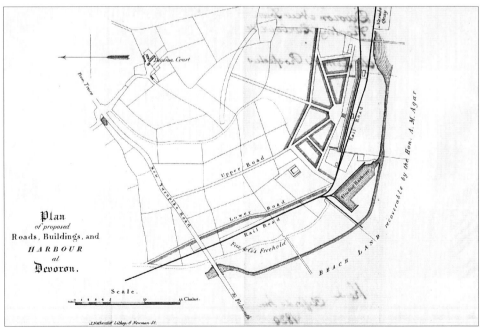

Plan
of proposed
Roads, Buildings, and
HARBOUR
at
Devoran.

Scale.

union of the violent and disaffected, the weak and the unprincipled.' Voting by secret ballot was still far in the future, and there were now many more votes that had to be bought.

James returned briefly to London where on 11 May 1832, in the church of St Clement in Fulham, he married his second wife, Elizabeth Butt.[398] We know nothing of their courtship or indeed of how they met. She was certainly no heiress, and it is possible, merely because of the coincidence of the surname, that she was the daughter of a fellow land agent with whom he had once crossed swords in the Warwick years (see Chapter 2). She being only 25, there was a 36-year difference in their ages (plate 16a). One likes to believe it was a love-match – he could certainly have been a persuasive suitor, even if a fairly impoverished one – and eighteen months after the wedding she would bear him a daughter, who was christened Anne.[399]

James and his young wife returned to Plasnewydd which, he had confided to Thomas Agar-Robartes, would now be his home for life. Agar-Robartes was not altogether delighted about this, commenting to his mother 'What do you think of that?' But at least she offered James the temporary agency at Devoran – perhaps as a sort of wedding present – and James expressed his humble thanks in a letter to Baugh Allen. 'Little indeed she knows how much she has obliged both myself and my distant, unprotected family, but heaven will reward her though I have not the power to serve her as I desired to do.' There were still many projects uncompleted and treaties unresolved. In August the Glynn estates were yet again put up for auction and yet again failed to reach their reserves; there were ongoing disputes with the turnpike trusts; his own railway schemes had got nowhere; he had achieved some improvements at Devoran but not all, for his great 'prospectus' had withered and the floating dock remained unbuilt.[400]

In 1833 James would encounter more bad luck, writing in March from the Falmouth Bathing House that he had had an unspecified but 'dreadful accident'. In June, however, he could report more optimistically that that he was 'engaged in the valuation of Chiverton and other estates of William Peter, MP for Bodmin'.[401] He could also tell Baugh Allen that Cornwall was now politically quiet and property prices were rising again. And in January 1834 he finally managed to sell the remainder of the Glynn estates, including the burnt-out mansion, to Sir Richard Hussey Vivian, for a compromise price of £29,000. Sir Richard was partly motivated by the belief that the purchase would assist the return of his son Charles Crespigny Vivian as one of the MPs for Bodmin, an ambition achieved in 1835 when Peter retired.

It appears that by 1834 James's association with Anna-Maria and Thomas Agar-Robartes was at an end. For the next two years we know little of his activities in Cornwall. Ellen Paine claimed that her father did more agency work for the Earl of Falmouth who was developing his estate at Tregothnan, but the details are unknown.[402] At least James should have received a commission of a few thousand pounds from the Glynn assignees which, if he managed to keep some of it out of the hands of his own assignees, would have made his life a little more comfortable.

* * * * *

JAMES was back in London in June 1836, when he was invited to appear as an expert witness before a select committee of the House of Lords. It was investigating that perpetual phobia, the potential fire hazards generated by locomotives both in built-up areas and 'in respect to plant-ations, cornfields, stack-yards and agricultural buildings in general'.[403] This invitation was highly significant on two counts. First, it was a ringing endorsement of James's status and reputation, and secondly it proved to be his last chance to meet the Stephensons and several of the distinguished engineers with whom he had last had discourse in 1830 at the opening of the Liverpool & Manchester. Evidence from sixteen witnesses was taken over a total of four days.

The first of the key witnesses, George Rennie, said that he knew of only two cases of fire damage from locomotives, both involving bales of cotton being set alight on waggons, probably from cinders dropped through the fire grate. He claimed that the fitting of 'the hood or cullender to the top of the chimney' had eliminated the problem of sparks arising from the 'violence of the draught'. He pointed out that neither Walter Hancock nor Goldsworthy Gurney, the most notable and successful of the steam road-carriage engineers, had ever had problems from sparks. He also extolled the merits of South Wales coal – 'there is no smoke from it or sparks' – though it was expensive and difficult to get going. Dr Dionysius Lardner, an early and sometimes erratic commentator on railway matters, came next and confirmed that a cornfield had been set alight on the Leicester & Swannington line and perhaps on the Stockton & Darlington, but there the construction of the locomotives was very 'rough'.

On the second day Robert Stephenson took the stand and gave an account of the experiments that he and his father had carried out on the Liverpool & Manchester engines, testing various meshes and gauzes in the chimneys to trap large cinders. With too fine a mesh the efficiency of the blast was affected, but he had found a satisfactory compromise in a spiral grid of wires at the top of the funnel. George Stephenson himself, by now at the pinnacle of his eminence, then recounted more of his own earlier experiments, including a shield shaped like an umbrella held a foot above the chimney and Venetian blinds up the inside, none of which had been successful. Charles Blunt CE quoted his experiences with locomotives on the continent, while John Rastrick said that from his observations, both on railways and in the iron industry, any sparks emitted from chimneys cooled down almost instantaneously, particularly when mixed with steam. A fireman from the London & Greenwich who had had his clothes burnt by sparks was also questioned.

James's testimony on the same day lasted for half an hour. When asked if he had considered the likely dangers of fire from locomotives, his reply was typically emphatic, not because he had heard about accidents arising from this cause, but because he had been engaged with 'all aspects of railways for a long time'. He recounted how he had been chairman of the Staffordshire Miners in 1816 and had 'considered it my duty to see all the railroads in England, in order if possible to introduce a new system by Engines . . . and thereby to improve the iron trade'. He went on to recount his three meetings with Blenkinsop at Leeds in 1816, followed by visits to Hedley and finally his encounters with George Stephenson at Killingworth, where he had seen 'the first Engine that I approved of'. On the specific question of danger from sparks and cinders, he replied that he believed there was 'none whatever, with proper caution', particularly if coke was used as the fuel and a 'hood was put over the top of the chimney'. When pressed on whether he had ever travelled on any 'great railroad', he stated he had been at the opening of the Liverpool & Manchester Railway – 'I was the projector; the original plan and survey was my work' – but had not made any subsequent journeys by rail.

Another aspect of the problem, and a slightly ironic one, arose from the evidence of James Walker CE, who had recently succeeded Thomas Telford as president of the Institution of Civil Engineers. He had been responsible for a number of large steam-powered water pumping stations within urban areas and, because of their large boilers and furnaces, he had enquired of various fire insurance offices what precautions they demanded to reduce the risks from chimney emissions. He had been surprised by their indifference. When pressed, one office had confided that if there were never any risks of fire damage they would be driven out of business!

The longest examination was reserved on the fourth day for Hardman Earle, the managing director of the Liverpool & Manchester and the man with the greatest experience of running a commercial passenger-carrying railway. He recounted how the company had paid out some compensation to genuine claimants and how the locomotives were being continually modified, although the Bolton line, which had running powers over their tracks, had been slow to adopt these improvements.

The following month the Duke of Richmond presented the report of the committee's findings. They made no recommendation for general legislation on the subject, but were 'of the opinion that no Railway Bill providing for the transit of locomotive Engines through populous places should be allowed to pass unless it contain clauses for making provision against the Danger of Fire from the chimneys and fire-places of the engine.'

A summary of the evidence of certain key witnesses was reported in the *Mechanics' Magazine* that summer, though not that of James. Indeed, he had contributed nothing material to the analysis of the problem. Nor did the editor bother to mention the contribution of another witness, the young rising star Isambard Kingdom Brunel, who actually made a very relevant point. He cited the experience of engines on the Dublin & Kingstown Railway where a sloping screen had been placed over the end of the tubes below the blast pipe, and also suggested that coke was more hazardous than coal as it was 'lighter and more frangible'.

One is left, tantalisingly, to speculate whether James managed to spend any time with Rastrick and the Stephensons, all witnesses on that second day of evidence. At the very least they must have met in the reception rooms, and perhaps they even dined together. Sadly we will never know.

This visit by James to the House of Lords had another implication. He took the opportunity to make himself familiar with the procedures for presenting a personal petition. Since Saxon times it had been an inalienable right of all citizens to petition the monarch on matters of personal grievance and the redressing of injustices, this right being enshrined both in Magna Carta and the 1688 Bill of Rights. Petitions were read prior to debates in Parliament and by the 1830s were taking up a considerable amount of time. Whereas in 1788 the annual total was only about 176, by 1832 this had increased to a veritable flood, and in that year a select committee recommended that most petitions should be filtered by examining committees.[404] The government did not completely remove petitions from the floor of the house, although they became increasingly rare. But one which did achieve this privileged status was that of William James, which was presented to the Commons by John Wilkes MP on 4 August 1836, and to the Lords on the following day by the Earl of Ripon.

It was cleverly worded. The preamble stated that he had personally spent over £10,000 on 'inventing, improving and carrying into execution various engines, plans, systems and works . . . for which he had never received the least remuneration or compensation'. But he was not seeking personal redress for this; the plank of his argument was that he had been a joint proprietor in George Stephenson and William Losh's locomotive patent, and that they had exploited his contribution to their agreement but not shared their rewards with him. Again he was not seeking personal recompense as such, but wished that the patent laws should be changed to give greater protection to inventors and prevent unscrupulous people from extracting and exploiting particular disclosures within a patent. And not only patents. He had suffered 'the mortification of seeing other persons taking up and adopting his inventions, *plans and sections*' and felt that his experiences were equally deterring 'many other inventors, engineers and men of science from promoting and publishing schemes for lessening labour, and otherwise advancing the great works now in contemplation throughout the kingdom.' He himself, he claimed, had two inventions in the pipeline 'by which the public might be greatly benefited', but he was reluctant to proceed for fear that his ideas would be stolen before he had any 'compensation and credit from his ingenuity and perseverance.' The penultimate paragraph stated that 'your Right Honourable House has recognised and protected *literary* property by the law of Copyright . . . providing not only against the piracy of the whole, but also against the abstraction of any of its parts.' His petition closed with the 'prayer' that Parliament should extend the law of copyright not only to patents but to 'plans, models and labours', providing compensation and remuneration to the originators when they were 'successfully appropriated by other persons'; and it cited the specific example of 'the success of your petitioner's project, the Liverpool & Manchester Railroad.'[405]

Parliament did nothing immediately to address James's complaint, but there was an interesting spin-off. In October the *Railway Magazine* carried an article headed 'The Original Projector of the Liverpool & Manchester Railway'.[406] The editor, John Herapath, was evidently not familiar with James, but had picked up on the petition 'in accordance with the spirit of our Magazine to notice every subject relating to railways.' Although surprised that James had remained 'so long in silence and in the shade', he felt that if his claims were indeed fact ('and we do not dispute it') he must be a person of a 'rather peculiar character'. Why had he been so modest and so self-effacing about his involvement in the Liverpool railway, when 'every other engineer has been ambitious to obtain even a feather of distinction from having been in the slightest way connected with this very successful undertaking?' Herapath would look into the matter and try to find 'the causes and motives of this extraordinary forbearance, so that justice at least may be done to his pretensions by an impartial public.' James's rejection by George Stephenson struck a personal chord, for Herapath had himself developed important theories about molecular motion in gases – later proved to be absolutely correct – which had been scorned and rejected by Humphrey Davy when president of the Royal Society in 1820. Davy's refusal to allow his paper to be published in the society's proceedings had had a negative impact on Herapath's own career as a scientist and teacher. One of the motives in founding his *Railway Magazine* was to give publicity to a range of related scientific matters, together with his own often idiosyncratic contributions.

This was a perfect cue for James himself to respond, and a long letter from him was published in the November issue.[407] Much of the content will now be familiar to readers of the present story – the surveys of his many railway schemes, the instigation and tribulations of the Liverpool project and so forth – but they may have come as a great surprise to many of Herapath's readers, who would have been particularly intrigued by one paragraph which showed that he still had surprises of his own in store. 'I owe to mankind the benefit of two other discoveries; one which will prove, in my estimation, of *far greater value than the engine railway system.*' What precisely this involved he was not prepared to say, except that he hoped to demonstrate it 'in Newhaven, as soon as from my own miserable resources I can find funds for models, surveys and subsistence.'[408]

Not that James had given up on some of his other dreams as well, and in September he was in correspondence with Lord Hatherton of Walsall, Staffordshire, about various new railway schemes. Hatherton replied that he was glad to see him 'at work again on the old ground'.[409] Then on 14 December he wrote from Bodmin to his former clerk and confidant John Kershaw. These are the last words that survive from his own pen, a sad blend of optimism and defeatism, stoicism and bitterness. They encapsulate much of James's own character, his feelings for his children and his attitude to loyalty.[410]

I feel I am taking a liberty in addressing you, but the claims of a tried friendship will I hope not be forgotten, and whatever difference there may be in our [mutual] esteem has, I trust, taken place. Although it is probable we may never meet again – my health, distance and debilitating years appear to announce that fact – yet I am desirous you should not be mistaken as to the motives of my conduct in respect of my own affairs, all power having been taken out of my hands and transferred to the Assignees and their solicitor by this most dreadful Commission. Having had every sovereign drained from me by my first family, how useless, how hopeless would have been any interference. My fine property, which under my own management I flattered myself would have given me an ample fortune, through expenses, debtors and other circumstances will not I hear pay the demands of my just creditors, which is to me a most affecting circumstance . . . I fear some unprincipled claims have been made and some errors exist as to the debts. I never saw a list nor any of the accounts, which I hear are to be audited on Saturday. I have written a letter to Messrs Corrie & Carter [his solicitors] for permission on my return eastward to examine and extract from these accounts, and I hope the creditors will pass a resolution to that effect. Will you have the goodness to use your interest for this purpose?

I have heard (though I know not the fact) that the Bankrupt is entitled to some allowance. When I came to be examined on the Whitman Jones business, the sum paid me was not sufficient to defray my expenses . . . Mr Corrie lent me £20 . . . but from the

advances to Walter and others . . . I was unable to repay it. Mr Bill also lent me £10 on another occasion. My situation even as a bankrupt is peculiarly unfortunate, not having any friend or advocate between myself and the Commissioners, who I am certain are disposed to do me justice. Permit me to request that friendly office of you at these two meetings. I have sustained most ruinous losses in Mr ****** and Mr ****** absconding to France, where they are living in style.[411]

His claims against them, he goes on, amount to at least £900, but he would settle for £500, the sum for which he could provide proof. He pleads with Kershaw to try to get him an advance of £100 against this claim and with it to repay Corrie and Bill and send him the balance. He concludes on a more optimistic note.

As to my General Prospect, I think it has much improved within the last 12 months. I open an office in London in January as a Land Agent and consulting Engineer. I have three views into futurity, which at present appear flattering, and as my unhappy children have disposed of every article of Furniture and memorial of my name and family, I am, as it were, sold out by them and must begin the world anew. Oh God! I have been most cruelly treated. But no more. I am truly rejoiced to hear of the Welfare and Respectability of your children, and of the health of yourself and your good Wife.

A postscript, however, shows the extent to which his natural self-confidence has been undermined by the process in Chancery.

In my Examination of Accounts, I merely want to ascertain the Amounts that the clear produce under the proper heads may be obtained by me, but if you think my personal offices may begrieve anyone, I do not urge it, or if I have the power to inspect and abstract, I would not urge it. The Advance is very material as my children in Birmingham are almost without the necessaries of life – God knows by their own folly. I have paid £50 from my quarterly payments on the day, besides a large advance to Walter. They would never be advised.

Even the outline of his financial entanglements being, at this distance, beyond recovery, some of the statements above are hard to understand. He does not know for sure if the bankrupt was entitled to an allowance (which in fact, after full disclosure of his affairs, he was); yet, according to his daughter Ellen, the court had earlier offered him an annual allowance of as much as £600, which he rejected.[412] Possibly he kept the true situation from her, for he was even now receiving quarterly payments which sound like an allowance. Whatever the exact truth, he was clearly, for a man of his background, on the breadline.

Although his wife was pregnant with their second child, he left her in Cornwall while he took the mail-coach up to Birmingham to spend Christmas 1836 with his son George Walter, mainly to consult him about his failing health.[413] He combined this with making his last journey into Wales, advising his friend Mr Binns about the management of his estate.[414] He also took the opportunity to visit Corrie again, and 'after expressions of the warmest feelings of friendship', his solicitor suggested that there was a good chance that James could still rescue as much as £30,000 for himself and his family – provided that he came back to Warwickshire and really got down to sorting out the chaos of his records.

But now a sequence of events set in which would make it too late. In the first week of the New Year James received an urgent letter infor-

ming him that his wife Elizabeth had gone into premature labour. He immediately headed back to Cornwall. There was no seat available within the mail-coach and he had to travel outside. It was a two-day journey, the weather was dreadful, and he was chilled to the bone. He probably had to walk the last mile through snow. There was at least good news when he arrived – the baby had been safely delivered and his wife had survived. The little girl would shortly be christened Winifred.[415]

When he left for Cornwall, James had already been 'in a state of extreme weakness'. Now he was seriously ill. The rigours of his last journey took a fatal toll and, three months short of his sixty-sixth birthday, he died of pneumonia on 10 March 1837.

*   *   *   *   *

THE tentacles of the railway network were spreading fast across the country. Over 500 miles had been built and a further 2,000 miles sanctioned. In another 22 years, Brunel's great bridge would be flung across the river Tamar and passengers could take a direct train from London to the heart of Cornwall with all the speed and comfort that had fuelled the dreams of a small-town Warwickshire lawyer.

TWENTY

The Battles
for Recognition

*'William James . . . spending his time and means for the public good,
died a poor and neglected man.'* [416]

ALFRED JENKIN wrote to Thomas Agar-Robartes on 20 March 1837, 'I observe that poor Wm James's death is confirmed by the newspaper'. A rather more fulsome obituary appeared in the *Gentleman's Magazine* for May, outlining the key facts of James's life and his membership of various notable societies and concluding with the following paragraph:

> He was the original projector of the
> Liverpool & Manchester and other
> railways, and may with truth be considered
> as the father of the railway system, as he
> surveyed numerous lines at his own
> expense at a time when such an innovation
> was generally ridiculed.

These words were echoed in a long-forgotten work, *Maunder's Biographical Treasury* of 1838. And that was it. No monument, no statue, not even a headstone, merely an unmarked grave in Bodmin churchyard. A week before he died James had written his last will, leaving everything he might possess in trust to his executors, to pay his debts and 'apply the residue for the use and benefit of my wife'.[417] Probate was granted at Bodmin on 11 July 1837, his effects being sworn at a value of under £1,500, of which his wife would have seen little or nothing since his debts were still in the hands of the Court of Chancery.

All of which doubtless left poor Elizabeth James in dire circumstances, with a newborn baby and a toddler. Perhaps she received some help from her husband's Masonic Lodge, the 'One and All' of Bodmin, even though their wish to bury him with full masonic honours was declined.[418] She soon returned to her parents in St Johns, Fulham, and it was here that Robert Stephenson went to see her to discuss some recognition from the Liverpool & Manchester directors for her late husband's contribution to this – by now – supremely successful company. By 1838 it was earning around £250,000 a year (of which passenger traffic, interestingly, accounted for more than half) and paying a dividend of 10 per cent. Stephenson told her in October that he had written to Joseph Sandars 'expressing my willingness to give any aid in my power',[419] though she had to wait until January for Sandars's reply. It brought the good news that the directors had awarded her an ex-gratia payment of £300.[420] It seems likely that James's bachelor brother Henry took her under his wing, because when he died at Leamington Spa on 28 November 1852 he left her the bulk of his estate, valued at nearly £4,000; and when she died 44 years later she was buried in the same grave.[421]

George Walter was the first of James's children to try to stir the public's attention to their plight and the way their father's memory was being overshadowed by George Stephenson. In May 1839 he placed an advertisement to this effect in the *Midland Counties Herald* and it was later reproduced in the *Mechanics' Magazine*, whose editor disapproved of the method employed, which 'put a clog to the publication of an apparently well-found claim', but suggested that surely Stephenson ought to share the merit he had achieved 'out of that stupendous system of internal communication which his partner, Mr James, projected.'[422] This was shortly followed by a brief sketch of James's life attributed merely to 'one of his relations'.[423] This was, almost certainly, James's daughter Ellen. George Walter, whose hat was already in the ring, had no need of anonymity, and the sketch reads like a summary of Ellen's later book.

The first person who tried to cash in on James's reputation by way of a public subscription was his youngest sister, Elizabeth Mudie, who had indirectly been one of the causes of her brother's ruin. In 1839 her spiteful and litigious husband, Peter Mudie, had resubmitted his claim for the imaginary dowry to the High Court, only to have it dismissed again. He finally took it to the Appeal Court in 1841, which closed the affair on the grounds of lack of evidence and 'want of good faith', and ordered Mudie to pay all costs.[424] That same year, Elizabeth had a memorial printed inviting 'any pecuniary aid that may be conferred on her', with the recommendation of fourteen eminent engineers and railway personalities, headed by Francis Giles, who had been one of the most prominent critics of George Stephenson over the 1825 Liverpool & Manchester Bill, and including Robert Stephenson, James Walker, Joseph Locke and Isambard Brunel.[425] The key paragraph stated that 'the system of railways, which her brother was the main instrument in bringing to bear, has been attended with vast public benefit and great pecuniary benefit to the undertakers of them; but in which his fortune was seriously impaired, his health injured and her own provision and prospects destroyed.' This sparked an outraged response from James's children, none of whom would benefit from this particular appeal. In July, William Henry James, together with 'several other gentlemen' petitioned the Lord Mayor of London to try to get it suppressed, but it was too late.[426] Considerable sums had already been pledged and the delegation was advised that the best course would be for them to publish their own case as quickly as possible.

But it was not until 1846 that the much more important 'Testimonial' was launched to promote 'a general subscription for the three sons and one daughter of William James . . . in consideration of their father's public services'. Many of these services were enumerated, ending with the compelling phrase 'it being an acknowledged fact that to their father's labours the *public are indebted for the establishment of the present railway system*'. This petition, a far more serious affair than Elizabeth Mudie's begging-bowl, was backed by a heavyweight committee and clearly intended to be presented to Parliament. By the 1840s the number of such petitions was running at over 30,000 a year, and the only way to establish a 'fast-track' priority was to obtain the endorsement of the Lord Mayor of London.[427] This was duly achieved by a declaration at Mansion House on 24 June 1846.[428]

The committee was headed by Robert Stephenson himself, and was supported by Locke, Brunel, George Rennie, Charles Vignoles and John Sylvester, along with ten other luminaries of the day, including Joseph Clinton Robertson who was a civil engineer and patent agent, and, more relevantly, the proprietor of the widely-read *Mechanics' Magazine*. Now at last James's contribution could be recognised before the world and his first family given some compensation; with such potent backing it could hardly fail. That at least was the belief of William Henry James and Ellen Paine. But their hopes were soon to be dashed. The Testimonial was effectively buried and never pushed through to a conclusion. Why?

Supporters of a conspiracy theory, like Ellen Paine, claimed the reason was that George Stephenson was 'exceedingly wroth' with his son for getting involved and had the document suppressed.[429] While his friend George Hudson was called the 'Railway King', George Stephenson was now referred to as the 'Father of the Railways', a title he relished. Nowhere, in any of his correspondence or public utterances, did George Stephenson give any credit or recognition to the help and assistance that he had received from his one-time partner. This did not go unnoticed. Edward Pease wrote in one of his very last letters, 'I continue to regret that so much merit should be so lightly rewarded by parties whom he so laudably endeavoured to serve.'[430] Robertson claimed in correspondence with Ellen Paine that the Testimonial had 'failed through mismanagement' (by implication, that of William Henry James), and was himself prepared to go into print in 1848 with an article which revived the controversy and took up the cudgels once more on James's behalf.[431] Reproducing the Testimonial in full, he added the following:

To this document, which assigns, with unimpeachable speciality and distinctness, to William James, that prominent place in railway history which George Stephenson was habitually fond of ascribing to himself . . . are subscribed the names of nearly all the most distinguished railway engineers of this railway era, including, in a foremost place, that of ROBERT STEPHENSON! . . . To our thinking, it is such as should set the question at rest for ever.

There were perhaps two other reasons why the Testimonial failed to get anywhere in 1846. This was the year of the great Railway Mania when the national economy was at risk from a tsunami of speculation. It has been estimated that at the close of 1845 there were no fewer than 620 proposed railway companies seeking an average of £900,000 each. A further 640 were preparing to apply to Parliament the following year. Promoters were competing with one another to try to raise a total of more than one billion pounds to build 50,000 miles of track, compared with the 2,800 miles constructed by 47 companies in the previous twenty years.[432] Parliament suddenly saw everyone to do with railways – and particularly the initiators of this hydra – as monsters rather than saints. Furthermore, Robert Stephenson and Locke were both about to embark on their own political careers, the former as Tory MP for Whitby and the latter as Reform MP for Honiton, and they may have felt that pressing the claims of a railway pioneer would not, at that moment, advance their prospects.

The loss of the Testimonial, on which he had set such store, was an especially cruel blow for William Henry James, who suffered an acute nervous breakdown as a result. But 1846 did witness one fine accolade to his father. In his Presidential Address to the Institution of Civil Engineers, Sir John Rennie gave a concise history of the early development of railways, ending with a list of 37 engineers who 'must be borne in mind as associated with the invention and propagation of the railway system'.[433] James's contribution and reputation still allowed his name to be prominent among the most famous of his contemporaries.[434]

Seven years after her father's death, Ellen James married a pharmacist in Rickmansworth named Trayton Paine. Their marriage was somewhat blighted by having to give a home to her brother Frederick, whom she described as 'never being able to support himself, through excessive nervous debility, and is supported by the charity of a brother-in-law. For 17 years, myself and my husband have had to maintain him in everything. It is a most cruel position for a married sister . . . causing misery on all sides.'[435]

When in June 1857 Samuel Smiles published his hagiography of George Stephenson, she was incensed that her father's memory had been besmirched and that his contribution to Stephenson's elevation had been belittled and virtually ignored. Worse still, Smiles had not taken the trouble to discover any details of her father's life after his bankruptcy, merely assuming that he had taken the coward's way and escaped to France. This was corrected in later editions, but by then Smiles had published his sanctimonious *Self Help; with illustrations of Character and Conduct*, and George Stephenson fitted his idealised role-model precisely: the poor, self-educated boy who pulled himself up by his bootstraps and achieved great public benefits solely through his own endeavours. To Smiles, James was the antithesis, a Regency character tainted with a bankruptcy caused not by entrepreneurial risk-taking but the sin of gambling. Perversely, but because they supported the credo of Self Help, Stephenson's failings were lauded as examples of his tenacity in the face of adversities; particularly where these could be laid at the door of men of better breeding. Over the next hundred years his biography would become the standard source for nearly all railway historians, but its success and popularity were largely due to its being extremely readable. More recent and more analytical critics concede that even 'if it lacked the philosophical power of Carlyle, the literary capability of Dickens or the scholarship of Macaulay, it had a little of each'.[436] And it did pay James one very significant compliment: 'Though he did not discover the locomotive, he did what was the next best thing to it, he discovered George Stephenson.'[437]

The first response to Smiles from the James family was a letter to the *Mining Journal* by William Henry James, printed on 14 November 1857. In setting out to answer the question 'who was the *bona fide* originator and founder of our modern Railway System?' he makes a concise and ardent case for his father being the 'first person to agitate and advocate throughout the length and breadth of the country the establishment of railways as a general means of transit . . . and the first person also to suggest, as practicable, the rapid conveyance of passengers and light goods by locomotive engines.' This, therefore, entitled him to a unique status in precedence to Gray, Pease, Sandars and Stephenson. Further letters printed on 5 and 27 December elaborated on all his father's railway schemes, highlighting the partnership agreement with Stephenson and Losh.

This was still not enough for James's daughter, Ellen Paine, whose resentment of Smiles's treatment of her father drove her to publish her own long-contemplated biography, *The Two James's and the Two Stephensons*. But it has all the elements of being thrown together in haste; it suffers from a maddening lack of any sequential time-line, and the narrative jumps backwards and forwards within a most confusing chapter structure, which makes it virtually unreadable. Her analysis of what she sees as her father's betrayal is both blinkered and biased; she has an axe to grind and is intent on burying it between the shoulder-blades of George Stephenson. And for the Victorian readers of Samuel Smiles, her timing and intent could not have been more unfortunate.

Her book was printed in 1861 by G. Phipps of Ranelagh Street, Eaton Square, London, the authorship being concealed under the anonymity of the initials E.M.S.P. Did she feel, like George Eliot and the Brontes, that it would be taken less seriously if people knew it had been written by a woman? Did she deliberately try to cloak it in an aura of mystery? She financed it by subscription, sending out copies to her father's patrons, friends and business associates and inviting donations. The final list of subscribers (see Appendix B) makes for interesting reading, not only for the names that are included but also for those that are not.[438] The contributions from the Greaves family and the Bagnalls are to be expected; several medical practitioners, perhaps friends of George Walter, were generous. Because the name of T. Bottley, the husband of Samuel Bill's daughter who 'showed great kindness to James's family after his death', is not recorded, it must be assumed that by 1861 he had died or gone abroad. Nor does the name of Kershaw figure. John Kershaw, her father's clerk and confidant, had died prior to 1861 – Ellen referred to him as 'the late Mr Kershaw' from whom she and her sister had received 'much kindness and sympathy'[439] – but there is no contribution from his son, who was by now a prominent cement manufacturer in the Midlands and a partner with the Greaves family in the quarries at Wilmcote. Nor is the Tarleton family represented, although Dinah James's great-nephew Henry Tarleton had been another of those who gave noteworthy support after William James's death.[440]

Ellen must have been pleased by the donations from Edward Pease's descendants and from T. R. Crampton, whose innovative locomotive designs had made such an impact, particularly in France. Sir Rowland Hill, the initiator of the Penny Post, was generous to the tune of £5, perhaps in recognition of the great benefits that railways had given to postal distribution and of James's part in their introduction. The Redesdale family remained supportive into the next generation, making the second largest contribution of £10 7s 6d, which was exceeded only by the £16 sent anonymously by 'A Good Engineer'. One might identify this man with Robert Stephenson,

who was only too well aware of the debt that he and his father owed to William James, had he not died in 1859. John Rastrick too had died in 1856, leaving Sir John Rennie as perhaps the most likely candidate.

The total subscription list generated £98. One hopes that Ellen more than covered her costs; she had been forced to publish it herself, she said, by the avarice of commercial publishers.

> Should a work sell for 15 shillings, the publisher takes 10 shillings, leaving the author 5 shillings out of which he has to pay for the printing, binding etc. No wonder that the publisher can vie with the nobility in their establishments and equipages![441]

Her own copy of the book has four letters stuck to the flyleaf, one of which was from Lord Redesdale: 'Your book proves that your late father had a greater claim to the title of 'Father of Railways' than either Mr Pease or George Stephenson.'[442]

For two years the Paines enjoyed rather more privacy, because Frederick was staying with George Walter James, possibly in some medical asylum under his supervision. Unfortunately Walter died in March 1865 and Frederick perforce returned to Rickmansworth. An increasingly desperate Ellen had received no subscription for her book from the 5th Earl of Dartmouth, so on 17 April 1866 she wrote to Lord Bagot, the Earl's cousin, enclosing a copy of the book and inviting him to subscribe. Getting no reply, she wrote again on 1 May, including the rather melo-dramatic words 'My dear father had the honour of being Agent to the 3rd and 4th Earl of Dartmouth and sank £15,000 or about that sum in proving coal upon their estate at Golden Hill, West Bromwich and never received any benefit therefrom, *although some of his family have died from starvation.*'[443] She is presumably referring to her sister Marianna; in her book, Ellen had been rather more restrained, saying that her elder sister 'being of a delicate constitution, soon sank under these great privations and misfortunes.'[444] This time her letter bore fruit and she received 10 shillings by return of post.[445]

What became of William James's offspring? The marriages of his daughters by his second wife have been touched on in Chapter 19. The lives of his surviving children by his first wife were more complicated. The first death in the Paine household was in fact Ellen's husband, Trayton, who was buried on 22 October 1868 aged 52. Ellen took over the pharmacy practice – the 1871 census gives her profession as 'chemist' –

Fig.14: **James's grandson, Henry Benson James** CE **(b.1835)**

and, despite her misery and ill health and the burden of supporting Frederick, she lived on until September 1882, leaving the house and personal effects to the value of £336 to her invalid brother.

William Henry James never made a fortune from any of his inventions and in 1846 suffered the apoplectic fit 'which affected him for many years, and from which he never wholly recovered'.[446] An eight-page 'Public Testimonial' on his behalf was drafted in November 1861, 'in recognition of his invaluable and unrequited services in connection with the founding of our magnificent railway system, by the gratuitous assistance he rendered to his late father . . . and for his having allowed the late George Stephenson and William Losh the liberty of introducing his invention of Tubes into the boilers of their locomotive engines'.[447] It elaborated on all his patents, his work on steam road carriages and how he had lost 'his patrimony of £50,000 as settled by [his father's] will, together with the whole of his private property, exceeding in value £20,000 more'. It minced no words about who was to blame – 'all the merits and profits of a world renowned undertaking . . . were carried off by W. James's successor, the late Mr George Stephenson'. Because the only known (hand-

written) copy names no specific backers, it was probably never printed and circulated. It appears that William Henry married, late in life, a woman called Mary Anne – the 1861 census has them living in Camberwell – but there is no evidence that he ever had any children. He died on 16 December 1873, supported by charity in the Dulwich College almshouses.[448]

John Henry James, the second son, died some time between 1851 and 1861.[449] He had followed a career as a civil engineer and married twice. By his first wife, Elizabeth, he had three daughters and four sons, two of whom (confusingly) were named William Henry (b.1827) and George Walter (b.1833). The former worked for the South Eastern Railway, becoming a stationmaster at Dorking in Surrey and then at Sturry in Kent; he had nine children by Harriet Mary Tarrant.[450] The latter emigrated to Australia in 1854, possibly with another of his brothers, and founded a whole new dynasty. Some became farmers, some traders and storekeepers, while others made careers on the burgeoning Australian rail network.[451] John Henry James's fourth son, Henry Benson (b.1836), also started his career on the South Eastern Railway, later becoming a distinguished civil engineer with his own consultancy operation in Victoria Street, London. He was at one time Master of the City Masons' Company. John Henry James's second wife, Sarah, bore him one son, Arthur (b.1855), who also became a civil engineer.

William James's third son, the doctor and surgeon George Walter James, spent most of his career in the Midlands and before 1851 married a woman named Emily. By 1861 he had moved to Woburn Park, Bedfordshire, where he died, apparently childless, in 1865.

Frederick Whitworth Tarleton James, who was the last surviving and saddest of William James's children by his first marriage, lingered on until his eightieth year and was buried at Rickmansworth on 26 July 1887.

A final attempt was made, in the last years of Victoria's reign, to reassert James's claim to be the true 'Father of Railways' and to erect a lasting memorial to his achievements. The torchbearer now was his grandson, Henry Benson James CE, who recruited to his cause the 'last railway king', Sir Edward William Watkin, together with the men who spearheaded the final great main line into London, Sir William Pollitt and his son Harry of the Great Central Railway. Blazing the trail was a certain R. R. Dodds, who in 1899 wrote a provocative article in the *Railway Magazine* headed 'Was Stephenson the Father of Railways?'[452] He recounted and re-examined the same facts that had been contained in William Henry James's letters to the *Mining Journal* in 1857, though – probably deliberately – he did not refer to Ellen Paine's book. He ended:

Men of the highest position and experience in the railway world are bethinking themselves of the duty that devolves upon them of recognising the genius and farsightedness of Mr William James as the pioneer of railway enterprise in this country ... It is proposed to erect a statue to Mr James's memory either in the City of Liverpool or the City of Manchester, which surely owe him a debt of the deepest gratitude.

An even greater honour, Dodds understood, was being sought from the authorities, namely a tablet in Westminster Abbey alongside Robert Stephenson's tomb. And he concluded that the answer to the question he had posed in the title of his article was a clear negative.

The article itself was widely reproduced and was favourably reviewed in both the *Liverpool Courier* and the *Manchester Courier*, which, Dodds concluded in a second article, was 'testimony in favour of Mr James of the highest possible value.'[453] Most illuminating was the reaction of the *Newcastle Leader*, a journal that might have been expected to take a partisan line. A piece entitled 'A rival to Stephenson' was generous in its assessment of James, warmly supporting the idea of the statue and the tablet.

No one will begrudge the memory of Mr James these tributes of honour ... The inception of the railway was an achievement of such merit that there is glory enough for all of those who had a share in the great work.

But sadly, like the 'Testimonial' of 1846, these grand proposals never went further. Next year the family shelved them because of public preoccupation with the Boer War.[454] Sir Edward Watkin had planned to read a paper to launch the appeal, but at the age of 80 his health was failing, and early in 1901 he died. Without his pugnacious and charismatic leadership, the project, and William James's reputation, evaporated.

TWENTY ONE

Re-assessment

HOSE who, like his daughter, look for a conspiracy theory behind James's historical eclipse can find much to support their case, with George Stephenson and Samuel Smiles as the main culprits. James showed Stephenson generous admiration and in return the latter ruthlessly exploited the openings that James made for him. But his crime was really only one of ingratitude; to people of James's background, Stephenson was guilty above all of bad manners.

If the alternative interpretation of history is based on the 'cock-up' theory, augmented by bad luck, James's life was littered with examples. His personal wealth was wrecked by the financial slump of 1816 and the subsequent restoration of convertibility, yet he did not try to escape the responsibilities arising from his bankruptcy. It was unfortunate that the revival of his fortunes was shattered by the economic meltdown of 1825. As Tom Rolt has pointed out, James was in some ways his own worst enemy.[455] On the one hand his actions were always inspired by the highest Christian (and masonic) motives, yet on the other hand he could be infuriatingly self-righteous. While he detested corruption, whether it was Vancouver's self-aggrandisement, auction rings, or Alfred Jenkin's double-dealing, his resentment often sounded sanctimonious.

Robert Stephenson, albeit one of James's greatest admirers, confided to Samuel Smiles that James was 'no thinker at all on the practical part of the subject he had taken up. It was the same with everything he touched. He never succeeded in anything.'[456] This is a gross over-simplification. An opposite and more recent view is that 'William James was a unique individual – he seemed to possess a genius in many areas of technological endeavour, and in the early years of his life undertook several successful projects.'[457] This echoes another opinion. 'He was not only one of the most successful men in his chosen profession and generally an astute business man,

but in his efforts to establish a railway system he took the trouble to acquaint himself with every new development or improvement in track and machinery.'[458]

But these things are relative, and it must be admitted that, as far as individual schemes were concerned, James's failures were greater than his successes. None the less, as Hugh Torrens points out in his foreword to this book, the study of failures is illuminating and instructive, not only to future pioneers but also to historians.

To what extent were James's failures his own fault? He was not, admittedly, a team player; he needed to be in sole charge of his endeavours. He succeeded on the Stratford Canal project where he had the authority of his majority shareholding. He was very successful on behalf of those land agency clients who could concentrate on the priorities which he had correctly identified. He would have been more successful in Cornwall if his plans had not been so ambitious, his patron less conservative, and her steward and her county neighbours less antagonistic.

His failure at Liverpool was due partly to factors outside his control, but also because he wilfully declined to concentrate on his brief, being diverted by his railway schemes at Bolton and elsewhere and by his investment in the Upper Avon. His physical absence from Canterbury meant that his sponsors came to a decision on their route which he would not have endorsed but which fitted in with George Stephenson's retrograde design philosophy. The Bexhill coal debacle was not his initiative, but one which he adopted as a response to a national emergency. His greatest project, the Central Junction Railway, was destroyed by lack of financial support and what would later be called the health-and-safety apparatchiks.

Above all, William James was a strategist, not a tactician. He would never have claimed to be an artisan. He painted on a broad canvas with a wide brush. His attitude to accounting, for example, was to concentrate on the pounds and to hell with the pence, a cavalier approach which certainly contributed to his bankruptcy and the misfortunes which subsequently afflicted him and his family. He tried, moreover, throughout his whole career, to juggle with too many balls at once. So did plenty of the great names who were his contemporaries. Among the good jugglers who succeeded, Telford and Robert Stephenson spring to mind. Among those who lacked the concentration or the knack, and who therefore dropped the balls, were Trevithick and James. The difference between these pairs is that, broadly speaking, Telford and Stephenson were executives who built to order, whereas Trevithick and James were visionaries whose executive capacity did not match their vision.

But all organisations – be they political, military or commercial – need people of vision, people who can anticipate the future and plan accordingly, people whose far-sightedness can inspire and motivate those responsible for executive action. Prophets can often be neglected by comparison with those who leave more tangible monuments of their achievements. In this respect I can do no better than quote Rolt's verdict on Ellen Paine's claim, endorsed by Edward Pease among others, that it was William James, not George Stephenson, who was the real Father of Railways.[459]

At a time when such a conception must have appeared to his contemporaries as fantastic as space travel, James had a clear vision of an England seamed with locomotive railways. Moreover he cried that vision in the wilderness with such fanatical persistence that willy-nilly he conditioned the minds of even the most sceptical Englishmen to accept the *idea* of railways. By doing so he undoubtedly paved the way for the railway revolution even though he played no part in that revolution when it came.

As it turned out, Ellen Paine's biography, written with the motive of restoring James's reputation, proved to be the biggest hurdle to achieving that end. Biased, embittered and unstructured, it has been the primary source for nearly all subsequent writers who have tried to put James into his historical perspective. He deserves better. If he did not succeed in his visionary projects, if he had all too many failures and disappointments, he should now be given due recognition – as he was in his lifetime – for his crusade to modernise the inland transport of the Industrial Revolution. One fact is undeniable. No other single person had a greater involvement in the gestation of the railway system during the crucial decade of 1820–1830. As a planner, promoter, surveyor, inventor, devisor of parliamentary Bills and advocate of steam locomotion, William James's contribution was unique. He was a giant, albeit with feet of clay, and he should be remembered as arguably the greatest visionary of his age.

APPENDIX A

The Patents

WILLIAM JAMES and his eldest son took out seven patents relating to improvements to railways and the use of steam power on roads, and five on unrelated topics. Apart from the first, they were filed in the name of William Henry James who was a qualified engineer, but there is little doubt that the inspiration for many of them came from his father.

Registering a patent for an invention protects the originator from plagiarists for a limited period of time; it also allows the inventor to make money by licencing its use to third parties. At the time we are concerned with, registration was an expensive business, costing £100 to cover England alone, with further charges for Scotland and Ireland, added to which was the cost of lithographic plates for diagrams. Nor did the Patent Office carry out any searches to establish whether the patent did or did not represent genuine novelty. The high cost was largely to deter time-wasting cranks. Until 1852, when a new Patent Act came into force, there were at least no annual renewal fees. After that date, the initial filing cost was reduced to £25 but an additional £150 was payable over the life of the patent – usually 17 years.

James saw that railways faced a number of operational problems which would only increase in magnitude as they developed, while his son concentrated on improving steam carriages on roads. The scope and ingenuity of their patents is remarkable and they deserve greater recognition. Most were, for their day, so impractical that only one was taken up during the inventors' lifetimes. But the concepts behind many of them were far ahead of their time and would later be incorporated in machinery that became accepted practice.

The following pages summarise only the most significant patents.[460] For the record, the following minor patents were also filed by William Henry James:

7520 (1837) Signalling apparatus (quickly superseded by the electric telegraph)

7637 (1838) Machines for weighing substances and liquids

7854 (1838) Apparatus for heating and cooling liquids

10,784 (1845) Manufacture of plates and vessels for heating purposes

14,283 (1852) Apparatus connected with heating and refrigeration¶

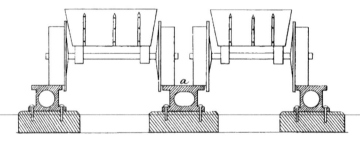

Patent No. 4913 (WJ 1824)
Hollow cast-iron rails and their uses

THE BASIS of this invention was to cast rails in the form of hollow tubes with a flat running surface. Cast iron being weak in tension but strong under compression, the tubular configuration, it was claimed, would markedly improve the load-bearing capability. The patent covered other ancillary advantages:

a) The top surface could be made wide enough to allow sets of waggon wheels (with inside bearings) to pass each other as they travelled in opposite directions. Supported by suitable frames, the hollow rail could also be used in monorails.

b) The continuous tube thus formed could be used to transport liquids (or even gases) like a conventional pipeline. James may have been influenced by the work of the Stone Pipe Company which had set up operations at a quarry above Cheltenham, on the route of his proposed branch off the Central Junction Railway.

The *Register of Arts and Sciences* for 26 March 1825, in a fulsome review of this patent, said that it was 'well entitled to the attentive consideration of the public', the patentee being 'a gentleman who has been for a series of years engaged in the construction of rail-road communications . . . and in the working of mines.' But this is a whimsical and surely expensive design, difficult to maintain, and by 1824 cast-iron rails were already outdated.

Patent No. 4957 (WHJ 1824)
Four-wheel drive for steam road carriages

THE PROBLEM addressed by this invention was the dragging of the outer wheel on a rigid-axle steam road carriage when going round any sort of corner, particularly when the radius was tight and the wheels had narrow treads. James's solution was to fit a separate steam engine (cylinder and crank-axle) to drive each wheel, with the added refinement of linking the regulator of each engine to the steering mechanism. His patent was rendered redundant by the invention of the differential gearbox, but the basic concept – using either electric or hydraulic motors – would be used in the 20th century for specialised vehicles, including the Moon Buggy. W. H. James reverted to the concept of a multi-cylinder divided-drive layout for his carriage built in 1829 for Sir James Anderson, but now the power was concentrated on the rear axle only (see Chapter 18).

Patent No. 5117 (WHJ 1825)
Construction of railway carriages and rails

THIS IS probably the Jameses' most far-sighted and visionary patent. Whereas the previous one was uniquely applicable to cornering road locomotives, there were related problems for railway locomotives and their trains as they became heavier and faster, with greater horsepower being delivered to the rails. Although contemporary locomotives travelled only at a fast walking pace, James could envisage that speeds of 30 mph would soon be possible, and this merely a stepping stone to very much higher ones when the frictional drag between wheel and rail on the outside of a curve, even of relatively large radius, would be significant, enough to damage the rail as the outer wheel on a rigid axle had to skid to catch up the shorter distance travelled by the inner wheel.

The solution proposed was to use profiled wheels incorporating three different diameters, riding on rails – at curves – with a complementary stepped profile. The Jameses were anticipating a problem that would be alleviated by the introduction of superelevation when laying high-speed track on curves, but the problem of the deterioration of rail surfaces due to the skidding of wheels (gauge-cracking) would become a very real concern, culminating in the notorious Hatfield crash of 2000.

The second problem addressed was that of distributing the power of a locomotive over a longer length of the track. As the weight and power of locomotives increased, it would be difficult to deliver this power to the track without either overloading or slipping. The solution was elegantly simple: distribute the power along the whole length of a train by driving every axle. This involved a series of longitudinal drive shafts supported by bearings under each waggon or carriage, with bevel gears to each axle and an ingenious form of universal joint where the vehicles were coupled together. Individual axle-loadings would be kept low while adhesion would be maximized, with potentially huge advantages for tackling gradients.

The original patent drawing showed no locomotive and a half-scale model, demonstrated at Mr Crowther's timber yard in Birmingham in 1825, was powered by a hand-crank.[461] The illustration in Elijah Galloway's *History of the Steam Engine* (1830), which is reproduced below, shows an imaginary locomotive as motive power. The model was capable of tackling gradients as steep as 1 in 12, and 'this mode of communicating the impulse of the prime mover to all the carriages of a train seems to be well deserving of the attention of engineers.'

In its original form, James's concept of 'all-wheel' drive would be accompanied by severe problems of friction, wear, and lubrication; but it would be the basis of every modern multiple-unit train powered by axle-hung electric motors, and in the steam era

A

B

C

D

Patent no. 5117

A: the carriage wheels are running in a straight line, consequently the peripheries are equal, and the bearings of the rail equal.

B: The wheels are making a curve equal to an increase of half an inch in a yard on the outer track.

C: The wheels and other parts are adapted to make a turn, where the curve makes a difference in the two lines of two-thirds of an inch in the yard.

D: A curve wherein the difference is one inch.

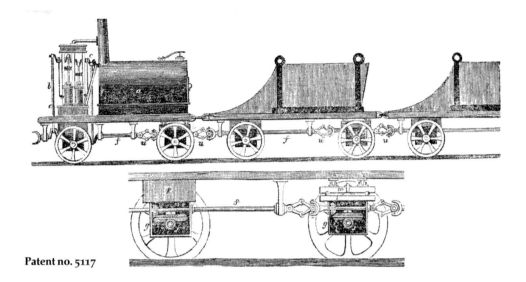

Patent no. 5117

was applied to the Shay, Climax and Heisler geared locomotives that powered the North American logging industry. William Henry James would return to the concept in his patent No. 10,411 of 1844

Patent No. 5176 (WHJ 1825)
Apparatus for diving underwater

THE CONSTRUCTION of docks, harbours and large bridges would be facilitated if men could work freely beneath the surface of the water, without the restrictions of a diving bell or air-lines from a supply on the surface. James's patent can be seen as the precursor of the modern scuba-diving, air-bottle apparatus. The diver would wear an integral copper helmet and rubberised jacket, made water/air tight by elasticated bands around the waist and the upper arms. Compressed air was contained in a large, doughnut shaped iron cylinder that was strapped around the diver's waist, with a breathing tube connected (via a valve at the diver's manual control) to a mouthpiece in the helmet. A spring-loaded valve on the top of the helmet was supposed to allow exhausted air to be blown out. The specification stated that the apparatus 'may be employed with perfect safety and great advantage in mines or other places filled with deleterious gases', but on land the weight of the compressed air vessel would have been intolerable.

Patent No. 5186 (WHJ 1825)
Self-cleaning water-tube boiler

WILLIAM HENRY JAMES realised that the boiler for a practical steam road-locomotive should be as light and compact as possible, while at the same time generating high-pressure steam with speed and safety. He was convinced, along with many other like-minded pioneers, that these objectives could best be met by water-tube boilers in which the steam pressure was contained within heated tubes rather than the boiler barrel itself. Even in the 1820s metal tubes could be made to contain pressures of 1,000psi or more, a figure unthinkable for conventional boilers.

The bugbear for all such boilers was that ordinary water deposits lime-scale when it boils, building up layers of encrustation which reduce thermal conductivity and block the flow of water – the common problem of furring in kettles and domestic hot-water systems. James's unique solution was to a boiler in which the tubes consisted of a series of interconnected circular rings with the furnace contained within, but mounted on slide bars so that the grate could be completely withdrawn when tube cleaning was necessary. Each tube would contain a quantity of 'scouring pebbles' and, when cleaning was required, the water and steam pipes would be disconnected, the furnace withdrawn and the whole assembly rotated and vibrated, so that the pebbles would break up the accumulated scale and the detritus could be flushed out with fresh water. This was the eventual outcome of the patent anticipated in the partnership agreement of 1821 with Losh and Stephenson (see Chapter 10).

James certainly incorporated a boiler of this design in his steam carriage built for Sir James Anderson in 1829, but the cleaning process, perhaps not surprisingly, did not work in practice. A subsidiary benefit of the design was that the steam generated would be very effectively superheated, imparting, to use James's own expression, greater 'elasticity'. Galloway claimed to have witnessed one of the boilers at work, measuring 3ft 6in by 20in diameter and generating steam at 150psi within 15 minutes of 'inserting the fire within the furnace.'

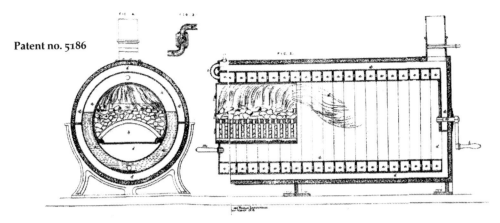

Patent no. 5186

Patent No. 6297 (WHJ 1832)
Improvements to the design of steam carriages etc

THE SPECIFICATION covers a number of distinct inventions within the overall design of a steam road tractor or tug:

a) Three separate drive-trains using continuous chains over pulleys of different diameters, thereby allowing three different gearing ratios to the rear wheels.[462] This anticipates to some extent the multi-gear mechanisms on modern bicycles, but gear-changing could only be performed when the vehicle was stationary.

b) Separate mechanical clutches activated automatically by the steering mechanism, so that on turning the front wheels the power is concentrated entirely on the driving-wheel on the outside of the curve. The concept is used in modern tanks and other tracked machinery, but with friction clutches or epicyclic gearboxes.

c) A water-tube boiler formed from several thick plates of iron with frequent holes drilled through them, connected in series by elbow joint tubes: a low-cost way of making a nest of closely-packed tubes without addressing the inherent problem of internal scaling.

Patent No. 9473 (WHJ 1842)
Elevated and pneumatic underground railways

THIS ELABORATE patent breaks completely novel ground, introducing concepts far removed from conventional rails laid at ground level. The first part deals with an elevated track consisting of multiple iron rods supported on iron or wooden frames over existing roads or railways. The rods are maintained in tension by heavy weights and pulleys, and in one version the weight of a standard-width carriage is spread over rollers rather than individual wheels. By tensioning the rail-rods rather like a guitar string,

Patent no. 6297
Elevation of James's
steam road-tug.
The 3-speed gearbox
included is believed to
be the earliest example
of such a device.

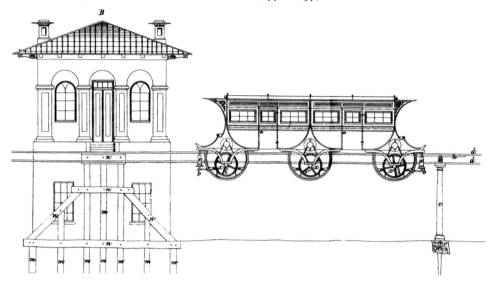

the need for continuous support was supposedly removed, resulting in a relatively light-weight support structure. The inherent drawbacks seem self-evident.

The second part concerns itself with the high-speed transmission of mail via parallel underground tubes between distant sites. Along the tube network a series of air-pumps would provide partial vacuum in advance of the mail 'shuttle' and positive pressure behind it. The tubes could be of any practical diameter, say 18 inches, and intermediate drop-off points could be achieved by appropriate valves, deflecting baffles and 'sidings'. This was no novelty. By 1842 the idea of the totally enclosed pneumatic tube had been around for over thirty years, and Samuda and Clegg's atmospheric railway had been under trial for two.

Patent No. 10,411 (WHJ 1844)
Regulating the speed of trains

EXCESSIVE SPEED and break-away carriages were already the cause of numerous contemporary accidents, spreading alarm among politicians and the travelling public. The problem was likely to be exacerbated on lines with relatively steep gradients. James's proposal was to use centrifugal governors (as used to control the speed of stationary steam engines) fitted to individual locomotives and/or carriages. In the case of the former, spring-loaded rods would be connected to the regulator, and in the latter case to the brakes. A particularly convenient drive to his governors could be taken off the transmission of his multiple-unit trains as proposed in patent no.5117.

This patent combines the use of proven components, the only novelty being the way they are made to interact with one another. The concept anticipates 'cruise-control' devices on modern cars. Perhaps the most intriguing aspect of the patent lies in the design of the locomotive shown in the accompanying drawing, with its four-cylinder 'V' configuration which anticipates the Heisler locomotives of Erie, Pennsylvania, by nearly 50 years.

APPENDIX B

Subscription list for 'ESMP'

Source: Ellen Paine to Lord Bagot, 1866,
Univ..of London Goldsmith's Library, I1.861

Name	£	s	d	Note
Lord Hatherton	1	11	0	
'A good Engineer'	16	0	0	
The Hon. Jack Percy	1	5	0	
Mrs J. E. Chambers	5	0	0	
Henry Adhams Esq.	5	0	0	
Frederick J. Welch Esq.	1	7	6	
E. Luchin (?)	1	0	0	
Talbot Dawes Esq. MD	1	0	0	1
J. B. Melsom Esq. MD		7	6	
Samuel Berry Esq. MD	1	0	0	
Lord Ebury	1	0	0	
W. Bagnall Esq.	1	0	0	2
James Bagnall Esq.	4	10	6	3
Thomas Bagnall Esq.	6	0	0	4
Mrs Hearson		8	6	5
R. Barnes Esq		10	6	6
Henry Pease MP		10	6	7
J. Pease JP		7	6	
Matthew Milchamp JP		7	6	
A. Greenaway Esq Banker		10	6	
Louis Lloyd Esq Banker		10	6	
Shelmore Ashby Banker		10	6	

Name	£	s	d	Note
Edward Greaves late MP	3	3	0	
J. Greaves JP		7	6	
R Greaves Esq Banker	1	0	0	8
J Smithson Esq	1	0	0	9
J Haunton	1	0	0	10
J G Wise	2	0	0	11
Lord Redesdale	10	7	6	
(6 members of Royal College of Surgeons)	3	17	6	
The Earl of Clarendon		10	6	
The Earl of Essex		10	6	
The Earl of Effingham		10	6	
The Earl of Verulam		10	6	
Lord Abergavenny		10	6	
Viscount Falmouth		10	6	
Lord Harris		7	6	
Lord Londis		10	6	
Lord Gage		10	6	
Lord Hardwicke	2	0	0	
Sir John Kirkland		7	6	
Lord Willoughby de Broke		10	6	
Lord Cathrope		10	6	
The Earl of Chichester		10	6	
The Earl of Shaftesbury	2	0	0	
T. E. Ewart MP		7	6	
William Ewart MP		7	6	
G. Glynn MP		10	6	12
Sir R Barry MP		10	6	
Sir Roland Hill	5	0	0	13
James Russell Esq.	1	0	0	
Wesley Richards Esq.	1	0	0	
John Hawkshaw Esq.		10	6	14
William Gale Esq.		10	6	15
W. H. Cutler Esq.		5	0	16
R. Rawlinson Esq.		10	6	17
Walter Gale Esq.	2	0	0	18
Samuel Briggs Esq.	1	1	0	
Jervis Smith Esq.		10	6	
T. R. Crampton Esq.		10	6	19
John Bragden Esq	1	0	0	
The Earl of Devon	1	0	0	
Thos. Davis MRCS	1	0	0	
Lord Bagot	1	0	0	
TOTAL	**£98**	**4**	**0**	

Notes

1 Coroner
2 Coal & Iron Master (1797–1863)
3 Coal & Iron Master (1804–1872)
4 Landed Gentleman of Newberries Park, Watford (1799–1863)
5 Late of Rickmansworth Park
6 The Grove, Rickmansworth
7 Son of Edward Pease
8 Son of John Greaves
9 The Priory, Warwick
10 Warwick
11 The Woodcotes, Warwick
12 Cornwall client.
13 Postal Reformer
14 Chartered Eng.
15 Chartered Eng.
16 Chartered Eng.
17 Chartered Eng.
18 Indian Peninsular Railway
19 Locomotive designer

Family Trees

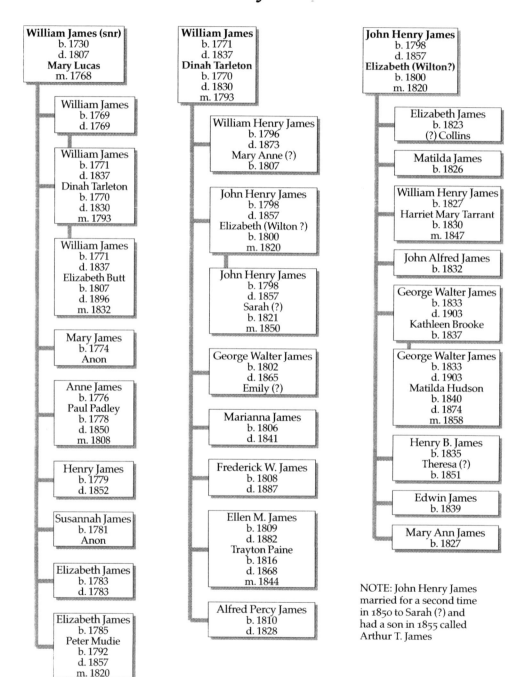

William James (snr)
b. 1730
d. 1807
Mary Lucas
m. 1768

William James
b. 1769
d. 1769

William James
b. 1771
d. 1837
Dinah Tarleton
b. 1770
d. 1830
m. 1793

William James
b. 1771
d. 1837
Elizabeth Butt
b. 1807
d. 1896
m. 1832

Mary James
b. 1774
Anon

Anne James
b. 1776
Paul Padley
b. 1778
d. 1850
m. 1808

Henry James
b. 1779
d. 1852

Susannah James
b. 1781
Anon

Elizabeth James
b. 1783
d. 1783

Elizabeth James
b. 1785
Peter Mudie
b. 1792
d. 1857
m. 1820

William James
b. 1771
d. 1837
Dinah Tarleton
b. 1770
d. 1830
m. 1793

William Henry James
b. 1796
d. 1873
Mary Anne (?)
b. 1807

John Henry James
b. 1798
d. 1857
Elizabeth (Wilton ?)
b. 1800
m. 1820

John Henry James
b. 1798
d. 1857
Sarah (?)
b. 1821
m. 1850

George Walter James
b. 1802
d. 1865
Emily (?)

Marianna James
b. 1806
d. 1841

Frederick W. James
b. 1808
d. 1887

Ellen M. James
b. 1809
d. 1882
Trayton Paine
b. 1816
d. 1868
m. 1844

Alfred Percy James
b. 1810
d. 1828

John Henry James
b. 1798
d. 1857
Elizabeth (Wilton?)
b. 1800
m. 1820

Elizabeth James
b. 1823
(?) Collins

Matilda James
b. 1826

William Henry James
b. 1827
Harriet Mary Tarrant
b. 1830
m. 1847

John Alfred James
b. 1832

George Walter James
b. 1833
d. 1903
Kathleen Brooke
b. 1837

George Walter James
b. 1833
d. 1903
Matilda Hudson
b. 1840
d. 1874
m. 1858

Henry B. James
b. 1835
Theresa (?)
b. 1851

Edwin James
b. 1839

Mary Ann James
b. 1827

NOTE: John Henry James married for a second time in 1850 to Sarah (?) and had a son in 1855 called Arthur T. James

Abbreviations used in the bibliography and references

BL   British Library
DNB   *Dictionary of National Biography*
EMSP   Biography of James by his daughter Ellen
    Matilda Steward James, pub'd 1861 – page 8
ER1   J. Rees and A. Guy (eds), *Early Railways 1*. 2001
ER2   M. J. T. Lewis (ed.), *Early Railways 2*. 2003
ER3   M. R. Bailey (ed.), *Early Railways 3*. 2006
LRO   Liverpool Record Office
NLW   National Library of Wales, Aberystwyth
PRO   Public Record Office (National Archives)
RCHS   Railway & Canal Historical Society
VCH   *Victoria County History*
WRO   Warwick Record Office

Adderley, H. A., *History of the Warwickshire Yeomanry Cavalry*, 1912

Addyman, J. and Haworth, V., *Robert Stephenson; Railway Engineer*, 2006

Albert, W., *The Turnpike Road System in England 1663–1840*, 1972

Atkinson, G., *The Canal Duke's Collieries*, 1998

Bailey, M. R. (ed.), *Robert Stephenson – The Eminent Engineer*, 2003

Barton, D. B., *Redruth & Chasewater Railway*, 1966

Basnett, L., 'The first public railway in Lancashire', *Trans. Lancashire and Cheshire Antiquarian Soc.*, Vol.62, 1951, pp.157–80

Baxter, B., *Stone Blocks and Iron Rails*, 1966

Bick, D., *The Gloucester & Cheltenham Tramroad*, 1987

Biddle, G., *The Railway Surveyors*, 1990

Billingham, N., *Stratford Canal*, 2002

Billingham, N., 'Andrew Yarranton and the Industrial Revolution', *Canal & Riverboat*, January 2004

Billingham, N., 'William James: the man who killed the canals', *Canal & Riverboat*, April 2004

Bird, A., *Roads & Vehicles*, 1969

Boase, G. C., *Collectanea Cornubiensia*, 1890

Bolton, R. & P., *A Wellesbourne Guide*, 1989

Boyes, G., 'The Exchequer Bill Loan Commissioners as a source of canal railway finance', *Jnl. RCHS*, Vol.24, 1978, pp.85–92

Boyes, G., 'Railway Bills not enacted, 1799–1830', *RCHS Tramroad Group Occasional Paper 85*, 1994

Boyes, G., 'An alternative railway technology', in *ER1*, 2001, pp.192–207

Boynton, J., *Shakespeare's Railways*, 1994

Broadbridge S. R., *The Birmingham Canal Navigations, Vol.1 1768–1846*, 1974

Buckley, J.A., *The Cornish Mining Industry*, 2002

Burton, A., *Richard Trevithick*, 2000

Burton, A., *The Rainhill Story*, 1980

Carlson, R. F., *The Liverpool & Manchester Railway Project 1821–31*, 1969

Charlton, L.G., *The First Locomotive Engineers*, 1974

Chester-Browne, R., *The other sixty miles*, 1991

Daunton, M.J., *Progress and Poverty*, 1995

Davies, H., *George Stephenson*, 1975

Davies, J., *Shakespeare's Avon*, 1996

Dickinson, H. W. and Lee, A., 'The Rastricks – Civil Engineers', *Trans. Newcomen Soc.*, Vol.4, 1923–4, pp.48–63

Donaghy, T. J., *Liverpool & Manchester Railway Operations 1831–1845*, 1972

Down, C. G. and Warrington, A. J., *The History of the Somerset Coalfield*, 1972

Ellis, C. Hamilton, *British Railway History 1830–1876*, 1954.

EMSP (Ellen Paine, née James), *The Two James's and The Two Stephensons*, 1861, reprint 1961

Evans, F. T., 'Steam Road Carriages of the 1830s: why did they fail?', *Trans. Newcomen Soc.*, Vol.70, 1998–9, pp.1–27

Evans, J., *A Lancashire Triangle*, 2003

Fellows, R. B., *History of the Canterbury & Whitstable Railway*, 1930

Fletcher, W., *Steam on Common Roads*; reprint 1972

Forbrooke, T. D., *Abstract of Records and Manuscripts respecting the County of Gloucester*, 1807

Fortesque, M. T., *History of Calwich Abbey*, 1915

Gale, W. K. V., *The British Iron and Steel Industry*, 1967

Garfield, S., *The Last Journey of William Huskisson*, 2002

Gibb, A., *The Story of Telford*, 1935

Girouard, M., *The English Town*, 1990

Gould, S., *The Somerset Coalfield*, 1999

Guy, A., 'North-Eastern locomotive pioneers 1805 to 1827', in *ER1*, pp.117–44

Hadfield, C. and Norris J., *Waterways to Stratford*, 1962

Hart, B., *The Canterbury & Whitstable Railway*, 1991

Haworth, V., 'George Stephenson, 1781–1848', in Jarvis A. (ed.), *Nineteenth Century Business Ethics: papers presented at the Merseyside Maritime Museum*, 1992

Haworth, V., *Robert Stephenson; the making of a prodigy*, 2004

Herold, C., *The Age of Napoleon*, 1963

Hilton, B., *Corn, Cash, Commerce*, 1977

Holt, J., *General View of the Agriculture of the County of Lancaster*, 1795

Hopkin, D. W., 'Reflections on the iconography of early railways', in *ER1*, pp.342–54

Jackman, W. T., *The development of Transportation in Modern England*, 1966

Jarvis, A., 'The story of the story of the life of George Stephenson', in D. Smith (ed.), *Perceptions of Great Engineers*, 1994, pp.35–45

Jastram, R., *The Golden Constant*, 1977

Jeaffreson, J. C., *Life of Robert Stephenson*, 1864

Jenkin, A., *News from Cornwall*, 1951

Jenkins, S. C. and Carpenter, R. S., *The Shipston-on-Stour Branch*, 1997

Johnson, P., *The Birth of the Modern – World Society 1815–1830*, 1991

Keast, J. *The King of Mid-Cornwall*, 1982

Kidner, R., 'Chirk Castle and the Tramroads', *RCHS Tramroad Group Occasional Paper 66*, 1990

Layson, J. F., *George Stephenson; the Locomotive and the Railway*, 1881

Lead, P., *Agents of Revolution*, 1989

Lee, C. E., *The Evolution of Railways*, 1943

Lee, C. E., *Early Railways in Surrey*, 1944

Lewis, J., 'What happened to the Glynns of Cardinham?', *Jnl. of Royal Institute of Cornwall*, 2002, pp.50–63

Lewis, M. J. T., *Early Wooden Railways*, 1970

Lewis, M. J. T., 'Bar to fish-belly: the evolution of the cast-iron edge rail', in *ER2*, 1970, pp.102–17

Macnair, M., 'The patents of William James and William Henry James', *Jnl. RCHS*, Vol.35, 2005, pp.194–6, and subsequent issues

Malet, H., *Coal, Cotton & Canals*, 1990

Marshall, C. F. Dendy, *A History of British Railways down to the year 1830*, 1938

Marshall, C. F. Dendy, *A History of Railway Locomotives down to the end of the year 1831*, 1953

Marshall, J., *Biographical Dictionary of Railway Engineers*, 2003

May, T. E., *The Constitutional History of Great Britain*, 3rd ed. 1871

Morgan, P., 'The Warwickshire Yeomanry in the 19th Century', *Dugdale Soc. Occ. Papers No. 36*, 1994

Mountford, C. E., 'The Hetton Railway', in *ER3*, pp.76–95

Norris, J., *The Stratford & Moreton Tramway*, 1987

Pearce, T. R., *The Locomotives of the Stockton & Darlington Railway*, 1996

Pease, A. E., *Diaries of Edward Pease*, 1907

Pendered, M. L. and J. Mallett, J., *Princess or Pretender*, 1939

Phillips, C. J., *History of the Sackville Family*, 1929

Pigott, H., *Private Correspondence of a Woman of Fashion*, 1832

Pocock, T., *The Terror before Trafalgar*, 2002

Priestley, J., *Historical Account of the Navigable Canals, Rivers and Railways of Great Britain*, 1831, reprint 1969

Rattenbury, G. and Lewis, M. J. T., *Merthyr Tydfil Tramroads and their Locomotives*, 2004

Rees, J., 'The Strange Story of the *Steam Elephant*', in *ER1*, pp.145–70

Rees, J. and Guy, A., 'Richard Trevithick & Pioneer Locomotives', in *ER3*, pp.191–220

Repcheck, J. *The Man who found Time*, 2003

Reynolds, P. R., 'Paul Padley', *Jnl RCHS*, Vol.23, 1977, pp.21–3

Rolt, L. T. C., *Thomas Telford*, 1958

Rolt, L. T. C., *George & Robert Stephenson – The Railway Revolution*, 1960

Rowson, S., 'When did the Merthyr Tramroad become the Penydarren Tramroad?', *Jnl RCHS*, Vol.34, 2003, pp.310–15

Serres, O. W., *Letters, Poems and Memoirs of Earl Broke of Warwick*, 1819

Simmons, J., 'For and against the locomotive', *Jnl of Transport History*, Vol.2, 1956, pp.144–51

Simmons, J. and Biddle, G (eds), *Oxford Companion to British Railway History*, 1956

Skeat, W., *George Stephenson – The engineer and his letters*, 1973

Smiles, S., *The Life of George Stephenson*, 1857 and many subsequent and differing editions including *Lives of the Engineers*, Vol.3, 1862, and the New York edition of 1868

Spring, D., 'English landowners and nineteenth-century industrialism', in Ward, J. T. and Wilson, R. G. (eds), *Land and Industry*, pp.12–62, 1857

Stevenson, R., *Report relative to various lines of Railway from the coal-field of Mid-Lothian*, Edinburgh, 1819

Stevenson, R. (ed.), 'Essays on Rail-roads', in *Prize-Essays and Transactions of the Highland Society*, Vol.6, 1819, pp.1–146

Symons, M. V., *Coal Mining in the Llanelli Area*, Vol.1, 1979

Thomas, D. St J., *Regional History of the Railways of Great Britain*, Vol.1, 1973

Thomas, G., *Records of the Militia from 1757*, 1993

Thomas, R. H. G., *The Liverpool & Manchester Railway*, 1980

Todd, A. C., *Beyond the Blaze, a biography of Davies Giddy (Gilbert)*, 1967

Toghill, P., *Geology of Britain*, 2000

Tomlinson, W. W., *The North Eastern Railway: its rise and development*, reprint 1967

Torrens, H., 'Coal hunting at Bexhill 1805–1811 – How the new science of stratigraphy was ignored', *Sussex Archaeological Collections*, Vol.136, 1998, pp.177–91

Torrens, H., *William Smith (1769–1839) and the search for raw materials*, 2003

Tyler, N. 'Trevithick's Circle', *Trans. Newcomen Soc.*, Vol.77, 2007, pp.101–13

Vancouver, J., *A Memoir*, 1825

Vaughn, A., *Railwaymen, Politics and Money*, 1997

Veitch, G. S., *The Struggle for the Liverpool & Manchester Railway*, 1930

Vivian, J. L., *The Visitations of Cornwall*, 1874

Ward, J. R., *The finance of canal building in the 18th century*, 1974

Warren J. G. H., *A Century of Locomotive Building*, reprint 1970

Webb, S. and B., *The Story of the King's Highway*, 1913, reprint 1963

Welham, R.C. *Henley-in-Arden; Life from the Past*, 1993

Whetmath, C. F. D., *The Bodmin & Wadebridge Railway*, 1994

Whishaw, F., *The Railways of Great Britain and Ireland*, 1840

Williams, E., *Early Holborn and the Legal Quarter of London*, 1927

Wood, N. A., *Practical Treatise on Railroads*, 1825

Worth, M. *Sweat and Inspiration*, 1999

Young, R., *Timothy Hackworth and the Locomotive*, 1975

INTRODUCTION
1. Ellis 1954, pp.432, 22
2. Biddle 1990, p.25
3. Simmons and Biddle 1997, p.237
4. Hadfield and Norris 1962, pp.85, 5
5. VCH Staffordshire, Vol.2, p.101
6. Vaughn 1997, p.50
7. Jackman 1966, p.509
8. Simmons 1956, p.144
9. Rolt 1958, p.157
10. Smiles 1857, p.158. By 1874 he had edited out most of the references to William James.
11. An exception is an article by Canon R. B. Fellows in The Locomotive, 15 March 1937

NOTES ON SOURCES
12. Jackman 1966, p.509

CHAPTER 1
13. A memorial plaque was unveiled by Prof Hugh Torrens on William James's birthday in 2003, in the presence of a number of his descendants. It can be seen on the exterior wall of the 'Yew Trees' on Henley-in-Arden High Street (plate 2b).
14. EMSP, p.7
15. LRO, 385JAM/5/1–7
16. ibid
17. EMSP, p7
18. Thomas 1980, p.247 n.5, quoting a biographical note of 1840 in the British Library.
19. Smiles 1862, p.190. 'Taking' is used in the sense of 'charming'.
20. LRO, 385JAM 6/4. Sir Edward Smythe was the second son of George Walter Smythe of Eske Hall, Co. Durham and Acton Burnell, Shropshire. He was four years older than James and in 1781 had married his cousin Catherine, the only child and heiress to Peter Holford of Wootton Hall.
21. EMSP, p.75
22. William James Snr sold the house and its estate to a Richard Williams (EMSP, p.6), who in turn sold it to a John Townshend of Chiswick some time before 1807 (Forbrooke 1807, pp.196–7). It is probable that at this time William James Snr also made over some properties in Warwick to his elder son.
23. Lead 1989, p.25
24. EMSP*, p.99
25. Fortesque 1915, p.38
26. Private communication from the Granville family
27. Little is known about the subsequent life of this child except that he became a civil engineer, married twice and had nine children (see Chapter 20).
28. EMSP*, pp.8–11

29. Girouard 1990, p.30
30. Jastram 1997, p.105–112

CHAPTER 2
31. WRO, CR1886
32. Serres 1819, p.4; WRO C920
33. Pendered and Mallett 1939, p.93
34. The addiction of the English gentry to gambling was a major factor in many a financial embarrassment. As an example of the sort of money staked on sporting events, the Sporting Magazine for July 1793 reported the results of a typical cricket match held at Lord's Ground, St Mary-le-bone, between teams arranged by Earl Winchilsea and G. Louch Esq for 1,000 guineas. The Earl's team won by three runs.
35. EMSP*, p.10
36. Adderley 1912, p.19; further background is given in Thomas 1993 and Morgan 1994. The Warwickshire Yeomanry were soon called into action to help suppress a bread riot at Pickard's Mill in Birmingham in June 1797. By 1800 they numbered 300 men and in September that year were again called out to quell another riot in Birmingham. The Regiment was to fight with great distinction in the South African War and both World Wars. In 1917, at Huj in Palestine, the Warwickshire Yeomanry conducted the last full-scale cavalry charge by any regiment in the British Army. The present author was privileged to serve with them for four years in the 1960s, buying his 'No. 1' uniform and spurs from the then Earl of Warwick.
37. EMSP, p.11. She had not been born by this time, so the tale may have been exaggerated in the telling.
38. EMSP*, p.11
39. WRO, CR1886/Box 418/TN293 (Letterbook A)
40. ibid
41. James was proposed by William Lester of Paddington Green and seconded by Joseph Champey and William Meredith. He paid a life subscription on 12 May 1802. His name last appears in the printed list for 1835. Address in 1808, Warwick and 5, New Boswell Court, Lincoln's Inn; from 1829, 3 Thavies Inn, London.
42. The site is now (2007) occupied by the Aylesford Hotel and Restaurant.
43. Confirmed by the Law Society and sundry correspondence of 1802–3 signed on behalf of 'James & Hughes'.
44. The Treaty with France, which was signed on 27 March at Amiens. It was rescinded in 1804
45. WRO, CR1886/Box 418/TN293 (Letterbook A)
46. Before the establishment of a

formal Stock Exchange, the sale of shares was arranged by adverts in local newspapers or by auctions conducted by specialist agents like Smith.
47. EMSP*, pp.13 and 20, confirmed by correspondence in WRO, CR1886/Box 418/TN293 (Letterbook A).
48. This trend accelerated in the second half of the 20th century. The 'Yew Trees' and its extensive gardens were bought by the Jewsbury family in 1944 for £12,000 and the house was sold in 1980 for £500,000. After a brief period as a hotel, it was divided into three residences. One of these was offered for sale in 2004 at £630,000.
49. WRO, CR1886/Box 418/TN1774 (First Letterbook)
50. EMSP, p.19
51. Atkinson 1998, p.5
52. ibid. By 1773, the combined population of Manchester and Salford stood at over 29,000 (Malet 1990, p.2).
53. Lead 1989, p.5
54. EMSP*, p.19
55. Atkinson 1998, p.14
56. EMSP, p.19
57. WRO, CR1886/Box 418/TN293 (Letterbook A)

CHAPTER 3
58. Henry Addington became Lord Sidmouth in 1805 and was Home Secretary at the time of the Peterloo massacre in 1819. J. Hiley Addington died of a 'mortification in his stomach' in June 1818 (Gentleman's Magazine that month).
59. This and all James's subsequent letters in this chapter are quoted from his two letterbooks 1802–06, WRO, CR1886/Box 418/ TN1774 and TN293, unless otherwise noted.
60. Anthony George Eckhardt was a prolific inventor, filing thirteen patents between 1771 and 1806. This particular invention may have been for 'Manufacturing pipes for conveyance of water underground'.
61. WRO, CR1886/Box 482A
62. There is a possibility that this man was the father of a daughter born in 1807: Elizabeth Butt was to play an important role in James's later life.
63. See also his letter to William Smith of 1801, quoted in Chapter 5. His opinion of some of his fellow land agents had not improved.
64. EMSP, p.96
65. John William Kershaw (Kirshaw). He was elected a member of the Geological Society in 1847 and became a part-owner of the Wilmcote quarries once owned by James.
66. Formerly known as Hooker's Court, it would later be pulled down

to make way for the Royal Courts of Justice.

67. WRO, CR1886 (James's expenses)

68. The following four paragraphs are based on James/Dartmouth correspondence in Stafford Record Office, D1778/V/1290 and D564/12/18, and WRO, CR1886/Box 418/TN293 (Letterbook A).

69. Symons 1979, pp.117–19, 206–7; Vancouver 1825, pp.58–68

70. WRO, CR1886/Box 420 (Statement of the Affairs of the Earl of Warwick)

71. This was one of the very earliest detailed maps of an English town, itemising each property by number with its owner and occupier. Copies are available (2007) from Warwick Record Office.

72. St John's House is now (2007) part of the County Museum and includes the museum of the Royal Warwickshire Regiment. James's fine house was demolished in the latter part of the 20th century. The only known photograph – of the frontage – is in *Around Warwick*, Frith Book Company, 2002, p.29.

73. Sale particulars prepared by James when he was considering putting it up for auction. Extracts by kind permission of the present owners.

74. EMSP, p.16. There is a slightly bizarre footnote to this saga. The *Gentleman's Magazine* for May 1808 records that 'John Smith, a fine youth about 16 years of age died of rabies in the house of Mr James at Trebinshun, having been bitten the previous January – along with ten other people – by a dog in Warwick'.

CHAPTER 4

75. Toghill 2000, introduction

76. Repcheck 2003. Hutton was a member of the respected Scottish Enlightenment group, but his radical theories did not receive greater attention at the time because his writing style was turgid. Even his supposedly popular work of the 1790s, *The Theory of the Earth*, was unreadable.

77. Torrens 1998, p.179

78. Given what was to happen later to William Smith and the way that unscrupulous people were to pirate his discoveries and claim them as their own, this warning was extraordinarily appropriate.

79. Torrens 1998, p.179

80. Much of the following saga is based on Torrens 1998. A summary of the entire episode was published in *The Standard*, 20 April 1889.

81. Gale 1967, pp.28–38. Worried about the potential shortage of timber for shipbuilding, successive governments had legislated to restrict the amount of wood used for charcoal burning. In most cases, however, the Wealden area was exempt.

82. James was appointed Gentleman Steward to the Manor of Bexhill in 1806. He continued to supervise annual Manor Courts until 1810 (private correspondence with William

F. Hedger, Bexhill historian).

83. Pocock 2002. Less flattering was the Prince of Wales's assessment of her as a 'very plain and cold-hearted woman' (Pigott 1832, Vol.1, p.110). Whitworth became a friend of the Duke of Dorset when the latter was ambassador to France in 1783, and later became a confidant of Marie-Antoinette.

84. Private correspondence with William F. Hedger. A letter from James to Forster dated 28 January 1806 (WRO, CR1886/Box 418/ TN293) suggests that a Mr G. Neville Thomson, a banker living in Andover, had expressed a wish to 'join a speculation' but subsequently declined to be involved in this one.

85. Centre for Kentish Studies, Maidstone, U269 E173/2

86. WRO, CR1886/Box 418/TN293

87. Torrens 1998, p.182

88. William Whitmore would later be James's chief engineer on the Stratford Canal. Correspondence between Sir Joseph Banks and Matthew Boulton in 1783 refers to Whitmore as being, among other things, a 'steel toy-maker' who had made the struts of a 'flying machine' for a Mr Miller (*Notes and Queries*, 24 February 1923).

89. Torrens 1998, note 80. Two years after James's death, Smith would write in his diary that he 'became acquainted with a Gentleman concerned for Lord Warwick's Clutton Colliery early in 1800 and permitted him to take a copy of my Geological Table 1799, but what use he made of it I never heard' (quoted by Torrens from W. Smith Archives, Oxford University Museum). In the light of the Bexhill debacle the answer might appear to be rather little, at least in the short term.

90. Phillips 1929, p.305

91. EMSP p.97. There is a minor mystery here. According to Ellen Paine, her father had 'possessed a large house' at Bexhill, but the property he advertised for sale in *Sussex Weekly Advertiser* on 17 July 1812 is more likely to have been Millbank House, possibly acquired by the mining company for James's accommodation, although during his intermittent visits to Sussex he probably stayed with Lord Whitworth and the Duchess.

92. Cambridge University Library, Add. MS 7918. The Geological Society had been founded more as a gentlemen's dining club than an association of scientists.

93. Stephen Winthrop, Scholar of St Johns College, Oxford; Lincolns Inn 1785; studied medicine Edinburgh and St Bartholomew's 1794–6; lived in Warwick 1803–10. He and Horner were in fact brothers-in-law, having both married daughters of Gamaliel Lloyd of Leeds.

94. Elected ordinary member 3 January 1812, admitted 21 February 1812, address (in 1820 list) 5 Boswell

Court, London, and West Bromwich, Staffs. Some writers have confused this election with another William James (1787–1861), fellow of Oriel College, Oxford. James contributed annually to the Society and donated a 'Section of the Strata at Wyken colliery, Coventry' 3 November 1815.

95. Torrens 2003, p.182

96. ibid p.165

CHAPTER 5

97. Webb 1963, Albert 1972. For coaches, Bird 1969

98. There were no really comparable organisations on the Continent, and the important role of the turnpike trusts in supporting the momentum of the Industrial Revolution in this country should not be underplayed.

99. Next year the figure was down below 6,000,000, and it declined every year after that, until the railways had achieved a complete monopoly. The last mail coach in the country made its final delivery at Thurso on 1 August 1874.

100. *VCH* Warwickshire, Vol.3, p.243

101. Marshall 1938, pp.175–81.

102. Worth 1999, p.21; Burton 2000, p.66–74; Fletcher 1891, p.48–57. As it turned out, steam haulage for passenger transport on common roads was to prove a blind alley because of opposition from vested competitive interests, crippling tolls imposed by the turnpike trusts, and the fear that it would frighten the horses, a mythology finally crystallised in the infamous Red Flag Acts of 1865 and 1878.

103. EMSP* p.18. She is referring to the diary then in the possession of her eldest brother but now sadly lost (see *Notes on Sources*).

104. For overviews, Lewis 1970, Marshall 1938, Lee 1943, Baxter 1966

105. Goodchild 2006, Lee 1944

106. Baxter 1966, pp.15, 34

107. EMSP*, pp.18–19

108. This statement came under searching scrutiny in *Backtrack*, Vol. 17 Nos 10–12, 2003. See also Rees and Guy 2006.

109. Its proper name is the Merthyr Tramroad, although popular parlance has long called it the Penydarren Tramroad as if it had been built and exclusively used by Penydarren ironworks; see Rowson 2003 for the background to the nomenclature.

110. The latest discussion of the evidence for the locomotive is Rattenbury and Lewis 2004, pp.51–5.

111. EMSP, p.37.

112. Smiles 1857, p.159

113. Tyler 2007

114. *Mechanics' Magazine*, Vol.46, 1847, p.308. The site was later covered by a building of University College, London, which bears an appropriate commemorative plaque.

115. Marshall 1953, pp.23–7. The locomotive was built by Hazeldine & Rastrick of Bridgnorth; John Urpeth Rastrick will figure again as the man

chosen 12 years later to build James's railway from Stratford-upon-Avon. See also Rees and Guy 2006, pp.197–9.
116. *The Engineer*, 4 March 1921, p.242
117. Todd 1967, p.91. The name *Catch-Me-Who-Can* is attributed to a suggestion from his heiress wife, for whom he changed his surname to Gilbert.
118. Apparently he did a detailed survey of a route in that year, but only in 1812 did James return to this project with a 'business plan'.
119. NLW, Chirk Castle MS F6053; EMSP*, pp.21; WRO CR1886/Box 418/TN293
120. EMSP, pp.21–2. Agar's widow, Anna-Maria Agar, will become a very important character in James's later career.
121. EMSP*, p.23

CHAPTER 6

122. WRO, CR1886/Box 482A
123. ibid
124. ibid
125. This may account for the fact that the Warwick archives still contain 190 of James's share certificates in the Stratford Canal dated 6 October 1813, plus ten 'Old Shares' on vellum with a note stating their value at the time was £1,500.
126. There would eventually be five collieries on the Earl of Warwick's estates around Clutton, two of importance (Frys Bottom and Greyfield) and three smaller (Burchells, Knapp Hill and Mooresland) (Down & Warrington 1972).
127. WRO, CR1886/BB813/Box 425
128. Serres 1819, p.40; WRO, C920. Olivia Serres was a controversial character, claiming to be the legitimate daughter of George III's, brother, the Duke of Cumberland. Another theory is that she was actually the daughter of the Earl of Warwick, swapped at birth for his first child born in 1771, who might have been in reality the boy-child of Robert Serres, an artist in Warwick.
129. WRO, Finch-Knightley papers, Packington 1977
130. EMSP p.16. She gives the sale value as £57,000. Unfortunately the manorial deeds were burnt in a fire at Packington Hall in the 20th century, so we have no further details of when James bought it. The sale particulars refer to the 'release from William James of Warwick Esq. and others', so James may have been the head of a syndicate rather than the sole proprietor.
131. 'Report on the mines and minerals existing in the estates of Tytherington and Itchington, the property of the Rt Hon Lord Willoughby de Broke,' 1809 (BL, Egerton MS2989)
132. LRO, 385JAM/3/1
133. LRO, 385JAM/5/7
134. Lee 1944
135. It was in fact extended, but only to Godstone, through a separate

company, the Croydon, Merstham & Godstone Railway authorised in 1803.
136. Priestley 1831, p.610
137. EMSP* p.22. Edward, 1st Baron Thurlow of Ashfield, 1731–1806
138. Lambeth Palace Archives, Doc 19 TR22. Over 70 letters to and from George Frere of Messrs Forster, Cooke and Frere, the Archbishop's solicitors, are in the Palace archives.
139. Nothing is known about the rest of his life, except that he died in 1828.
140. Sutro Library, San Francisco, Lib SG 2:9 1/3

CHAPTER 7

141. Billingham 2004a
142. Davies 1996, p.49
143. Hadfield and Norris 1962, Billingham 2002. See also Billingham 2004b
144. Broadbridge 1974, pp.22–4
145. Shakespeare Centre, Stratford-upon-Avon, Stratford Canal Papers, letter from S. Butler to J. Hill, 31 July 1792
146. Billingham 2002, p.124. The initial shareholder register makes interesting reading. No individual was allocated more than ten shares. Among them were the Duke of Dorset (who owned considerable land along the route), Court Dewes of Wellesbourne (though not at that stage Bernard Dewes), the Earl of Plymouth, and Sir Edward Smythe of Wootton Hall. Four members of the Perrott family at Fladbury owned twenty shares between them. John Tarleton, Dinah James's brother, owned five, while another William James of Henley-in-Arden, an innkeeper, one.
147. Stratford-upon-Avon RO, DR574/548
148. WRO, CR1886/Box 418 (James Letterbook)
149. Priestley 1831, p.603. This classic work of reference was based on a study of all the relevant Acts of Parliament, not on fieldwork. Priestley describes these branches as if they had been built.
150. *Mining Journal*, 26 December 1857. James had had a major fall-out with the Birmingham company about an alternative canal route along the river Tame from his South Staffordshire mines. They had promised to promote this link if James relinquished his interest, but when the enabling Bill was presented to Parliament they emasculated it to such an extent that it failed.
151. 'Report of the Committee of Works of the Stratford Canal Navigation.' The original is in the possession of the Canal Association; extracts are quoted by kind permission of the chairman, Clive Henderson.
152. His daughter wrote that he had spent £20,000 on the Stratford Canal (EMSP, p.15). This was probably an exaggeration. His shares would have cost him approximately £8,580 – if he had paid all his calls – though it is not known how many debentures he may have subscribed to as well. His

certificates for 171 of the 'new' £30 shares, bearing the date 1813, still lie in the WRO, CR1886/BB703, items 501–6. There are also 10 'old shares' in his name (numbers 514–523) with a handwritten note to say that they were 'worth £1,500'. This too is an exaggeration; the figure is what they had cost him.
153. Ward 1974, p.123
154. PRO, RAIL 875/3, various entries
155. PRO, RAIL 875/3
156. In 2001 this original plaque broke and fell off onto the A3400, luckily in the middle of the night. British Waterways restored the main structure in 2002–3 and mounted a cast-aluminium replica in its place. The original has been relocated on a wall alongside the canal.
157. The cast-iron plates from which the troughs were constructed are assumed to have been supplied by William Whitmore & Sons in Birmingham. A short branch off the Birmingham & Fazeley canal between Farmer's Bridge locks 7 and 8 led right into the Whitmore foundry on Newhall Street (Chester-Browne 1991, p.11).
158. Herold 1963, p.367
159. EMSP, p.98. It is possible that the Emperor may have heard of James in correspondence with Lord Whitworth.
160. Smiles 1857, p.160; EMSP*, p.72; *Railway Times*, 26 October 1839; *Mechanics' Magazine*, 7 September 1848, p.500
161. Hadfield and Norris 1962, p.90
162. ibid, p.88

CHAPTER 8

163. George Legge, Viscount Lewisham, 3rd Earl of Dartmouth (1755–1810). He married Lady Frances Finch, daughter of the Earl of Aylesford.
164. EMSP, p.24. This is probably another example of the daughter wishing to extol the father's high-minded character; the Earl probably never intended the offer to be a gift. Furthermore, Samuel Fereday had been mining into this seam at Ettingshall by the end of the previous century.
165. *VCH* Staffordshire, Vol.2, p.107. Sandwell Park was the Earl's seat.
166. EMSP*, p.95
167. Sale particulars, *Aris's Birmingham Gazette*, 26 April 1824
168. *Mechanics' Magazine*, Vol.31, 1839, pp.474–8
169. EMSP, p.16
170. LRO, 385JAM/6/1
171. Pease 1907, p.60
172. Hilton 1977, p.13. In 1812, the average price of corn had reached 126s per quarter, but an abundant harvest in 1813 meant that prices the following year fell to 74s. The intervention price of 80s was broached in the two years following the disastrous harvests of 1816, but over the next sixteen years general deflation kept market prices around 60s.
173. The significance of this initiative,

particularly as it affected canal and railway finance, is discussed authoritatively in Boyes 1978.

174. In the light of present-day obsessions with political correctness and politicians' conflicts of interest, it is amusing to speculate whether Vansittart declared his own interests in this respect.

175. WRO, CR1886/Box 902/32. Later documents show that by 1883 the net income had hardly increased at all, standing at £18,336, generated from 8,262 acres in Warwickshire and 1,840 in Somerset (*Burke's Peerage*)

176. *Trans. Soc. of Arts*, Vol.38, 1819, p.58. Later in the century, new owners would extend the quarries and supply the flooring slabs for Pugin's House of Lords at Westminster.

177. PRO, RAIL 875/3, various entries

178. Evidence to House of Lords Select Committee, June 1836 (see Chapter 22)

179. Outside the dreams of starry-eyed projectors, there had hitherto been only one such practical if unfulfilled proposal, a 125-mile line from Berwick to Glasgow surveyed by Telford in 1809–10 (Gibb 1935, pp.143–7).

CHAPTER 9

180. EMSP, p.31

181. Stratford Record Office, ER8/1/14 (list of landowners along the route)

182. Norris 1987, p.11

183. EMSP*, p.25

184. Others had dreamed of long-distance steam railways in England, particularly Sir Richard Phillips in 1813 and Thomas Gray in 1820, but both had envisaged Blenkinsop's cogged rail system which would have kept speeds to a minimum.

185. 2 Geo IV cap.36

186. A series of articles by Robin Barnes in *Backtrack*, Vol.17, Nos 9–11, 2003

187. The best overview of early locomotives is still perhaps Marshall 1953.

188. During the period under discussion, 1810–20, Trevithick used pressures as high as 150psi for some of his stationary engines, but there is no certainty that he ever designed another locomotive after 1808. For possible examples, Rees and Guy 2006.

CHAPTER 10

189. Stevenson 1819, p.26. Though often referred to as the '1818 Report' it was actually published in 1819.

190. Tomlinson 1915, pp.15–16; Marshall 1938, pp.151–4

191. Warren 1923, pp.29–30. The letter is written from Chipping Norton, which suggests that he was in the process of extending his survey beyond Moreton-in-Marsh towards Oxford.

192. Christopher Blackett, owner of Wylam colliery and (with his viewer William Hedley) a very early promoter of steam locomotion. John Buddle was the viewer at Heaton and Lambton collieries and another staunch advocate of mechanisation. The fact that James links Buddle with Chapman suggests that he may have seen the monstrous six-wheeled *Steam Elephant* locomotive now attributed to them, of which a replica was built in 2001 (Rees 2001). Chapman never built another locomotive.

193. LRO, 385JAM/1/5/5. EMSP, p.45 is certainly wrong in claiming that it was her father who introduced Stephenson to Pease and that this was another of his achievements that was usurped.

194. Private communication from Nick Billingham. Smiles 1857, p.179 records that James was accompanied by two of his sons, one of whom was very alarmed by the 'snorting monster'. This may have been his fourth son, Frederick James, then aged 13, who was to suffer from nerves all his life. Smiles 1857 is confused over the dates of the visits; Smiles 1862 even more so.

195. Smiles 1862, p.190

196. Warren 1923, p.45

197. *Mechanics' Magazine*, Vol.49, 1848, p.500, which is an editorial following up a letter (p.401) from an anonymous 'Coal & Ironmaster of Staffordshire' who may have been either Samuel Bill or John Kershaw. It reproduces only the first section; the only known sources for the complete document are *Mining Journal*, 26 December 1857 and EMSP*, pp.84–5. The three sources have minor variations of wording.

198. Warren 1923, p.30

199. EMSP*, p.85

200. Several road carriage builders of the time, such as Goldsworthy Gurney, were preoccupied with water-tube boilers. Ellen Paine (EMSP, pp.86–7) tried to make an issue of her interpretation that the fire-tube boiler eventually incorporated in *Rocket* had been suggested by her brother, when in fact the concept had been around for a quarter of a century. John Stevens had patented it in America in 1791 and in Britain in 1805 (Addyman and Haworth 2006, p.38).

201. Smiles 1857, p.179

202. Jeaffreson 1864, vol.1 pp.53–4

203. Victoria Haworth, private communication 2003

204. PRO, RAIL 673/1 (S&M Railway Minute Book)

205. This far-sighted suggestion of welded rails was not original to James but borrowed from Birkinshaw's patent of 1820.

206. Nowadays this is accepted practice in the railway, airline, construction and computer industries, and gives us yet another example of James's financial prescience.

207. Skeat 1973, p.48

208. LRO, 385JAM/1/5/1

209. Priestley 1831, p.297

210. LRO, 385JAM/1/5/1. Three locomotives mentioned were for the Hetton Railway.

211. Bick 1987, pp.68–9

212. Hilton 1977, p.165; *DNB*

213. EMSP*, p.31. A search in Gloucester Record Office and contemporary newspapers has failed to reveal anything more about this advertisement.

214. *Mining Journal*, 15 December 1857.

215. PRO, RAIL 875/3, p.359

216. PRO, RAIL 673/1. The anonymous engineer was probably John Urpeth Rastrick, who was building ironworks near Stourbridge for the Earl of Dudley around this time. Although the famed Shutt End Railway opened only in 1829, he may have built a predecessor (Dickinson and Lee 1923–4, p.56; *Locomotive Magazine*, 14 May 1910).

217. Warren 1923, pp.30–1

218. WRO, CR271/Box 3; Simmons 1956, p.147

219. This supports the view that Greaves carried out his field work alone, without the assistance of 'an expert engineer'.

220. Boyes 2001. Palmer, 27 years old, was working as Telford's assistant. He published some interesting studies of rolling resistance on tramways, based on experiments on the Gloucester & Cheltenham. Two short and short-lived lines based on his patent were built in 1824. Like many other nine-day wonders of the time, publication of the patent, which included reference to wind- and sail-power, sparked rapturous but ill-informed comment in the press.

221. PRO, RAIL 673/1

CHAPTER 11

222. Thomas 1980, p.13. It is unclear how much influence James and Gray had on each other's thinking. Neither made any reference to the other in any surviving correspondence.

223. Veitch 1930, p.24

224. LRO, 385JAM 4/1, reproduced in Thomas 1980, p.14

225. EMSP* p.39, summarised in Carlson 1969 p.55

226. Opponents of railway privatisation in the UK in the1990s, with the separation of track ownership (Railtrack) from the train operators, claimed there was no precedent for such a concept. They were wrong to the extent that the Stockton & Darlington was indeed originally set up on precisely this principle. It created total chaos, and all operations were soon integrated under one authority.

227. Davies 1975, p.123

228. Later in his distinguished career he would become MP for Whitby.

229. *Trans. Manchester Assn. of Engineers*, 1889, pp.23–29. Such light tramways laid on nearby Trafford Moss at least 27 years earlier (Holt 1795, p.97) had conceivably inspired James's own temporary Stratford line. Stannard would later be appointed the contractor for this section of the Liverpool & Manchester Railway,

bringing with him the expertise to float the line across Chat Moss. George Stephenson initially opposed this solution, but later claimed it as his own initiative.
230. EMSP*, p.115, quoting *Mechanics Magazine*, Vol.31, 1839, p.476.

CHAPTER 12
231. Priestley 1831, pp.424–7
232. EMSP*, pp.32–5
233. EMSP*, pp.35–6. The seat of Lord Hardwicke, a former Lord Lieutenant of Ireland , was Wimpole Hall between Cambridge and Royston.
234. EMSP*, p.22, undated, but apparently belonging to this period.
235. *Mining Journal*, 26 December 1857. See also EMSP, p.68.
236. Smiles 1857, p.181
237. Guy 2001, p.131
238. Davies 1996, p.53
239. EMSP*, p.82
240. NLW, Chirk Castle MS E3033
241. NLW, Chirk Castle MS E3034
242. NLW, Chirk Castle MS E3027
243. LRO, 385 JAM 1/5/6
244. LRO, 385 JAM 1/6/2. Frederick Whitworth Tarleton James, the fourth son, was then aged 14, and his father was giving him practical experience as part of his apprenticeship.
245. Biddle 1990, pp.76–80
246. NLW, Chirk Castle MS E3031
247. EMSP*, p.27
248. Rastrick would go on to greater things. He designed and built many bridges, forges and engineering works, as well as a few locomotives. One of these, the *Stourbridge Lion*, was the first to be exported to the USA in 1829, while the similar *Agenoria*, now preserved at the NRM, was provided for the Shutt End Railway. His staunch advocacy of steam locomotion helped many railways to obtain their Acts, including the Liverpool & Manchester in 1826. He would be a judge at the Rainhill trials in 1829, but his most famous achievement was building the London & Brighton Railway in 1836.
249. LRO, 385 JAM 1/5/3
250. LRO, 385 JAM 16/3
251. EMSP, p.31. No record of this proposed railway survives in the Blenheim archives.
252. Stevenson 1824, pp.140–1. *Encyclopaedia Edinensis*, Vol.6, 1827, p.9, and *Edinburgh Encyclopaedia*, Vol.17, 1830, p.208 also use the phrase *skeleton railway*, but borrowed from Stevenson.
253. LRO, 385 JAM 1/6/4
254. NLW, Chirk Castle MS E3035
255. LRO, 385 JAM 1/3/1
256. LRO 385, JAM 4/2
257. LRO 385, JAM 4/3
258. LRO 385, JAM 1/5/4
259. LRO 385 JAM 1/6/5
260. NLW, Chirk Castle MS E3028
261. EMSP*, p.44
262. LRO, 385 JAM 1/1/1
263. Smiles 1868, p.254, quoted in Carlson 1969, p.57
264. May 1871, vol. III, chapter XI, p.25

CHAPTER 13
265. Lewis 2002. Much of the saga of James and the Glynn estates derives from this article and private correspondence with the author.
266. LRO, 385JAM/1/5/5
267. LRO, 385JAM/1/6/5
268. LRO, 385JAM/1/5/6.
269. LRO, 385JAM/1/5/7
270. James never got round to writing the other eleven essays. The first is extremely rare, a copy being sold in 1986 for £325. Another in the library of the Institute of Civil Engineers. There is a fuller summary in Lee 1944.
271. EMSP*, p.56
272. EMSP*, pp.63–6
273. PRO, PRIS 4/35 p.42
274. EMSP*, p.57
275. It seems reasonable to assume that Miss M'George was the landlady of the office James had rented. Should there be a default on the rent, the contents would not be secure. Or was it a codename for George Stephenson, or even Robert? John Copner Williams was the agent of the Chirk Castle estate, cited in the previous chapter apropos the proposed railway from Chirk to Chester. James's team were on their way to do the detailed survey for his railway from Chirk to Chester.
276. Reynolds 1977, p.22
277. EMSP, p.99. She claims he sold it Furnival, who was later involved with the British Rock and Patent Salt company at Stoke Prior, Droitwich. James may never have been paid. He possibly purchased it from Rufford, another salt entrepreneur who would appear as a major creditor at James's bankruptcy. It had been James's intention to evaporate brine in steam-heated pans invented by his son.
278. EMSP*, p.73
279. For the background to the railway, Fellows 1930, Hart 1991
280. PRO, PRIS 4/35, p.170
281. Stratford Record Office, ER8/1/109 and 111. Roe was a contractor from Moreton-in-Marsh, Bradley was the Stourbridge firm of Bradley, Foster, Rastrick & Co in which J. U. Rastrick was a partner.
282. Norris 1987, p.17
283. Warren 1923, p.67
284. PRO, B5/15, p.281
285. Padley had possibly played the leading role in bailing his brother-in-law out from his previous incarcerations for debt.
286. EMSP, p.76
287. EMSP*, p.62
288. EMSP*, p.88
289. EMSP*, p.68
290. EMSP*, pp.55–6, frequently quoted in biographies of Robert Stephenson.
291. EMSP, p.75
292. PRO, RAIL 673/1
293. PRO, PRIS 4/35
294. She had inherited the land from an uncle and in 1804 married Charles Agar, who died in 1811 leaving her with the responsibility of an infant child, Thomas James, and the entire Cornish estates

295. The correspondence quoted here and in later chapters between James, Anna-Maria Agar, Alfred Jenkin and Baugh Allen is mainly in the Cornwall Record Office (CL339–342) but some in the archives at Lanhydrock, quoted here by kind permission of the senior archivist and the National Trust. Other letters from Alfred Jenkin are in the Courtney Library, Truro.
296. Courtney Library, Truro, Jenkin letterbook 7 April 1806
297. Thomas 1973, p.161. The directors' saloon, possibly the oldest railway carriage in the world, is exhibited at the Royal Cornwall Museum in Truro.
298. Locomotives would not be used on the line until 1854.
299. Courtney Library, Truro, Jenkin letterbook 1 December 1823.
300. Carlson 1969, p.60

CHAPTER 14
301. LRO, 385JAM/1/7/1. This duplication of names has caused confusion among historians, even the renowned Tom Rolt (1960, p.96).
302. Warren 1923, p.34. Robert Stephenson Snr was dismissed from Hetton in Sept. 1823. Locomotives were only used on the relatively level sections either side of the Warden Law bank (Mountford 2006).
303. Jackman 1966, p.466; Boyes 1994; Simmons 1997, p.311
304. EMSP, p.14
305. The only known copy is a manuscript, now in a private collection, addressed to John Crowley of Wolverhampton with an attached note from the company solicitor, George Barker: 'The Committee do not think it right to publish these resolutions until a personal communication has taken place between them and the Gentlemen of Manchester and Liverpool.'
306. Hopkin 2001, p.348
307. Lanhydrock archives, quoted by kind permission of the senior archivist and the National Trust
308. Carlson 1969, pp.62–4. The other members were Lister Ellis, Henry Booth and John Kennedy.
309. EMSP*, p.59
310. Cornwall Record Office, CL339 and CL319
311. Thomas 1980, pp.18–19 wrongly puts James in prison for the third time between 14 May and 18 August 1824. This was a different William James, with different creditors. Our James has a cast-iron alibi for several dates in this period, when he was clearly not in gaol.
312. Barton 1966. The total length, including branches to individual mines south of Redruth, was 14 1/4 miles and it was laid with edge rails to a gauge of 4ft. It cost £22,500 including dredging operations at Point Quay.
313. Overend, Gurney & Co would, in the future, help finance many railway schemes. In 1865 it floated on the Stock Market, and its failure on 'Black Monday', 11 May 1866, was the single

definitive cause of Bank Rate being raised to 10 per cent and the subsequent crash of 1866.
314. EMSP*, p.60
315. EMSP*, p.61
316. EMSP, p.74
317. EMSP*, p.66
318. Haworth 1992
319. LRO, 385JAM/1/7/2. Robert Stephenson Snr had married his brother George's housekeeper Ann Snaith in 1808. She was then acting as foster-mother to the five-year-old Robert, while his father was working on a three-year assignment in Scotland.
320. BL, Add MS 38781 f.4. It was quite a lengthy residence, for he was still receiving correspondence at Stratford in November 1826. His patent granted in January 1826 (No. 5325, 'Axletrees to Remedy the Friction on Curves to Waggons etc') gives his address as Bridge Town, Old Stratford, Warwicks. This is the invention referred to in George's letter to James of 16 January 1823. It consisted of mounting each wheel of a waggon on its own full-gauge axle, so that it rotated independently without requiring a double-framed axle box. It was never adopted.
321. EMSP*, pp.29–30
322. PRO, RAIL 673/1
323. Warren 1923, p.162
324. Skeat 1973, p.63
325. Vaughn 1997, pp.51–2
326. Fellows 1930, p.84
327. Hart 1991, p.8
328. Fellows 1930, pp.15–20
329. Haworth 2004, p.15
330. Bailey 2003, p.22

CHAPTER 15
331. Robert Wilson had no connection with the firm of Losh, Bell & Wilson.
332. BL, Add MS 38781 f.4
333. ibid f.24
334. Young 1923, p.140
335. Presumably this refers to the Birmingham & Liverpool project. The promoters must have been very confident of raising their capital and getting a Bill through parliament to have ordered their first locomotive.
336. Fletcher 1891, p.75
337. Smiles 1857, p.325. The route of the main line had been surveyed by Paul Padley and George Hamilton (Cheshire Record Office, QDP60).
338. Johnson 1991, p.887
339. Basnett 1950–1; Evans 2003
340. Lancashire Record Office, Preston, PDR 131
341. Lancashire Record Office, Preston, DDHU 6/5
342. Warren 1923, p.38
343. Priestley 1831, p.138
344. Centre for Kentish Studies, Maidstone, Plans Q/Rum 74
345. EMSP*, p.97
346. LRO, 385JAM/1/4
347. Worcester Record Office, 338/37.3–37.5
348. Keast 1982, p.33
349. Whetmath 1994, p.5

CHAPTER 16
350. Fellows 1930, p.83
351. PRO, RAIL 673
352. London Jnl. of Arts, Vol.10, 1825, pp.310–12. For details, see Appendix A.
353. Many books describe the events of this day, e.g. Rolt 1960, pp.84–6.
354. PRO, RAIL 673
355. Fellows 1930, p.84
356. Hart 1991, p.10
357. EMSP*, pp.89–90
358. EMSP*, p.47
359. Young 1923, p.385. The letter is also quoted by Hart, though he omits this important paragraph.
360. He was finally declared redundant on 30 August 1826, when George Stephenson ordered his brother up to Bolton (PRO, RAIL 673).
361. PRO, RAIL 673
362. Rolt 1960, p.114
363. Garfield 2002, p.98
364. Jenkins and Carpenter 1997, p.6. This book is also a comprehensive history of the entire Stratford & Moreton Railway. On p.10 is a good illustration of the design of the original rails and sleepers.
365. Boynton 1994, p.7
366. Letter to Ellen Paine in 1857 quoted by EMSP*, p.47
367. Fellows 1930, p.87
368. EMSP*, pp.92–4

CHAPTER 17
369. Spring 1971, pp.27–8. For the main sources for Cornish material, see Chap.15 note 3.
370. WRO, CR1886/733/1
371. Lancashire Record Office, Preston, DDHU/21
372. The name is derived from the notorious Witches of Pendle, tried for witchcraft and murder in 1612.
373. This can be deduced from James's letter to Anna-Maria Agar of 15 April 1829. In 1841 the property was owned by the Bodmin Corporation, who may well have been James's landlord.
374. EMSP*, p.91
375. Bailey 2003, p.213; Haworth 2004, p.36 attributes his 'conversion' not only to James but to an incident when he was shipwrecked on his way from Cartagena to New York.
376. Todd 1967, p.215
377. Burton 2000, pp.216–218
378. No evidence of correspondence between Davies and James has yet been discovered.
379. EMSP, p.102
380. EMSP, p.92
381. EMSP, p.76
382. Williams 1927, p.833. Thavies was originally an Inn of Chancery, a preparatory place of legal education subordinate to Lincoln's Inn. It was Paul Padley's address on his lithograph of the Redruth & Chasewater Railway and James's address for correspondence at the period. It was also William Henry James's address on one of his later patents.

CHAPTER 18
383. Wood 1825, p.32
384. If a tube burst, the water and steam would be sprayed inside the fire chamber. This would tend to quench the fire and certainly cause some hazard from steam escaping through the firing hole, but nothing compared to the bursting of a conventional boiler which would explode like a shrapnel bomb.
385. Rolt 1960, p.147
386. The final flowering of William Henry James's concept was the steam railcar built by the Besler brothers in 1935 for the New York, New Haven & Hartford Railroad. This incorporated an oil-fired flash water-tube boiler with three series of coils for successively heating, boiling and superheating. Steam at a pressure of 1200psi was passed to a four-cylinder compound power truck, the exhaust steam being then recirculated through a condenser. It proved to be unreliable in service and was withdrawn in 1943 (my thanks to Alan M. Levitt for pointing out to me this latterday connection).
387. Mechanics' Magazine, Vol.12, 1829, pp.194–9. Sir James Anderson, of Buttevant Castle, was an eccentric Irish baronet who financed W. H. James's steam carriages until he went bankrupt in 1832. By 1838 he had raised more capital and continued with his own projects, building a number of road steamers in both Manchester and Dublin.
388. Using Phillipson's standard formula, the tractive effort of the James's carriage was about 450lb, compared to 382lb for Novelty, 694lb for Sans Pareil and 826lb for Rocket. The higher figures for the last two were entirely due to the much larger cylinders. If the weight of James's carriage really was only 1¼ tons, it would certainly have travelled much faster than Novelty, which weighed 2¾ tons.
389. Fellows 1930, p.41
390. This gap was then only 4ft 8¾in, the same as the track gauge, the concept being that extra-wide loads could be carried on trucks straddling two lines. It would soon be increased to the familiar '6-foot way'. A recent and very readable account of the tragedy is Garfield 2003.
391. Both quoted in Rolt 1960, pp.189–92
392. Quoted in Ludovic Kennedy (ed.), A Book of Railway Journeys, 1980, p.5
393. For example Thomas 1980, p.241
394. Gore's Directory and View of Liverpool for 1832. George Rennie and his brother John had been joint chief engineers on the railway during the interregnum of 1824–6, between George Stephenson's two appointments. George Buchanan and Thomas Grainger were responsible for many early railways in Scotland, especially around Glasgow.
395. Discovered at 5 Rochester Road,

Coventry, the home of Mr T. H. Bushill. James's elder daughter by his second wife married into the Bushill family. The collection was auctioned by Sotheby's on 3 July 1973, most of the items being purchased by the Liverpool Record Office, becoming LRO, 385JAM. The print of the L&MR was purchased and resold by Francis Edwards, bookseller, but the present owner is unknown.
396. *Liverpool Times & Billinge's Advertiser*

CHAPTER 19
397. Courtney Library, Truro, Jenkin letterbook 31 March 1832. Trelissick house and gardens now belongs to the National Trust.
398. LRO, 385JAM/5/7. She was the daughter of a John Butt, who did not attend the wedding, implying that either he was dead or disapproved of the marriage. Her mother, another Elizabeth, was one of the witnesses along with a Thomas Hackman
399. Anne James married a Coventry solicitor, Thomas Bushill, on 2 April 1857. Over the next fifteen years they had nine children.
400. Devoran eventually became one of the Agar-Robartes's most rewarding properties. In 1846 they gave the inhabitants land for a church and endowed it with £60 per annum.
401. EMSP, p.91 erroneously assigns Peter to the aristocratic Petre family, possible because Edward Robert Petre was an MP in 1832, but for York, not Bodmin. She may also have been misled by the fact that Edmund Glynn's eldest daughter Elizabeth Anne had married Henry William Petre, a grandson of the 9th Baron Petre. Chiverton is in Perranzabuloe about six miles north-west of Truro.
402. EMSP, p.91. Edward Boscawen, a committed opponent of what he saw as the 'dreaded liberal' policies of Canning and Huskisson, gained notoriety by standing as second to Lord Winchilsea in his famous duel with the Duke of Wellington in 1829 (*DNB*).
403. House of Lords Record Office, Session 1836/L2/14226
404. House of Commons Information Office, Fact-sheet P7 – Procedure Series. The average annual number of petitions in 1811–15 was 1,100; by 1837–41 it had risen to 17,600, and in 1843 peaked at 33,898.
405. The Copyright Act of 1767 did cover published maps, charts and plans, and the amending Act of 1842 introduced the concept of protection for unpublished material if it was registered.
406. New series vol.1, 1836, pp.303–5. The *Railway Magazine* was launched as a monthly journal by John Herapath (1790–1851) in May 1835, almost simultaneously with the *Railway Gazette*. Whereas the latter expired after only a few issues, the *Railway Magazine* survived, under a variety of titles and formats, until 1894.
407. New series vol.1, 1836, pp.363–7

408. Given the coastal location of Newhaven, it might have involved the diving apparatus patented in the name of William Henry James in 1825 (see Appendix A). Another possibility is the novel type of dock gate, referred to in his *Report or Essay* of 1823, which had been first used at Sebastopol in the Crimea.
409. EMSP, p.91
410. *The Engineer*, 11 June 1926, p.617
411. The names of these two men (probably Fereday and Furnival), which must have been spelled out in the original letter, were presumably asterisked by the editor.
412. EMSP, p.74
413. EMSP, p.101. Pigot's *National Commercial Directory of Staffordshire*, 1828–9, gives George Walter's address as Hill Top, West Bromwich. This may have been the second house that William James owned in the town, later occupied by a sister of Thomas Attwood MP (EMSP, p.96). Pigot's 1837 Birmingham directory shows him operating as a surgeon in Great Hampton Street. He next appears in 1850 as a surgeon in Soho Street, Handsworth (*Kelly's Directory of Staffordshire*).
414. EMSP, p.100
415. She was born on 7 January 1837. On 21 July 1858 she married Joseph Norman Lockyer in Leamington Spa. They had eight children.

CHAPTER 20
416. Whishaw 1840, p.50
417. LRO, 385JAM/6
418. EMSP, p.100
419. LRO, 385JAM/2/2/1
420. LRO, 385JAM/2/1
421. LRO, 385JAM/5/7
422. *Mechanics' Magazine*, Vol.31, 1839, pp.156–7
423. *ibid*, pp.474–8
424. *Warwick Advertiser*, 31 July 1841
425. Science Museum Library. She received £5 from the directors of both the London & Birmingham Railway and the Great Western Railway (Thomas 1980, p.254 chap.13 note 1).
426. *Warwick Advertiser*, 31 July 1841
427. House of Commons Information Office; Fact-sheet P7 – Procedure Series
428. EMSP, pp.105–107
429. EMSP, pp.109–10. Robert Stephenson had been the crucial influence in encouraging William Henry James to launch the memorial, writing to him on 7 November 1844, 'I believe your late father was the original projector of the Liverpool and Manchester railway' (EMSP*, p105).
430. EMSP, p.109
431. *Mechanics' Magazine*, Vol.49, 1848, p.500
432. *Scripophily, Journal of the International Bond & Share Society*, September 2001, p.8
433. *Proc. Inst. Civil Engineers*, Vol.5, 1846, p.77
434. It is of little consolation to James's memory that a few names on Rennie's list – Barnes, Curr, Good and

Lambourt – do not rate inclusion in Marshall 2003. At least James and his eldest son have full if not wholly accurate entries there.
435. University of London, Goldsmith's Library, I1.861, letter to Lord Bagot, 17 April 1866. Frederick appears at their address in two censuses. In 1861 both he and Ellen give their place of birth, erroneously, as Trebinshun, Wales. In 1861 she gives West Bromwich, he Wyken, Coventry; again both are wrong.
436. Jarvis 1994, p.40
437. Smiles 1857, p.158
438. University of London, Goldsmith's Library, I1.861
439. EMSP, p.103
440. By a remarkable coincidence, the author's present house near Henley-in-Arden was once the property of another of Dinah James's great nephews, John Tarleton, who sold it 1861.
441. University of London, Goldsmith's Library, I1.861, letter Ellen Paine to Lord Bagot, April 1866
442. BL, Woodcroft Collection, Add MS 14612. The author's copy has a rubber stamp of H.B. James, and a bookplate of Sir Edward Watkin.
443. University of London, Goldsmith's Library, I1.861
444. EMSP, pp.102–3, implying that she had died around 1839–40. The death of a Marianna James is recorded in Birmingham in the first quarter of 1841.
445. University of London, Goldsmith's Library, I1.861
446. EMSP, p.111
447. BL, Woodcroft Collection, Add MS 14612. It may have been timed to coincide with the publication of EMSP.
448. *DNB*
449. He appears in the 1851 census living in Deptford, but not in the 1861 census.
450. Private communications with his great-great-granddaughters in England
451. Private communications with his descendants still living in Australia
452. *Railway Magazine*, Vol.5, 1899, pp.33–42
453. *ibid*, pp.364–8
454. *Railway Magazine*, Vol.6, 1900, p.409

CHAPTER 21
455. Introduction to the reprint of EMSP, 1961, p.vii
456. Smiles 1862, p.190
457. Donaghy 1972, p.15
458. Thomas 1980, p.12
459. Introduction to the reprint of EMSP, 1961, p.v

APPENDIX A
460. Fuller details may be found in Macnair 2005
461. *Encyclopedia Edinensis*, Vol.6, 1827, p.13; *London Journal of Arts and Sciences*, Vol.10, 1825, 310–12
462. A model of James's proposed 'tug' with change-speed gears is illustrated in Evans 1998–9, Fig.9.